W9-BUO-651

"If you read only one book about the Middle Ages, Eric Jager's thriller is the one to read."

—Steven Ozment, author of *A Mighty Fortress*
and *The Burgermeister's Daughter*

"Breathes astonishing vigor, realism and a remarkable modernity into a celebrated trial by combat in 1386 that effectively ended legally sanctioned duels as a means of Parisian justice . . . a taut page-turner with all the hallmarks of a good historical thriller: superb pacing, plot twists, dramatic tension and a fully fleshed cast of characters. Jager's spectacularly rendered portrait of the end of an era desperately in need of the approaching Renaissance is not a glimpse into the past but an enriching total immersion."

—*The Orlando Sentinel*

"An enthralling story that reads like fiction but is based on reliable sources. A world of passion, cruelty, and mismanaged law."

—Norman Cantor, author of
Inventing the Middle Ages and
In the Wake of the Plague

"Jager provides an excellent depiction of feudal society, placing the reader into the lives of knights and nobles, detailing their relationships with each other and to their lords. . . . The story of the duel and the rivalry leading up to it make for quick reading as enthralling and engrossing as any about a high-profile celebrity scandal today."

—*Booklist*

"Jager uses the historical record to marvelous effect when recounting the riveting story of two men locked in mortal combat . . . and who we deem the true victor is brilliantly left open to interpretation in Jager's engrossing tale."

—Margaret F. Rosenthal, author of
The Honest Courtesan

"Jager knows his territory well; we learn a good deal about medieval armor and weaponry, fashion and custom, the legal system and sexual idea, court politics and religion. His skillful prose quickly ensnares readers in the web of the characters' invention, allowing no escape until very near the end. . . . Sex, savagery, and high-level political maneuvers energize a splendid piece of popular history."

—*Kirkus Reviews*

"A spectacular panorama of the late Middle Ages, a golden glimpse into military, legal, religious, and domestic life at every social level, *The Last Duel* is an historical thriller, a can't-put-down kind of book that leaves us with the impression of having known and lived in another world. It combines the vivid erudition of Barbara Tuchman's *Distant Mirror* with the suspense and drama of Umberto Eco's *The Name of the Rose*. Eric Jager has invented a genre that reminds us that human nature has not changed very much over the ages and that sometimes reality is bigger than life and more riveting than fiction."

—R. Howard Bloch, Augustus R. Street
Professor of French, Yale University

"[A] vivid re-creation of 'the last judicial duel sanctioned by the Parlement of Paris' and a painstakingly documented picture of courtly love, pride, dishonor, and judgment in 14th century France."

—*Library Journal*

"Recounting a little known judicial combat from 1386, this is the best book about a single historical duel I've yet read. . . . For once a historian also manages to get it right when it comes to descriptions of the arms and armor as well as the combat itself. . . . Jager does a thorough job of laying out the circumstances of the conflict while in the process retrieving from history's dusty memory a description of an event worth reading about. The effort will prove interesting not just to students of medieval history, but anyone who enjoys great historical tales."

—J. Clements, The Association for Renaissance Martial Arts

"[A] thoroughly engrossing narrative, a story of honor, love, and valor that one might find in a medieval romance by Chrétien de Troyes."

—Bloomberg.com

"*The Last Duel* is popular history at its very best . . . Jager manages to encapsulate the complex world of 14th century France into a manageable backdrop for staging the heart of the story, a human drama made all the more thrilling for the fact that it is truth, not fiction."

—*The Advocate* (Tennessee)

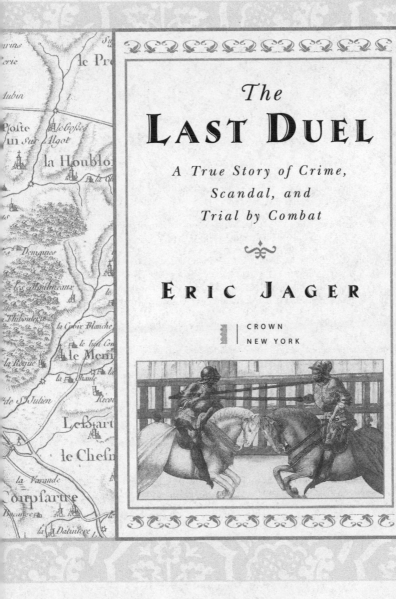

The
LAST DUEL

A True Story of Crime,
Scandal, and
Trial by Combat

ERIC JAGER

CROWN
NEW YORK

FOR PEG

sine qua non

2021 Crown Trade Paperback Edition

Copyright © 2004 by Eric Jager

Published in the United States by Crown, an imprint of Random House,
a division of Penguin Random House LLC, New York.

Crown and the Crown colophon are registered trademarks of
Penguin Random House LLC.

Originally published in hardcover in the United States by Crown, an imprint of
Random House, a division of Penguin Random House LLC, New York, in 2004,
and subsequently published in paperback by Broadway Books, an imprint of
Random House, a division of Penguin Random House LLC, New York, in 2005.

Library of Congress Cataloging-in-Publication Data
Jager, Eric
The last duel: a true story of crime, scandal, and trial by combat/Eric Jager.
p. cm.
Includes bibliographical references and index.
1. Wager of battle—France—History—To 1500.
2. Dueling—France—History—To 1500. 3. Crime—France—History—To 1500.
4. Scandals—France—History—To 1500. I. Title.
KJV8690.A82J34 2004
394'.8'09440902—dc22
2004045747

ISBN 9780593240885
Ebook ISBN 9780767919616

Printed in the United States of America on acid-free paper

crownpublishing.com

2 4 6 8 9 7 5 3 1

Book design by Deborah Kerner/Dancing Bears Design
Maps illustrated by John Burgoyne

The elaborate rules of judicial combat
left nothing to chance—except,
of course, the outcome itself.

—MARTIN MONESTIER,
Duels: les combats singuliers

This duel was the last one ever decreed
by order of the Parlement of Paris.

—J. A. BUCHON, EDITOR OF
JEAN FROISSART'S *Chronicles*

No one really knew the truth of the matter.

—JEAN LE COQ, PARISIAN LAWYER,
LATE FOURTEENTH CENTURY

CONTENTS

AUTHOR'S NOTE

The idea for this book first occurred to me ten years ago while reading a medieval account of the legendary quarrel between Jean de Carrouges and Jacques Le Gris. Fascinated by the story, I began collecting everything I could find about the Carrouges–Le Gris affair. Eventually I traveled to Normandy and Paris to explore manuscript archives and experience the places where the drama unfolded more than six hundred years ago. The resulting book is a true story based on original sources: chronicles, legal records, and other surviving documents. All persons, places, dates, and many other details—including what people said and did, their often contradictory claims in court, sums of money paid or received, even the weather—are real and based on the sources. Where the sources disagree, I give the most likely account of events. Where the historical record is silent, I use my own invention to fill in some of the gaps, while always listening closely to the voices of the past.

PROLOGUE

On a cold morning a few days after Christmas in 1386, thousands of people packed a large open space behind a monastery in Paris to watch two knights fight a duel to the death. The rectangular field of battle was enclosed by a high wooden wall, and the wall was surrounded by guards armed with spears. Charles VI, the eighteen-year-old king of France, sat with his court in colorful viewing stands along one side, while the huge throng of spectators crowded all around the field.

The two combatants, in full armor, swords and daggers at their belts, sat facing each other across the length of the field on thronelike chairs placed just outside the heavy gates at either end. Attendants held a stamping warhorse ready by each gate, as priests hurriedly cleared the field of the altar and crucifix on which the two enemies had just sworn their oaths.

At the marshal's signal, the knights would mount their horses, seize their lances, and charge onto the field. The guards would then slam the gates shut, imprisoning the two men inside the heavy stockade. There they would fight without quarter, and without any chance of escape, until one killed the other, thus proving his charges and revealing God's verdict on their quarrel.

The excited crowd was watching not only the two fierce warriors, and the youthful king amid his splendid court, but also the beautiful young woman sitting alone on a black-draped scaffold overlooking the field, dressed from head to toe in mourning, and also surrounded by guards.

Feeling the eyes of the crowd upon her and bracing herself for the coming ordeal, she stared ahead at the flat, smooth field where her fate would soon be written in blood.

If her champion won the judicial combat and killed his opponent, she would go free. But if he were slain, she would pay with her life for having sworn a false oath.

It was the feast day of the martyred saint Thomas Becket, the crowd was in a holiday mood, and she knew that many were eager to see not only a man slain in mortal combat but also a woman put to death.

As the bells of Paris tolled the hour, the king's marshal strode onto the field and held up a hand for silence. The trial by combat was about to begin.

PART ONE

1

CARROUGES

In the fourteenth century it took several months for knights and
pilgrims to travel from Paris or Rome to the Holy Land, and a
year or more for friars and traders to journey across Europe
and all the way to China along the Silk Road. Asia, Africa, and the still-
undiscovered Americas had not yet been colonized by Europeans.
And Europe itself had been nearly conquered by Muslim horsemen,
who stormed out of Arabia in the seventh century, sailed from Africa
to capture Sicily and Spain, and crossed swords with Christians as far
north as Tours, France, before being turned back. By the fourteenth
century, Christendom had faced the Muslim threat for more than six
hundred years, launching repeated crusades against the infidel.

When not united against its common foe, Christendom was often
at war with itself. The kings and queens of Europe, a large extended
family of brothers and sisters and intermarried cousins, squabbled and
fought with one another continually over thrones and territory. The
frequent wars among Europe's feuding monarchs reduced towns and
farmland to smoking ruins, killed or starved the people, and left rulers
with huge debts that they paid by raising taxes, debasing the coinage,
or simply seizing the wealth of convenient victims like Jews.

At the center of Europe lay the Kingdom of France, a vast realm
that took twenty-two days to cross from north to south, and sixteen

SOLDIERS PILLAGE A HOUSE.

English soldiers plundered many parts of France during the Hundred Years' War. Chronique du Religieux de Saint-Denys.

MS. Royal 20 C VII., fol. 41v. By permission of the British Library.

days from east to west. France, the forge of feudalism, had endured for nearly ten centuries. Founded amid the ruins of Roman Gaul in the fifth century, it had been Charlemagne's fortress against Islamic Spain in the ninth, and it was Europe's richest, most powerful nation at the start of the fourteenth. But within a few decades Fortune had turned against France, and the nation was now desperately fighting for its survival.

In 1339 the English crossed the Channel and invaded France, beginning the long, ruinous conflict that would be known as the Hundred Years' War. After cutting down the flower of French chivalry at Crécy in 1346, the English captured Calais. A decade later at Poitiers, amid another great slaughter of French knights, the English seized King Jean and took him to London, releasing their royal prisoner only in exchange for vast French territories, many noble hostages, and promises to pay a colossal ransom of three million gold *écus*.

Stunned by the loss of its king and what it cost to buy him back, France fell into civil war. Rebellious nobles betrayed King Jean and joined with the English invaders, peasants enraged by new taxes rose up to murder their lords, and the volatile citizens of Paris split into feuding factions and butchered one another in the streets. Chronic droughts and crop failures added to the misery of the people. And the Great Plague that carried off a third of Europe in 1348–49, leaving unburied corpses scattered over fields and stacked in the streets, kept returning every decade or so for another grim harvest.

As Death stalked the land, pictured by artists of the time as a shrouded skeleton wielding a great scythe, and as black warning flags flew from belfries in plague-stricken villages, God Himself seemed to have abandoned France. When the Great Schism shook Europe in 1378, dividing Christendom into two warring camps led by rival popes in Rome and Avignon, the Roman pope blessed England's cruel and mercenary war of conquest in France, as English clerics preached a new "crusade" and sold indulgences to finance the slaughter of French "heretics."

Conquering English armies were followed into France by criminals and outlaws from all over Europe, bands of savage men known as *routiers*, or "the scourge of God," who roamed the countryside looting towns and villages and extorting tribute from the terrorized people. Amid the violence and the anarchy, France threw itself into a frenzy of fortification. Frightened villagers built earthen walls and dug defensive ditches. Desperate farmers surrounded their houses and barns with stone towers and water-filled moats. Towns and monasteries raised and thickened their walls. Churches were fortified until they resembled castles.

The bloodlust of war and the crusading spirit kindled by the Great Schism led to many atrocities. Not even nunneries were sacred. In July 1380 English troops mounted a brutal raid on Brittany during which they "stormed a convent and raped and tortured the nuns, carrying off some of the unfortunate women to amuse them for the rest of the raid."

In the autumn of 1380 King Charles V died, leaving the realm to his eleven-year-old son, Charles VI. France was then just two-thirds its modern size and less a unified nation than a loose patchwork of separate fiefdoms. Large territories were held by the young king's four jealous uncles, who had been appointed regents during his minority; others were occupied by enemy troops. Burgundy belonged to Philip the Bold, the most powerful royal uncle and founder of a dynasty that soon would rival France itself. Anjou belonged to another royal uncle, Duke Louis. Provence was a separate county, not yet part of France, and parts of Guyenne were held by the English. Brittany was a nearly independent dukedom, while Normandy was also infested by the English, who used it to launch raids on the rest of France, recruiting many renegade Normans to their cause. The strategic port of Calais, long an English stronghold bristling with men and arms, was pointed like a dagger at the nation's heart, Paris.

Surrounded by rivals and enemies, the boy-king in theory ruled over about ten million people. His subjects belonged to three main *estates* or social classes—warriors, priests, and laborers, or "those who fight, those who pray, and those who work." The vast majority were laborers, some of whom lived in towns where they kept shops, but most of whom were peasants or *villeins,* farming the manorial estates of their local lords or *seigneurs.* In exchange for protection in time of war and a strip of land for their own use, they plowed and harvested their lord's fields, cut firewood for his hearth, and yielded up shares of produce and livestock. Bound to the land from birth, they spoke local dialects, lived by provincial customs, and had next to no sense of national identity.

As the peasant served his lord, so the lord in turn served his overlord. The minor lord might be a knight holding a fief or two, the greater lord a count or a duke with many fiefs—lands held in exchange for service. A vassal—any man sworn to serve another—bound

FRANCE IN 1380.

King Charles VI, crowned at the age of eleven in 1380, inherited a loose patchwork of feudal territories, many held by powerful relatives or overrun by enemy troops.

himself to his lord by the act of homage and the oath of fealty.* The vassal knelt with his hands clasped between his lord's, saying, "Lord, I become your man." Then he rose, received a kiss on the mouth, and swore to serve his lord for life. These rituals cemented the mutual bonds holding society together.

The lifelong bond between lord and vassal was based chiefly on land. As feudal law decreed, "No lord without land; no land without a lord." Land yielded life-sustaining crops as well as lucrative rents, in either coin or kind, along with levies of mail-fisted knights and men-at-arms. Land was thus the feudal nobility's main source of wealth, power, and prestige—and the most enduring thing a man could pass down, with the family name, to his heirs. Valuable and coveted, land was also the cause of many quarrels and deadly feuds.

Nowhere did men fight over land more fiercely than in Normandy, a bloody crossroads of war since antiquity. The Celts had fought the Romans there; the Romans, the Franks; and the Franks, the Vikings, before the French and the English clashed there during the Hundred Years' War. The Vikings—or Northmen, *Normanni*—had eventually settled, taking Frankish land and wives and turning themselves into French-speaking Normans. The dukes of Normandy, a line founded in 911, became vassals to the kings of France.

In 1066 Duke William of Normandy crossed the Channel with an army of knights, fought and defeated King Harold at the Battle of Hastings, crowned himself king of England, and became known to history as William the Conqueror. As king of England, the Duke of Normandy now rivaled the king of France. For the next century and a half Normandy, with its prosperous towns and wealthy monasteries, remained a possession of the English crown.

In the early 1200s the king of France won most of Normandy back from the king of England in a hard-fought campaign. But English kings, being of Norman blood, still dreamed of Normandy. And many

---

* The term *homage* comes from French *homme*, "man," and *fealty* comes from *fealte*, "faith."

of Normandy's great families, Normans before they were French, kept an opportunistic eye toward England, always sniffing the air for winds of change.

When the Hundred Years' War began, and the English started reconquering Normandy, many Norman nobles betrayed the French king and allied themselves with the English invaders.

The loyal Normans who swore fealty to the young King Charles in 1380 included an old noble family by the name of Carrouges. Sir Jean de Carrouges III, by then in his sixties, had come of age near the start of the Hundred Years' War and fought in many campaigns against the English. The knight was a vassal to the Count of Perche, who had appointed him the military captain of Bellême, an important and coveted castle. He was also Viscount of Bellême, the king's local official—equivalent to an English shire reeve, or sheriff. In 1364 he had helped raise money for King Jean's ransom. The respected knight was married to Nicole de Buchard, a well-born lady with whom he had at least three children. The family's ancestral home was the fortified hilltop town of Carrouges, about fifteen miles northwest of Alençon.

According to legend, the Carrouges line was born of blood and violence. One story tells of an ancestor named Count Ralph who fell in love with a sorceress and kept trysts with her near a fountain in a forest glade, until one night his jealous wife surprised the two lovers there with a dagger. The next day the count was found with his throat cut. The countess escaped suspicion despite a mysterious red mark on her face. Soon afterward she bore a son named Karle, on whom the same red mark appeared when he turned seven, earning him the name Karle le Rouge. For seven generations all the family's children had this red mark, until the sorceress's anger was appeased. The name Karle le Rouge eventually became Carrouges, or so the story goes. The color red also figured in the family arms: a crimson field sown with silver fleurs-de-lis.

The family's violent past may have been folklore, but from Carrouges blood sprang a line of fierce warriors. One early lord of Car-

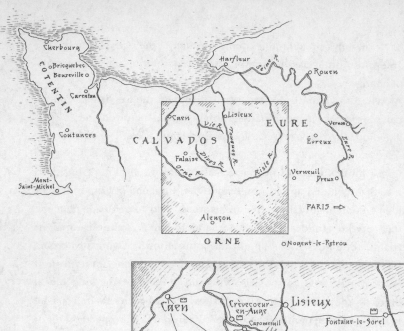

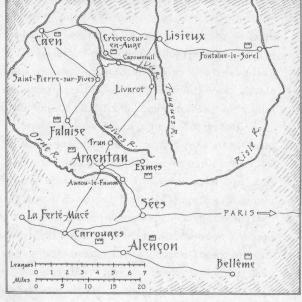

NORMANDY IN 1380.

The Carrouges family, vassals to the counts of Perche and Alençon, held lands in the parts of Normandy now known as Calvados and the Orne. The roads shown here are medieval routes.

rouges, Sir Robert de Villers, fought under King Philip II in the early 1200s to win Normandy back for France. In 1287 one of his descendants, Richard de Carrouges, served as a pledge in a judicial duel, swearing to fight in the principal's place if he failed to appear for battle.

Jean III's eldest son, Jean IV, was a born warrior. His warlike visage once stared from the wall of Saint-Étienne's abbey in Caen, where a mural showed him standing in full armor next to his heavy warhorse, sword and lance at the ready. But his image has long since faded into oblivion, and with it the tough, determined features of a warrior descended from the fierce Northmen. Brought up in the saddle, the younger Jean probably had little education, since surviving documents bear only his seal and not his signature. In 1380 he held the rank of squire.* Rather than the "gallant youth" this term often brings to mind, he was a battle-hardened veteran already in his forties, one of those "mature men of a rather heavy type—knights in all but name." He seems to have been a hard, ambitious, even ruthless man, given to angry outbursts if thwarted in his aims, and capable of holding a grudge for years.

By 1380, Jean IV commanded his own troop of squires, numbering from four to as many as nine, in the campaigns to rid Normandy of the English. In war he sought to burnish his name and enrich himself by seizing booty and capturing prisoners to hold for ransom, a lucrative business in the fourteenth century. He may also have sought a knighthood, which would have doubled his pay on campaign. The Carrouges family estate probably yielded 400 or 500 livres per year in rents, at a time when a knight's daily pay on campaign was one livre, while a squire received half that.

Jean had come into part of his inheritance, including some rent-producing land, at twenty-one. Upon his father's death he would get the rest, except for the smaller legacies left to his two siblings, his

---

* There were three main ranks of nobility—baron (*pair*), knight (*chevalier*), and squire or esquire (*escuier*). The counts of Perche belonged to the first rank, Jean III to the second, and his son, Jean IV, to the third.

younger brother Robert and his sister Jeanne. Robert, like many second sons of the nobility, could hope for only a small inheritance and so entered the priesthood. Jeanne married a knight, taking a portion of her father's land with her as a dowry. Their mother, Nicole, held some lands in her own name and would retain these and their rents if her husband died before her. But the rest would go to Jean, who had to ensure the survival of the Carrouges family name and pass the estate on to his own heir.

Jean's chief legacy was the castle and lands at Carrouges. The hilltop town commanded a broad plain of fertile farmland stretching northeast toward Argentan. A castle was first built at Carrouges in 1032 by Robert I, Duke of Normandy, father of William the Conqueror, and had been the site of several sieges. Located at a major crossroads and lying on a pilgrimage route to Mont-Saint-Michel, Carrouges was also the prosperous center for annual regional fairs.

By 1380 the Carrouges family had abandoned the castle in town— attacked and burned by the English—for another fort nearby. They built this later fort sometime after 1367 at the order of King Charles V to strengthen Normandy against the English—another sign of the family's loyalty to the crown. The imposing *donjon* or keep still survives as part of the elegant Château de Carrouges, most of which dates from later.

The old keep is more than fifty feet high, with granite walls ten feet thick at its base. It still has many of its original defenses—including a sloping base to deflect assaults, *meurtrières* or elongated arrow slits for firing down upon the enemy, and an overhanging parapet with slots in its floor for dropping projectiles or boiling liquids onto besiegers below. The upper floors of this *logis-tour*, or residential keep, included a kitchen, living areas, servants' quarters, and a latrine that discharged through one of the walls. An interior well assured a water supply during attack or siege. Other buildings to either side of the keep housed additional servants and the garrison. The keep itself consists of two adjoining square towers, and within its massive basement walls is a clever arrangement of doorways and arrow slits that enabled the defenders

Carrouges.

The Carrouges family built this formidable donjon *or keep to guard their lands from English troops. Fifty feet high and with walls ten feet thick at their base, it has a parapet with holes for dropping projectiles.* Archives Photographiques, Coll. M.A.P.(c) CMN, Paris.

to retreat from a larger chamber into a smaller one and shoot bolts and arrows into the space just vacated. The military architecture offers mute but powerful testimony to the dire conditions that the feudal nobility endured as enemy armies rampaged across Normandy and bands of robbers pillaged the countryside.

Besides the castle and lands at Carrouges, Jean also expected to inherit his father's coveted captaincy at Bellême and perhaps even his prestigious post as viscount. Bellême, a stronghold founded in the eleventh century on a hilltop site about forty miles east of Carrouges, had been an English possession until 1229, when it was recaptured by the French during a brutally cold winter siege. The French crown awarded Bellême to the counts of Perche, who could bestow the captaincy of this key fort as they saw fit.

As Jean awaited the rest of his inheritance, he enhanced his wealth and standing through a strategic marriage. His bride, Jeanne de Tilly, was the daughter of the wealthy lord of Chambois, whose great square fortress had walls twelve feet thick and ninety feet high. Jeanne brought some of her father's land and money to the union, enriching Jean and improving his connections among the Norman nobility. And well before Jean came into his full inheritance, Jeanne provided him with an heir—a son, probably born in the late 1370s.

Jean IV and his father loyally served their lord, Count Robert of Perche, who had inherited his domain in 1367. The count, fourth son of Charles of Valois, was a member of the French royal family and a cousin to several kings. He kept court at Nogent-le-Retrou, a fortified town about ten miles southeast of Bellême and the ancient capital of Perche. When Robert became Count of Perche in his early twenties, the Carrouges men, both father and son, knelt in the court before their much younger lord to do homage, saying, "Lord, I become your man," afterward receiving a kiss on the mouth and swearing the oath of fealty. For the next decade they attended their lord at court, yielding up their annual rents, helping to enforce his decrees, and answering his military call-ups to fight the English.

In 1377, however, Count Robert suddenly died while still in his thirties and without leaving an heir. Under feudal law, control of Robert's lands and castles in Perche reverted to his overlord, King Charles V. Following custom, the king granted Perche to Robert's older brother, Count Pierre of Alençon. Virtually overnight Jean and his father were bound to a new lord, to whom they had to do homage and swear fealty, placing their lives and destinies largely under his control.

Count Pierre of Alençon was one of the richest, most powerful barons in France. The third son of Charles of Valois, Pierre, too, was a cousin to many kings. In 1363, while in his early twenties, he was sent to England as a hostage along with other young French nobles to ensure the payment of King Jean's ransom. Pierre remained in England for over a year, returning to France in 1364, after King Jean's death.

As a third son, Pierre originally stood little chance of succeeding his father as count. But soon after he returned from England, a sudden turn of Fortune's wheel carried him aloft to great wealth and status, as his two oldest brothers entered the church, both quickly rising to great power there as archbishops but having to renounce their inherited lands and titles. In 1367, still in his twenties, Pierre became Count of Alençon and lord of a great domain. In 1371 he doubled his holdings by marrying Marie Chamaillart, a viscountess who brought him five more fiefs. Over time Count Pierre acquired still more lands, growing very rich from annual rents. When his brother Robert died in 1377, Pierre received all the holdings of Perche as well, including the fortress at Bellême and another at Exmes.

But Pierre's great wealth did not quench his lust for land, and he set about purchasing still more territory. His most important acquisition was Argentan, the fortified hilltop town about twenty-five miles north of Alençon. A beautiful town in a strategic location, Argentan had been a favorite residence of King Henry II when the English still held Normandy. Count Pierre set his heart upon having it. In 1372 he bought the town, the château, and the surrounding lands for 6,000 livres in gold.

Pierre immediately rebuilt the old palace at Argentan and took up residence there, moving his entire court from Alençon. The palace, an imposing four-story structure with Romanesque windows and three square towers topped by sharply angled roofs, still stands today. On its second floor is a great hall where the count held court, sitting in an ornately carved chair amid walls adorned by rich tapestries as he is-sued commands, presided over tribunals, and received visitors. To-ward noon trestle tables were set up in the hall, and the count dined there with his knights, squires, clerics, and guests. Here, it is rumored, he also entertained his mistresses, including Jeanne de Maugastel, the wife of one of his own vassals, with whom he fathered a bastard son. Count Pierre also fulfilled his conjugal duties to his wife, Marie, siring eight children during their first fourteen years of marriage.

Not that Count Pierre could spend all his time enlarging his do-main, enjoying his many fine possessions, and siring heirs along with the occasional bastard. As a royal cousin and a prince of the blood, Count Pierre was one of the French king's most trusted vassals in Nor-mandy, sworn to provide regular military service with the army of knights, squires, and other men-at-arms drawn from his vast domain. He fought in many royal campaigns, was seriously wounded at one siege, and for a time served as the king's lieutenant in lower Nor-mandy—all of the province lying west of the Seine.

Jean IV and his father, as Count Pierre's newly sworn vassals, made periodic visits to Argentan to attend their new lord, take part in the proceedings of the seigneurial court, and answer military call-ups in time of war. When not away for court business or campaigns, Jean III spent most of his time at Bellême, where as captain of the fortress he had to maintain the defenses and see to its supplies and garrison, numbering a few dozen men-at-arms. For this reason the knight made Bellême his main residence, living there with his wife Nicole.

The squire, who lived with his wife Jeanne and young son at the family seat in Carrouges, with his own retinue of men-at-arms, spent more time than his father at the court in Argentan. Carrouges lay much closer to Argentan than Bellême did—a little more than twelve miles compared with nearly forty, or an hour or two by horse compared with almost a full day's ride. In addition, Jean held the office of chamberlain to Count Pierre, a post to which he was appointed soon after he joined the count's service in 1377.

A chamberlain originally attended his lord in private, a role of great intimacy and trust. But over time the office became more honorary than practical. Still, as an officer of the court, the squire might be summoned on short notice to serve his lord on a special errand, or to be present for an important occasion. For serving his lord as chamberlain, Jean received a small bonus each year along with the distinction of belonging, at least in name, to Count Pierre's inner circle of courtiers and advisers.

One of Jean's fellow chamberlains in Count Pierre's court at Argentan was another squire, Jacques Le Gris. Le Gris was about the same age as Carrouges, and the two men were old friends. Their friendship had been formed in the service of the Count of Perche, for Le Gris, too, had been one of Count Robert's vassals until 1377, when Robert died and his lands and men were transferred to Count Pierre. So the two squires had arrived together at Argentan, new vassals to Count Pierre, both eager to prove their worth in loyal service to their new lord.

Although Le Gris held noble rank, his family was of humble origin, and their name was not nearly as old or distinguished as Carrouges. Its first written trace dates to 1325, when Guillaume Le Gris, Jacques's father, is mentioned in a charter. But over the next half century this family of shrewd and ambitious social climbers grew rich in land and other wealth, acquiring many valuable fiefs in Normandy and rising steadily in the ranks of the nobility. The Le Gris family arms bore the same colors as those of Carrouges, but in reverse—a silver field slashed with a crimson stripe.*

Jacques Le Gris was a large and powerful man, known for his

---

* Both coats-of-arms suggest the family name by the color of the field (background), red (*rouge*) for Carrouges, and silver or gray (*gris*) for Le Gris.

strength of arm and viselike grip. A squire and a man-at-arms, he had been captain of the key fortress at Exmes since 1370. Le Gris, unlike his fellow squire and friend, was also educated, being a cleric in minor orders—meaning that he could read and was trained to assist at the mass, although he had not taken the vow of celibacy. Indeed, Le Gris was married and had fathered several sons. There are hints that he was also known for seducing women—not unusual for either squires or clerics—and for joining in Count Pierre's revels with his mistresses.

Jacques Le Gris's friendship with Jean de Carrouges went back for many years, and at the time the two men joined Count Pierre's service they were on terms of great warmth and trust. When Jean's wife Jeanne gave birth to their son, Jean asked Jacques to stand as godfather. This was a great honor in the Middle Ages, especially among the nobility, for whom a godparent was virtually a family member. At the christening, conducted as soon as possible after the infant's birth to guard its vulnerable soul, Jacques held the child in his arms at the baptismal font. As the priest immersed the boy in the consecrated water, Le Gris swore to guard him from the Devil and protect him for seven years "from water, fire, horse's foot, and hound's tooth."

If Jacques Le Gris had prospered under Count Robert, his fortunes soared under Count Pierre. Like his old friend Carrouges, Le Gris was named one of Count Pierre's chamberlains soon after joining his service. But the wealthy squire quickly made himself so useful, at one point even lending Count Pierre nearly 3,000 francs, that his grateful lord singled him out for special favor.

In 1378, just one year after the two squires joined his court, Count Pierre gave Le Gris a very lavish gift: a large and valuable estate, Aunou-le-Faucon, that Pierre had only recently acquired himself. The gift compensated Le Gris for his loyal service to the count, including his recent and surprisingly large loan. Since the gift of land quickly followed the loan, it is even possible that Le Gris's money enabled Count Pierre to buy Aunou-le-Faucon in the first place—that Le Gris, in effect, helped Count Pierre finance the deal.

Such an ostentatious gift of land inevitably sparked jealousy and envy among the other courtiers at Argentan, all rivals for the count's patronage. It must have especially displeased Jacques Le Gris's old friend and fellow courtier, Jean de Carrouges. Jean's family was much older and more distinguished than Jacques's, but clearly Le Gris's star was rising much faster in Count Pierre's court. Both men were chamberlains, but only Le Gris was captain of a fort, Exmes. As Count Pierre's protégé, Le Gris also frequented the royal court in Paris. And as the count's new favorite, he was rapidly growing even richer. Despite the long and warm friendship between the two squires, Le Gris's success and prosperity rankled Jean de Carrouges, and relations between the two men began to cool.

Sometime in the late 1370s, not long after the two squires swore fealty to Count Pierre and joined his court at Argentan, Jean de Carrouges suffered a calamitous loss: his wife Jeanne fell sick and died. This terrible blow was soon followed by another catastrophe, as the son born to the couple several years earlier—Jacques Le Gris's godchild—also died. At nearly one stroke, Jean was suddenly deprived of his wife and his only living heir.

The cause of Jean's grievous double loss could have been any of the numerous diseases that ravaged medieval Europe and swept through the populace with devastating regularity—including plague, typhus, cholera, smallpox, and dysentery—for which there was no known cure. Possibly Jeanne died in childbirth, a frequent cause of death among medieval women, who gave birth in highly unsanitary conditions and without any medical recourse if there were complications, as there often were. Many women simply died of infection after giving birth.

Soon after losing his family, Jean de Carrouges left home to risk his own life in battle. In 1379 the ailing Charles V resolved to drive the English from Normandy before leaving the kingdom to his son, still only ten years old, and he raised an army under the command of Sir Jean de Vienne, the renowned admiral of France. Jean de Carrouges joined the royal campaign in the autumn of 1379, serving under Admiral Vienne in lower Normandy with his own paid troop of other squires. Like Jean, each man had to outfit himself with armor, weapons, servants, and horses, receiving a daily wage of half a livre.

The campaign lasted nearly five months and took Carrouges all over the Cotentin peninsula, which the English had been looting from their stronghold at Cherbourg. Various *montres* or musters dating from late October 1379 to early March 1380 show Jean and his troops moving jaggedly through the Cotentin in a sideways Z—from Beuzeville in the northeast, then south to Carentan, then northwest to Briquebec, near Cherbourg, and finally south to Coutances, about halfway between Cherbourg and Mont-Saint-Michel. Carrouges's command grew from four squires in October to nine in January, then fell again to only four in March, perhaps because of casualties.

Despite the inevitable danger, Jean de Carrouges probably welcomed the chance to go to war. The Cotentin campaign took the widowed squire away from his lonely life at Carrouges and threw him into the familiar excitement of battle and adventure with his comrades-in-arms, men from his household retinue or others whom he must have known quite well.

But as Carrouges repeatedly risked his life fighting the English, even losing some of his men in battle, he knew that he also risked the extinction of his name and family line. If he were killed, his name would die out and his estate would pass out of the Carrouges line. If he survived, he had to marry again—and marry well—as soon as possible. His brother was a priest and would leave no legitimate heirs; his sister had lost the family name upon marrying. It was up to Jean to ensure the survival of the Carrouges legacy.

As Jean traveled about the Cotentin, stopping between battles at towns and castles such as Beuzeville, Carentan, and Coutances, he kept his eye out for eligible young noblewomen. As an occasional guest in the great hall of the local lord or the captain of a fort, the squire had a chance to meet young women of the Norman nobility at table and to size them up as potential marriage partners.

Behind the smiles and compliments of courtship lay the serious business of feudal matrimony, which was not mainly about love or romance but about land, money, power, family alliances, and the production of heirs. The squire's ideal bride would be of noble descent and wealthy, with a dowry that would enrich him and enlarge his estate. She had to be young and fertile as well, to provide healthy sons, although there was no way to guarantee that with a virgin. And she had to be virtuous and chaste to ensure legitimate heirs. If the girl was pretty, too, there was no harm in that.

2

THE FEUD

❧

In 1380, the year that France crowned a new king, Jean de Carrouges successfully ended his quest for a new wife. Not long after he returned from the Cotentin campaign, the widowed squire married an heiress named Marguerite. The only daughter of an old Norman family, Marguerite had never been married before and was perhaps still in her late teens at the time of her betrothal. Young, noble, wealthy, and also very beautiful, she seemed the ideal bride for a nobleman eager to secure his family name and estate. As her father's sole heir, Marguerite would bring a rich dowry and eventually inherit still more land and wealth.

By all accounts, Marguerite was an exquisite young woman. One chronicler describes her as "young, beautiful, good, sensible, and modest"—the last term implying that despite her beauty she was no flirt or coquette. Another portrays her as "a very beautiful and courageous woman." Only one account, written by a monk deeply suspicious of women in general, fails to praise Marguerite's beauty or character. Jean de Carrouges himself later testified in court that his second wife was "young and beautiful" as well as "virtuous and chaste," although clearly he was a biased witness who by then had a legal ax to grind.

Marguerite's portrait once graced the same abbey wall in Caen that showed her warlike husband, but her face, too, has been erased by time, and no detailed physical description of her survives. However, authors and artists left many accounts of what they admired in female beauty. An ideal lady of northern France had light-colored hair, a gleaming white forehead, arched eyebrows, blue-gray eyes, a shapely nose, a small mouth with full red lips, sweet breath, and a dimpled chin. She also had a slender neck, a snow-white bosom, and "a body well-made and svelte." She wore a long linen gown or *chainse*, ordinarily white but brightly colored for festive occasions. Most noblewomen wore jewelry, too—a brooch or a necklace, and perhaps a gold ring set with gems.

As the lady of the castle, or *châtelaine*, Marguerite was expected to manage the household and to help her husband govern his estate. Although perhaps still in her teens, she would take charge of the castle during Jean's frequent absences to visit court or go to war, wearing at the waist of her long trailing gown a great bunch of keys that opened the cellars, chests, and storerooms. She would direct the servants in their daily tasks, supervise the child-rearing, and see to the comfort of any guests, as well as preside at the high table over the communal meals in the great hall. And at least privately, she might also advise her husband on the business of the court and other matters, since she had political influence among her own noble relatives and friends.

Marguerite was also supposed to maintain a ladylike demeanor and behave with perfect propriety. She had to be courteous, pious, charitable (showing what is still called noblesse oblige), discreet, and above all loyal to her husband. For the purity of aristocratic bloodlines, it was crucial that "a wife receive only one seed, that of her husband, lest intruders issued from another man's blood take their place among the claimants to the ancestral inheritance." Whatever liberties noblemen allowed themselves with peasant women on their estates or mistresses in town, they insisted on absolute chastity in their own wives.

In marrying a well-bred girl who combined beauty with virtue, Jean de Carrouges had some assurance that Marguerite would be a loyal wife and bear him legitimate heirs. Marguerite was many years Jean's junior, and the squire had doubtless heard the popular saying that warned, "An old man seldom has a young wife to himself." Still, older noblemen often married much younger women, since youth implied fertility and was thought to promise healthy heirs.

Marguerite had only one real fault that at first may have caused Jean some doubts about marrying her. She was the daughter of the infamous Robert de Thibouville, a Norman knight who had twice betrayed the kings of France. Sir Robert's twin acts of treason had taken place well before Marguerite was born in the early 1360s. But his treachery had left a cloud over the family, and Marguerite had grown up as "a traitor's daughter."

The Thibouville name is even older than Carrouges, and like Carrouges it still marks the Normandy landscape. Marguerite's family came from the Eure, the wet and fertile region just south of where the Seine loops past Vernon and Les Andelys on its way to Rouen and the sea. Her father's castle, Fontaine-le-Sorel, stood in the pretty valley of the river Risle, near the old Roman road running west from Évreux to Lisieux.

From this place came the first Robert de Thibouville, whose son served under William the Conqueror at the Battle of Hastings. In 1200, Robert de Thibouville II served as a sworn pledge—or second—in a judicial duel. Around this time the Thibouville family arms were established: a silver field split by a horizontal band of blue, bordered above and below by a row of three red ermines—a heraldic device resembling an inverted fleur-de-lis.

Marguerite's father, Robert de Thibouville V, nearly lost the rich family patrimony carefully built up over three centuries when he joined with other Norman rebels and fought against King Philip VI in the 1340s. Captured in battle and summoned before the king and his Parlement to answer charges of treason, Sir Robert barely escaped with his life and spent three miserable years in prison. Despite his brush with death and dishonor, he revoked his oath of fealty again a decade later—this time to King Jean—and fought for Charles the Bad, king of

Navarre, a rival claimant to the French throne. But once more Sir Robert cheated the king's headsman, and he was pardoned along with more than three hundred other Norman rebels in 1360.

Sir Robert soon reestablished himself. By 1370 he was military captain of Vernon, a key fortress guarding the Seine about thirty miles south of Rouen, with a great round tower seventy-five feet high. In the same year Sir Robert married Marie de Claire, indicating that by this time his first wife had died, leaving Marguerite motherless while still a child of perhaps only eight or ten.

Marguerite was born after her father's imprisonment, but losing her mother at an early age and growing up in a household governed by her stepmother must have left deep marks on her. Her father's remarriage also reduced her inheritance, since her stepmother, Marie, acquired a claim to some of the Thibouville estate. As Sir Robert's only child, however, Marguerite would still bring a large dowry and inherit a good deal of land and money.

Jean de Carrouges likely met Marguerite through her cousin, Guillaume de Thibouville, who was lord of Crèvecoeur-en-Auge, an important fort a few miles north of Capomesnil, one of the Carrouges family estates. Marguerite's wealth must have powerfully attracted Jean, perhaps even more than her beauty or nobility. Still, at first Jean may have hesitated to betroth himself to Marguerite because of her family's checkered history, worrying that he might jeopardize his standing with his new lord, Count Pierre, whose court he had joined only three years earlier. As a wartime hostage and the king's cousin, Pierre doubtless scorned the pardoned Norman rebels. And he may have wondered why Jean de Carrouges, his valued chamberlain and trusted vassal, was now marrying one of the Thibouvilles, who had twice betrayed the kings of France, treacherously serving their enemies.

But one of Pierre's fellow hostages in England had been a Thibouville. And Pierre himself had recently purchased Aunou-le-Faucon— the estate he gave to Jacques Le Gris—from none other than Marguerite's father. Perhaps Pierre's desire for this valuable land, which bordered his domain, overcame his scruples about doing business with an old enemy. Or perhaps he was willing to honor the spirit of the royal pardon granted to Sir Robert some twenty years earlier, if doing so greased the way to an attractive business deal. In any case, there is no evidence that Count Pierre opposed his vassal's marriage.

Jean and Marguerite's wedding took place in the spring of 1380. The setting was very likely Sainte-Marguerite-de-Carrouges, the parish church just two miles from Jean's castle and with a name that honored the bride's own. Saint Margaret was a beautiful girl in third-century Antioch who was said to have remained chaste in the face of temptations and threats from an evil governor and who, when the Devil appeared to her as a dragon and swallowed her whole, burst free by making the sign of the cross. She was also the patron saint of women in childbirth and thus auspicious for fertility.

Sainte-Marguerite's church was laid out in the form of a Latin cross, with rounded Roman-style windows and a square Norman steeple. Here Jean and Marguerite stood before an altar lit by tallow candles and perfumed with incense, their right hands clasped together, a crowd of relatives and friends looking on. The priest, holding an open prayer book, made the sign of the cross over the couple three times as he chanted the words that sanctified their union: *"Ego conjungo vos in matrimonium, in nomine Patris, et Filii, et Spiritus Sancti. Amen."** The mass was followed by a more worldly feast in the great hall of the groom's castle, with minstrels and dancing and many guests and much wine, after which the bride's maids finally prepared Marguerite for her waiting husband, and the priest blessed the bed to ensure fertility.

The nuptial mass and the wedding festivities were preceded by another important ceremony. This was the civil marriage, which traditionally took place beforehand outside the church, on its porch, where the partners publicly stated their consent, exchanged rings and

---

* "I join you in holy matrimony, in the name of the Father and of the Son and of the Holy Spirit. Amen."

BANQUET WITH MUSICIANS.

A wedding between noble families was usually celebrated with a great feast.

MS. Harley 1527, fol. 36v. By permission of the British Library.

kisses, and endowed each other with land and wealth. The act of endowment, or *dotation*, assured both Jean and Marguerite of inheritance rights in case of the other's death, cementing the agreement struck at the time of the betrothal. The propertied nobility saw the legally binding exchange of land and wealth outside the church as prior, in every sense, to the priestly blessing at the altar inside.

Despite Jean's delight at marrying the young, beautiful, and wealthy Marguerite, his mood on his wedding day may have been sobered by the terms of the marriage contract sealed on the church porch. His bride's dowry, however attractive, lacked a certain piece of land that Jean coveted. This was Aunou-le-Faucon, which Marguerite's father had sold to Count Pierre of Alençon in 1377 and which the count gave to Jacques Le Gris the following year. The sale brought Marguerite's father more than 8,000 livres and may have fattened Marguerite's dowry, but the loss of the land itself—and the potential rents, and the inheritance rights—angered the squire.

Two years earlier Jean de Carrouges had recognized that the gift of Aunou-le-Faucon showed Count Pierre's preference for Le Gris over himself and marked him as the new court favorite. But Jean hardly suspected at the time that Le Gris's good fortune would come at his own expense. Only after he decided to marry Marguerite, raising the question of her dowry, did he realize that Aunou-le-Faucon had slipped through his own fingers and into the hands of his rival.

When Jean saw that he could have acquired this fief himself as part of his wife's dowry, he took action. Starting a lawsuit to recover the land, he challenged the sale and transfer of Aunou-le-Faucon, despite the fact that Le Gris had already possessed it for some time. By May 1380, the quarrel over this piece of land had grown so loud and bitter that it came to the ears of the French king.

In the spring of 1380, Charles V had but a few months to live and would soon bequeath his war-torn and heavily taxed nation to his underage son. Weighed down by the endless war with England, the huge unpaid ransom for his father, popular revolts against new taxes, and many other crises in his realm, Charles received a petition from Count Pierre asking him to guarantee a gift of land to one of his vassals. The count, for his part, wanted to quash the dispute over Aunou-le-Faucon once and for all by obtaining royal approval for the gift. The ailing and preoccupied king, presented with this request from Count Pierre, his cousin and also one of his most powerful lieutenants in Normandy, readily complied.

On May 29, 1380, at the royal château of Beauté-sur-Marne, just outside Paris, the king presented Count Pierre with a charter confirming the count's gift of Aunou-le-Faucon to Jacques Le Gris. The royal charter specified that the land had compensated the squire for his many loyal services to the count, including the recent loan of 2,920 gold francs—a sum specified in the document. The estate was "an irrevocable gift" that Count Pierre promised to "guarantee, defend and deliver" against all others—a legal allusion to the suit raised by Jean de Carrouges. The king signed the charter, sealed it with green wax, and ordered it to be read aloud to the inhabitants of Aunou, leaving them in no doubt as to their true lord and master. This public declaration took place on June 10 at the Aunou parish church before an audience of thirty-nine people. Jean de Carrouges clearly had lost his case. The royal charter separated him from the coveted fief as firmly as a high, thick wall.

The risks of marrying a traitor's daughter were minor compared with the damage Jean inflicted on himself by quarreling over Aunou-le-Faucon. He had offended and alienated his old friend and fellow chamberlain Jacques Le Gris, while failing to reclaim the lost fief. He had opposed Count Pierre, his liege lord and main source of patronage and protection. And he had raised unpleasant associations with his name in the royal court as well. After only three years in Count Pierre's service, Jean had already marked himself as a jealous and contentious man, even by Norman standards.

The friendship between Carrouges and Le Gris had weakened in recent years amid their rivalry at Count Pierre's court, and the quarrel over Aunou-le-Faucon now drove a powerful wedge between them.

Evidence of a break is the fact that Le Gris, who had once stood god-father to Jean's son, a sign of great warmth and trust, did not attend his old friend's wedding and was conspicuously absent from the crowd of well-wishers who fêted the newly wed couple afterward. Le Gris may have been away on business of his own, but it seems more likely that he was not even invited to the celebration. For Jacques Le Gris not only missed the wedding; he did not actually meet Marguerite herself until much later.

Over the next few years Jean's fortunes in Count Pierre's court sank further, while Jacques Le Gris's continued to rise. In August 1381, Count Pierre visited the royal court in Paris, taking Le Gris with him in his retinue. There Le Gris attended a high-level council with the king's uncle, Duke Louis of Anjou. The council met to discuss the Kingdom of Naples, whose throne the rapacious duke would soon claim at the head of a crusade blessed by the Avignon pope. Jean Le Fèvre, bishop of Chartres, attended the council and mentioned Le Gris in a journal entry dated August 23 that places the squire of humble birth in very exalted company—"my lord the Duke of Anjou; myself, the Bishop of Chartres; the Lord of Châteaufromond; the Lord of Bueul; Sir Raymond Bardille; Sir Raymond Bernard; and Jacques Le Gris, squire to the Count of Alençon."

Count Pierre himself did not attend the council, sending Le Gris instead as his personal representative, a sign of the great trust he placed in his favorite. Le Gris, although only a squire from a recently ennobled family, was now gaining access to the very highest circles of the royal court as Count Pierre's protégé. Around this time Le Gris was also named a personal squire to the king—a largely honorary post that reflected the squire's value to Count Pierre, the king's cousin.

As for Jean de Carrouges, he was not even invited to Paris. After the bitter quarrel over Aunou-le-Faucon, Count Pierre had little reason to include the troublesome squire in his entourage while traveling or visiting the royal court. Carrouges, scion of a distinguished noble family and heir to a large sense of entitlement, had to stand by and watch as his old friend Le Gris, of lower birth but with a much shrewder sense of court politics, rose higher and higher in the world as his own fortunes continued to sink.

In 1382 a second and even angrier quarrel broke out between Jean de Carrouges and Count Pierre. In that year Jean's father died, leaving his lands to his son and vacating the captaincy of Bellême, the prestigious post he had held for the last twenty years of his life. Jean expected to inherit his father's post, since captaincies often descended from father to son. But it was not to be. Count Pierre, who had acquired rights to Bellême from his deceased brother Robert and so now could appoint its captain, entrusted the important castle to another man.

When Jean learned that he had been passed over for this coveted post, he was furious. Whereas the lost fief of Aunou-le-Faucon had originally been held by the Thibouvilles, Bellême had belonged to his own father, so Jean felt even more strongly that he had been unjustly deprived of a legacy. Count Pierre's decision not only reduced Jean's power and prestige; it was also a very public slap in the face. It suggested to the court at Argentan and the local nobility that Jean was not worthy to follow in his father's footsteps and take charge of the famous old fortress and its garrison. What made the insult even more galling was that Jacques Le Gris himself had long been captain of another key fort, Exmes, so that in being deprived of Bellême, Jean sank even further below Le Gris in Count Pierre's court.

So angry did Jean de Carrouges become about Bellême that he again brought suit against Count Pierre. The Middle Ages were a litigious time, the nobles of Normandy were more litigious than most, and it was not unheard of for a Norman vassal to appeal his lord's decision to a higher court, as Jean had already done in the Aunou-le-Faucon affair. Still, this second lawsuit was a risky course of action for Jean to embark on, one that would shape his life and destiny for years to come.

For a second time Carrouges failed to win his case. And once again his lawsuit only alienated him further from Count Pierre, in an age when the bond between lord and vassal was the bedrock of society and the foundation of a nobleman's career. The quarrel over Bellême did not directly involve Jacques Le Gris, but after the dispute over Aunou-le-Faucon, Le Gris doubtless sided with his lord and patron. So this second quarrel only worsened relations between Carrouges and Le Gris.

Not long after the dispute over Bellême, yet another quarrel broke out between Jean de Carrouges and Count Pierre—Jean's third quarrel with his lord in as many years, and one that directly entangled Jacques Le Gris as well, driving the two squires even further apart. This new quarrel originated when Jean made another miscalculated bid for land and power.

Eager to make good his recent losses, and having some ready cash on hand, perhaps from Marguerite's dowry, Jean decided to buy some land. On March 11, 1383, he purchased two fiefs, Cuigny and Plainville, from a knight named Jean de Vauloger. Both estates, one near Argentan and the other to the north in the region now known as Calvados, were choice farmlands promising rich harvests and excellent rents. So Jean's wish to acquire them is no surprise, although Cuigny's location—directly between Count Pierre's and Jacques Le Gris's own lands—may have been a danger sign that he ignored.

Soon the deal went sour. On March 23, 1383, only twelve days after the sale, Count Pierre asserted his prior legal claim to both estates and demanded that Carrouges yield them up.* Was Jean not aware at the time of his purchase that the lands were encumbered? Or did he actually know of the count's prior claim and simply go ahead with the deal anyway? Given the squire's contentious nature, he may have done just that. The combativeness that made him a fierce warrior and that may have saved his life many times on the battlefield was precisely his

---

* Under feudal law, hereditary fiefs held in vassalage from a lord could not be bought or sold out of the family without the lord's permission. If such lands fell vacant—that is, if the tenant died without heir—they reverted to the lord, who could then grant them to another vassal.

undoing in the court at Argentan, where tact and diplomacy advanced a man faster than sheer bravado or brute strength.

As a result of Count Pierre's prior claim, Jean de Carrouges had to yield up Cuigny and Plainville before he had taken full possession of them. Count Pierre refunded the sums that the squire had paid for these lands. But this setback for Carrouges cost him not just the land, and the rents he would have received from these valuable estates, and the right to bequeath the lands to his heirs, but also another embarrassing loss of face in the court at Argentan.

Outraged at Count Pierre's high-handed action but forced to bow to his lord's will, Jean de Carrouges vented his anger at his rival. Carrouges already resented Le Gris for ingratiating himself with Count Pierre, for insinuating himself as the new court favorite, and for enjoying the count's lavish patronage. Le Gris was captain of the fort at Exmes, while Carrouges had been deprived of Bellême. Le Gris had gone to Paris and been made a royal squire, while Carrouges had been left behind. Worst of all, Le Gris had received the valuable estate of Aunou-le-Faucon as an outright gift from the count, while Carrouges had had to buy costly land at his own expense, only to have it summarily reclaimed by his lord.

Confounded by Le Gris's success at court and his own failure, Carrouges became convinced that Le Gris had been plotting against him behind his back. All along, he concluded, Le Gris had been secretly urging Count Pierre to act against him, even benefiting personally as a result. The reason Count Pierre had seized Jean's rightful property three times in as many years—first Aunou-le-Faucon, then Bellême, and now Cuigny and Plainville—was the evil advice Le Gris had been whispering in his ear. To the bitter and suspicious Carrouges, his string of losses pointed to one conclusion: his old friend, in whom he had once trusted and confided, had treacherously betrayed him in order to advance himself. Le Gris had risen in the court by stepping on Carrouges.

Jean's third quarrel with Count Pierre, and his animosity toward Jacques Le Gris, tore away the last shreds of friendship between the two squires. Carrouges, blaming his old friend for his misfortunes, "now began to hate and despise Le Gris." Jean seems to have complained to others about his hated rival. He may even have openly blamed Le Gris in the court at Argentan, hurling angry accusations in his face.

Jean's resentful behavior only worsened his reputation as a jealous, contentious, irascible man, and he withdrew from the court. Although still officially one of the count's chamberlains, he became virtually persona non grata. For the next year or more Jean avoided the court at Argentan, which lay just twelve miles from his castle at Carrouges but from which he was now separated by a wide and bitter gulf. Called up in August 1383 to serve Count Pierre in Flanders, Jean left the campaign after only eight days in the field—a further hint of his estrangement from his lord.

This must have been a difficult time for Marguerite, scarcely three years into her marriage with Jean, as her angry and ill-tempered husband cut himself off from the court and sat in his castle keep, brooding over his misfortunes behind its high, thick walls. No doubt she got an earful about Jacques Le Gris, of whom she had heard a good deal over the past few years, but whom she still had never met.

Jean's alienation from the court, and from both Count Pierre and Jacques Le Gris, stretched out to a year or more. Not until 1384, when the feud may have entered its second year, was there any sort of rapprochement. The event that broke Jean out of his self-imposed exile from Count Pierre's court probably took place in the autumn of that year or even close to Christmas.

All across Normandy apple orchards had lost their leaves and been picked clean of fruit, and many stubbled fields lay fallow, although some were planted with winter wheat. Autumn brings cold, rainy weather to Normandy, and winter brings worse. The rain turns to snow and ice, making a muddy hash of the roads and plunging the land into a long winter freeze from which people seek shelter and one another's company around the hearth. The huge log-fed fireplaces in the great halls of Norman castles stand as tall as a man and at least as wide to warm the high, drafty rooms enclosed by thick stone walls that often remain cold and damp year round.*

Late in 1384, as the weather grew bitterly cold, Jean de Carrouges received an invitation from an old friend, a squire by the name of Jean Crespin. Crespin's wife had recently borne a son, and to mark the child's christening and his wife's fortunate rising from childbed, Crespin invited his friends and relatives to a celebration at his home. Crespin lived about ten miles west of Carrouges, near La Ferté-Macé, a town bordered by a royal forest where he served as a warden, protecting game and maintaining the royal timber supply.

Jean took Marguerite with him to join the celebration. After his angry retreat from the court at Argentan, this may have been one of his few social appearances that year. Marguerite, who had fewer opportunities than her husband to leave the castle at Carrouges, and who had spent the last year or more listening to him complain about his troubles, was probably even more eager than Jean to get away from home and mingle in the society of a cheerful crowd. At Crespin's she could count on seeing some familiar faces, as well as meeting new people, since only four years earlier she had left her father's castle far to the north to come to live with her husband.

Besides Jean and Marguerite, the invited guests included "many other noble and esteemed persons." Crespin, well connected at the royal court in Paris, also knew Count Pierre. Yet La Ferté-Macé lay a fair distance from Argentan, on the other side of Carrouges, and Jean was not likely to see many fellow courtiers there. Still bruised by his series of costly and embarrassing quarrels with Count Pierre, he may have accepted Crespin's invitation for this very reason.

And yet when Jean arrived at Crespin's and entered the great hall of the château with Marguerite at his side, there was Jacques Le Gris in the crowd, drinking wine and celebrating with the other guests. Marguerite, of course, had never met the squire. And what she knew

---

* Chronicles indicate that during the early to mid-1380s, Normandy experienced a number of harsh winters, with frequent snowfalls.

of him she had learned mainly from her husband, who had had nothing good to say.

Carrouges and Le Gris—once close friends, then rivals, and now enemies—caught each other's eye across the room. Other guests who noticed the exchange of glances paused in their merriment, like people who have seen lightning and are waiting for the thunderclap. The rivalry between the two squires had been a lively subject of gossip, and their acrimonious falling-out in Count Pierre's court over land, titles, and patronage was well known among the local nobility.

But there was no angry outburst, no exchange of insults, no challenge or threat. Nor was there a nonchalant attempt to ignore each other's awkward presence in the room. Rather, the two squires began moving toward each other, helped along by the good cheer all around them and the abundantly flowing wine. The chatter and laughter in the torchlit hall died down, as all eyes turned their way.

For the festive occasion, each squire wore a short jacket or doublet slashed with his family color—red for Carrouges, gray for Le Gris. The two men stopped near the center of the hall, face-to-face but a few feet apart, watching each other carefully.

Jean stepped forward first, his right hand extended. Le Gris met him halfway, moving quickly on his feet for his size, and seized Jean's offered hand in his powerful grip.

"Carrouges!" said the squire in gray, smiling.

"Le Gris!" said the squire in red, smiling back.

Greeting each other and clasping hands, the two squires put an end to their quarrel and made peace. The tension in the room dissolved. The nobles watching from around the hall shouted their approval while the ladies clapped, and Crespin stepped forward to congratulate the two men.

It is hard to believe that this was purely a chance encounter. Crespin knew both Carrouges and Le Gris, and perhaps he acted at Count Pierre's behest to help reconcile the two feuding squires. Carrouges, capable of holding a grudge for years, finally may have recognized while brooding in his castle that prolonging his quarrel with Le Gris would only hurt him further. And perhaps Le Gris, after several years of worsening relations with Carrouges and then their bitter falling-out, was willing to try to patch things up.

Whatever lay behind the encounter, something even more surprising happened next. After greeting and embracing Le Gris, Jean turned to Marguerite and told her to kiss the squire as a sign of renewed peace and friendship. Marguerite, bejeweled and elegantly dressed for the celebration in a long, flowing gown, stepped forward to greet Jacques Le Gris and kissed him on the mouth, as was the custom. The surviving account leaves no doubt about the fact that it was *she* who kissed *him*.

Given her husband's bitter falling-out with his fellow squire, Marguerite is not likely to have felt much goodwill toward Le Gris. Over the past several years Jean had painted Le Gris in the worst possible hues, adding for Marguerite's benefit some of the hearsay about his womanizing. The squire's scandalous conduct, even if only rumored, hardly recommended him to the young married woman as a friend or acquaintance. So Jean's command to Marguerite to kiss Le Gris, his hated rival and the man whom he had long blamed for his many misfortunes, may have surprised her. Even if the reconciliation had been prearranged and Marguerite knew about it in advance, she may have felt that Jean's telling her to kiss Jacques Le Gris was going a little too far—an impulsive gesture fueled by too much wine and one that he might later regret.

Jacques Le Gris was probably just as surprised as Marguerite. Hardly had he reconciled with Carrouges, after years of bitter quarreling and estrangement, than Jean's beautiful young wife suddenly stepped forward and kissed him on the lips. Over the previous few years, Le Gris had heard reports of Marguerite's great beauty, for Jean's marriage to the young heiress had been a lively topic at court. But Le Gris had never met Marguerite, nor had he ever seen her for himself, until now.

Marguerite's beauty doubtless made a strong impression on Le

Gris, as it did on everyone else who saw her. And if the squire with a reputation for scandal was on the lookout for new conquests, he may have been suddenly and powerfully attracted to the stunning young woman who briefly pressed her lips to his. It is likely that Le Gris's interest in Marguerite began at this precise moment.

3

BATTLE
AND SIEGE

The following spring, still smarting from his many setbacks in
Count Pierre's court and despite his recent reconciliation
with Jacques Le Gris, Jean de Carrouges decided to leave Normandy for a while and seek wealth and advancement abroad by joining a French military expedition to Scotland. The expedition,
launched in May 1385, was commissioned by the king of France. An
army of French knights and men-at-arms would sail to Edinburgh, join
forces there with the Scots, and then march south to slash and burn
their way through English lands, plundering towns and castles and destroying farms and villages just as crops were ripening for harvest.

Leading the expedition was Sir Jean de Vienne, the renowned military commander. Appointed the admiral of France in 1373 at the age
of thirty-two, Vienne had overhauled the French navy, organized the
coastal defenses, and led a series of celebrated naval raids against
the English. He also helped defeat Charles the Bad in 1378 and led
the Cotentin campaign in 1379, when Jean de Carrouges had served
under him for several months.

The admiral's army consisted of more than a thousand knights and
squires, plus twice that number of crossbowmen and "sturdy varlets,"
servants who also carried weapons, bringing the total French fighting
force to about three thousand men. The expedition attracted nobles

from all over France, and Jean de Carrouges joined up with a troop of nine other squires under his command.

Carrouges was by nature "much inclined toward adventure," and the campaign gave him a chance to abandon for a while the scene of his recent embarrassments at Count Pierre's court in Argentan. A display of valor on a foreign field might even earn him a knighthood. Above all, Carrouges hoped to profit from the expedition—to bring back enough wealth plundered from English towns and castles to offset his recent losses of land and revenue at home.

Before departing, Carrouges first had to ask his lord to release him from his regular military service. Count Pierre readily granted this request. After his many quarrels with Carrouges over the previous few years, the count was only too glad to be rid of his troublesome vassal for a while. Perhaps he even hoped that Carrouges would fail to return, since the squire was still without an heir, and some of his lands would revert to Count Pierre, who could then bestow them on more favored members of his court.

Jean also had to see to his wife's safety and comfort during his absence. Enemy troops and robbers still roamed Normandy, and Marguerite may not have wanted to remain at Carrouges during her husband's absence. Or perhaps Jean did not completely trust his beautiful young wife. Men from the garrison were always about, and Carrouges lay within easy reach of other castles and courts like Count Pierre's.

So before departing on campaign, Jean took Marguerite to her father's château at Fontaine-le-Sorel, about twenty miles southwest of Rouen. Marguerite had grown up there, leaving home only five years earlier to marry Jean. Fontaine-le-Sorel may have been her own choice, even though her stepmother was now mistress there. The other alternative was staying with her widowed mother-in-law, a less attractive option.

This would be Marguerite's longest separation from Jean since their wedding, and his departure may have filled her with foreboding. Perhaps she wondered if Jean had grown tired of her after five years of marriage, or if she had displeased him in some way. She still had not provided him with any new heirs, one of his main reasons for marrying her in the first place.

But Jean himself later claimed that up to the time of his departure, the two of them, husband and wife, "dearly loved each other and lived chastely and peacefully with each other." Jean also seems to have been on good terms with Marguerite's family. When the couple arrived at Fontaine-le-Sorel, probably in April, they were joined there by Marguerite's cousin, Robert de Thibouville, one of the nine squires who would accompany Jean on campaign.

Soon afterward Marguerite saw her husband off to war. She also bade her cousin farewell. She knew that the two men would face many dangers at sea and on foreign battlefields, and she likely wondered if she would ever see either of them again.

To join the expedition, Jean and Robert had to journey with their comrades from Normandy to Sluys, a key French port on the Flemish coast where Admiral Vienne was gathering his army and assembling a fleet.

Jean and his men arrived at the bustling port in late April or early May to see the harbor lined with nearly two hundred hulks and cogs—the deep, round-hulled vessels used for sailing northern waters. Dockhands were busily loading the ships with armor and weapons, including primitive cannons, along with the huge store of other supplies needed for up to a year of campaigning abroad. Many men shipped over their horses as well—for battle, riding, and transporting baggage. The ships were also loaded with lavish gifts for the Scots, including fifty suits of armor and 50,000 gold francs locked up in sturdy chests.

Before setting sail, Admiral Vienne paid the entire army in advance for two months' service. A roll call or *revue* of the troops, conducted on May 8, 1385, shows that *"Jean de Carouges, escuier,"* was present at Sluys with the nine squires under his command, and that he was paid 320 livres—half a livre per day for each man.

On May 20 the admiral gave orders for the fleet to depart. The weather was fair and the winds favorable. The French sailed along the Flemish coast northward from Sluys past Zeeland, Holland, and Friesland, then turned west toward Scotland and the Firth of Forth.

When the French put in at Leith near Edinburgh, word quickly spread that a large foreign army had arrived, and the Scots began to complain, saying: "What devil has brought them here? Who has sent for them? Can we not fight the English ourselves? Let them go back where they came from, for we can fight our own battles."

King Robert of Scotland, not to be outdone by his people, refused now to march on England until he had been paid a large bribe. Stonewalled by the Scots and having no other choice, Admiral Vienne agreed to King Robert's outrageous demands. Otherwise he would have had no help from his allies.

The combined army of French and Scots, about five thousand strong, finally marched from Edinburgh in early July. Proceeding south, they crossed the river Tweed and headed east, burning farms and villages as they advanced toward the sea. Eventually they called a halt at Wark, a fortress built on a rocky outcrop above the Tweed.

Castle Wark had a massive keep four stories high, each with "great vaults of stone" around its entrance and "five great murder holes"—openings above from which projectiles could be dropped or shot. Wark was held by Sir John Lussebourne, who had with him there his wife and children. Forewarned of the enemy's approach, Sir John had reinforced his garrison and placed "great bombards"—heavy cannons—on the castle walls. Besides the crossbows and cannons defending the battlements, the castle had great ditches on all sides to slow down the attackers and make them better targets from above.

Admiral Vienne sent forward a herald demanding that Sir John surrender the fortress or suffer a siege. In reply, Sir John shouted insults from atop the wall, warning the admiral that he had better retreat with his troops before he fell prey to the tricks of the untrustworthy Scots. After this parley, the assault began.

The Siege of Wark Castle (1385).

As part of a French campaign in Britain, Jean de Carrouges helped capture and destroy English castles. Froissart, Chroniques. MS. Royal 18 E.I, fol. 345.
By permission of the British Library.

As a fast-moving raiding party given to slash-and-burn tactics, the French and Scots were not equipped with any heavy siege engines, such as the trebuchet, which hurled great stone balls over castle walls onto enemy roofs. Nor were their small, portable cannons capable of knocking down the thick stone walls. The castle's solid rock foundation prevented mining—digging tunnels under the walls to cause their collapse. And the need for haste left no time to starve out the well-provisioned garrison.

So the admiral ordered an escalade. His men lashed together long poles to make ladders and prepared to scramble up the castle walls, the bravest first, followed pell-mell by their fellows. Fixing their ladders under the walls, the French "performed many gallant deeds, ascending to the battlements and there fighting hand to hand, dagger to dagger, with the garrison. Sir John Lussebourne showed himself a good knight and powerful in arms by engaging the French knights as they mounted the ladders."

The attackers faced boiling liquids, burning sand, or quicklime thrown down from the walls, as well as lethal bolts shot at close range from armor-piercing crossbows. An unlucky attacker scrambling up the ladder could also miss his footing and fall to his death in his heavy armor, or find his ladder thrown back into thin air by defenders wielding long poles just as he and his comrades neared the top.

The Scots refused to take part in the siege, but French crossbowmen posted around the castle steadily picked off the English garrison with their deadly bolts, "promptly transfixing every head that appeared above the battlements." And the French attackers "were so numerous, and the attack so often renewed, that finally the castle was taken, and the knight, his wife, and children, who were within it. The French who first entered made upwards of forty prisoners. The castle was then burnt and destroyed, for they saw they could not keep nor guard it, being so far advanced in England."

Proceeding south along the coast, the invaders next marched into lands belonging to Henry Percy, Earl of Northumberland, where they destroyed more villages and farms, burning everything in their track.

As fear and alarm galloped everywhere, Jean de Carrouges and his comrades threw themselves into the maelstrom of war, slaughtering enemy soldiers and civilians alike, seizing livestock, and carrying off any valuables. A French chronicler reports that his countrymen brought "murder, pillage and fire" to the land, "destroying all by sword or fire, mercilessly cutting the throats of peasants and anyone else they met, sparing no one on account of rank, age, or sex, not even the elderly or the infant at the breast."

The English lords whose lands and castles had been laid waste soon mobilized for a counterattack. The young King Richard II, incensed at the ferocious attack on his backside, hastened north from London with another army, vowing to annihilate the French invaders and burn Edinburgh in order to punish the Scots.

The French and the Scots learned of the approaching English through spies. Admiral Vienne was as eager as King Richard for a pitched battle. But the Scots, alarmed by reports about the size of the English army and concerned about supplies, urged a retreat to Scotland so as to have their own country at their backs when facing the enemy. Admiral Vienne, not wanting to lose his Scottish allies, agreed.

Once the English crossed the Tweed, they began retaliating in kind, "giving free and uninterrupted play to slaughter, rapine, and fire-raising all along a six-mile front and leaving the entire countryside in ruins behind them."

The Scots, to the amazement of the French, let the enemy devastate their lands without putting up a fight, even granting the English free passage through their lands to save them from destruction. Admiral Vienne, dismayed by this fresh betrayal, sent word to the Scots, saying, "What are your allies, whom you called to your aid, to do now?" To which the Scots replied, "Whatever they wish."

The admiral ordered his men to arm themselves, saddle their horses, and await his signal. That night the English army encamped a few miles south of Edinburgh and fell into an exhausted sleep, posting few sentinels. At the admiral's order, the entire French army stole away under the cover of darkness, giving the slumbering English camp a wide berth as they marched quietly south.

When the English awoke the next morning and approached Edinburgh, they found its gates unlocked, its streets empty, its inhabitants fled. While the French had secretly decamped by night, the Scots in that locality had emptied the town of goods and cattle, disappearing into the surrounding country.

Not for several days did Richard learn that the French had marched back into England to burn and pillage his lands again. Enraged, he ordered his men to put Edinburgh to the torch. On August 11 the English reduced the town to ashes, although the hilltop fortress survived the flames. Then Richard led his army up the coast as far as Aberdeen, laying waste to everything as he went.

A hundred and fifty miles to the south, the French and some of their still loyal Scottish allies were wreaking havoc in Cumberland, the green and hilly county just north of the Lake District. Jean de Carrouges and his men hoped to enrich themselves further with plunder and prisoners during this second raid deep into England.

Descending along the coast, the French and the Scots destroyed everything in their path. The invaders met little opposition—"as the country was drained, and all men-at-arms were with the English king on his expedition"—until, circling back, they came to Carlisle.

Carlisle had once been a fort on the Roman frontier and an anchor for Hadrian's Wall, whose remnants still stretched over the moors all the way to Newcastle and the other coast. Now an English stronghold, the town was heavily fortified with walls, towers, and ditches and well provisioned against siege.

On September 7 the French and Scots attacked the town, bringing up ladders to scale the walls "and mustering powerful forces in a busy attempt either to destroy it altogether or take it by storm." But the vigorous attack failed. Faced with an obstacle they could not easily penetrate, pillage, or destroy, and fearing attack while deep in enemy territory, the invaders decided to call an end to their fruitless siege.

As the French and Scots headed back north, slowed down by another huge haul of plunder, disaster struck. Sir Henry Percy, son and heir of the Earl of Northumberland, suddenly attacked from the rear. The young Percy—known as Hotspur for his speed and ferocity on horseback—fell upon the invaders by night, "killing many of them and putting numbers to flight," besides taking prisoner "twenty-six persons of substance."

Jean de Carrouges and Robert de Thibouville were fortunate not to be among those captured or killed. Not all of their comrades were so lucky. A *revue* of the admiral's army conducted a little over a month later, on October 28, shows that Jean had lost five of his nine comrades. Some may have been killed in earlier battles or fallen prey to disease. But some may have been lost during Hotspur's ferocious surprise attack on the retreating French army, which proved to be the last battle of the campaign.

As the season for war drew to a close, the various armies retired from the field, and Admiral Vienne decided to winter with his tattered army in Edinburgh. Jean de Carrouges had been away from home now for more than six months, and it looked as if he and his war-torn remnant would remain in Scotland until at least the following spring.

But the Scots were no more hospitable to the French than before: "The admiral, with his barons, knights and squires, suffered much from famine, as they could scarcely procure provision for their money. They had but little wine, beer, barley, bread, or oats; and their horses, therefore, perished from hunger, or were ruined through fatigue."

The admiral made a bad situation even worse by starting an illicit affair with a princess at the Scottish court, and threats were made against his life. Many French nobles now refused to stay on until spring, saying they feared they would either die of poverty or be murdered by the Scots. Reluctantly, the admiral gave permission for any to depart who wished to.

Having come to fight the English, the French left seething with

anger against the Scots. "They obtained passage to France and returned through Flanders, or wherever they could land, famished, and
without arms and horses, cursing Scotland, and the hour they had set
foot there."

On returning to France, many knights and men-at-arms "were so
poor they knew not how to remount themselves," and some "seized
the laboring horses wherever they found them in the fields," strag-
gling home without their warhorses and riding instead on the backs of
beasts accustomed to pulling plows and wagons.

Jean de Carrouges returned to Normandy in late 1385, his coffers
emptied and his health in ruins. He had spent a fortune equipping
himself for his foreign adventure, expecting his investment to pay off
richly in the form of plunder—gold, silver, horses, and other valuables. But he might as well have thrown his money into one of the peat
bogs of Scotland. Like many of the French, he also came back sick—
with a chronic fever that left him feeling weak and exhausted, and
given to constant shakes and sweats.

Having lost his health, a great deal of money, and five comrades-in-
arms, as well as the six months he had spent abroad on the fruitless expedition, Jean de Carrouges returned with only one real prize to show
for all his trouble: a knighthood. The review of the battered French
army conducted after their return to Scotland, in late October, lists
him as "Sir Jean de Carrouges, knight"—indicating that he earned this
distinction on campaign that summer or fall.

Jean de Carrouges was nearly fifty, and so far a knighthood had escaped him in Count Pierre's court. His new rank entitled him to be
known from now on as *chevalier*, as he would no doubt insist on being
called when he returned to the court in Argentan. It also doubled his
pay to one livre per day, although he still had not collected the full
amount due to him for the campaign, so badly were the wages in arrears.

When Jean disembarked at Sluys—or Harfleur, or one of the other
French ports—he hastened to Fontaine-le-Sorel, where he had left

Marguerite seven months earlier in her father's care. Accompanying him was Marguerite's cousin, Robert, who had also survived the dangers of battle, disease, and crossings by sea.

By the time the two men arrived at Fontaine-le-Sorel, Christmas was approaching. Marguerite may have looked forward to spending another few weeks at her father's castle with her newly returned husband and her cousin. Both men were worn out by the campaign, Jean was seriously ill, and the roads were bad in wintertime.

But the knight would not linger, staying for only a brief visit. After just a few days he left again, this time taking Marguerite with him, to go and visit his mother, who also had not seen him since his departure for Scotland many months earlier.

Nicole de Carrouges, now a widow, lived at Capomesnil, a family estate about thirty-five miles west of Fontaine-le-Sorel in Calvados. Nicole had moved to Capomesnil after the death of her husband three years earlier, when Count Pierre denied her son the captaincy of Bellême. For some reason, the widow had not come to live with her son and his wife at Carrouges. Perhaps she did not wish to share the castle there with her new daughter-in-law. Or perhaps Jean and Marguerite themselves preferred things this way.

Leaving Fontaine-le-Sorel, the couple followed the old Roman road running west to Lisieux. In winter, when the roads were often muddy and slippery with snow or ice, the journey probably took them at least two days, with overnight stays in towns along the way or at the châteaux of friends. The bad roads would have slowed down even a man traveling alone on a strong horse. And the winter of 1385–86, according to a French chronicle, was "wonderfully evil and hard." Marguerite rode warmly wrapped on a well-padded palfrey, or perhaps seated more comfortably in an enclosed carriage. She was attended by two or three maidservants, while several male servants took charge of the baggage train.

Riding in front of the little household procession, the knight wore his sword and kept his other weapons handy, while his men were armed with knives and cudgels to help keep robbers or brigands at bay. They were also on guard against *routiers,* the free companies or mercenary bands that lived off the land between the intermittent battles of the Hundred Years' War, prowling the countryside in search of prey and making even well-traveled highways unsafe. Encumbered by their baggage and on guard against ambush, the couple slowly made their way through the freezing Normandy countryside.

4

THE CRIME OF
CRIMES

M arguerite was hardly pleased to leave her father's castle and travel over rough and difficult roads in the dead of winter in order to visit her mother-in-law. Nicole's lonely château at Capomesnil did not offer the comforts or diversions of Fontaine-le-Sorel. In addition, there was her husband's health to think of. After months of campaigning and a sea crossing, and now with his chronic fever, Jean badly needed a rest instead of another midwinter journey. As the couple and their retinue bumped along the rutted, snow-streaked roads toward Capomesnil, Marguerite also may have felt a sense of foreboding about how Nicole would receive her. After more than five years of marriage, she still had not borne Jean any heirs, something her mother-in-law might fault her for during the visit.

Dame Nicole had never forgiven her son for rashly marrying the traitor's daughter some five years before, and for joining the illustrious name of Carrouges to the dishonored name of Thibouville. She knew, of course, that Jean had been smitten by Marguerite's beauty and attracted by her father's great wealth. Land and money were always to be desired, and Marguerite would inherit still more property upon her father's death. But a noble family's reputation was priceless, especially in Normandy, long a hotbed of conspiracy and rebellion, where the wrong alliance could sink a family's fortunes. A few years after the wedding, when Nicole's husband died, had not Count Pierre denied her son the captaincy of Bellême that was his by rights? Why, Dame Nicole, now nearly seventy, could have lived out her days in the splendid fortress once held by Saint Louis instead of her modest retreat at Capomesnil, if her headstrong son had not angered the count by marrying Marguerite. At Bêlleme everyone had paid court to her as Sir Jean's lady-wife. No one came to visit her now at Capomesnil except peddlers and lepers, and Nicole blamed her exile there in no small part on Marguerite, mistress of the larger and finer castle at Carrouges.

After Jean and Marguerite passed through Lisieux, a cathedral town where they may have stopped for the night with their servants, they left the old Roman highway and turned onto a country road running southwest toward the abbey town of Saint-Pierre-sur-Dives. About eight miles from Lisieux, a little over halfway to Saint-Pierre, they crossed the river Vie at the village of Saint-Julien-le-Faucon. There they turned onto a narrow track running west along the river's south bank.

After a few miles they came to a bluff overlooking the river, and a cluster of ten or twelve thatched houses inhabited mainly by farmers and tenants who worked the land. This humble place was Capomesnil. Near the hamlet, but standing by itself farther up the riverbank, was the lonely old château where Nicole lived.

The château was not large, having a main hall on the ground floor, a kitchen and servants' quarters in back, and upstairs living quarters consisting of several rooms reached by an internal stairway. It also had a sturdy keep or *donjon* for protection, but no encircling walls of any height, or defensive towers, and it was "situated in open country and far removed from any fortified place." The château no longer exists, having been demolished soon after the French Revolution, but it resembled many of the other small châteaux or manor houses that still dot the Normandy landscape. In this remote and unfrequented spot, Nicole lived quietly with a few servants and very few visitors. The near-

CAPOMESNIL.

Jean left Marguerite at his mother's modest château, situated on the south bank of the river Vie, when he went to Paris in January 1386. Detail from Cassini de Thury, Carte de France, *no. 61 (ca. 1759).* Charles Stuart de Rothesay Papers, Department of Special Collections, Charles E. Young Research Library, UCLA.

est inhabited place, besides the hamlet, was the village of Saint-Crespin, across the river and on the crest of a hill nearly a mile to the north.

Marguerite probably hoped that her stay at Capomesnil would not last very long, and that after a few days she and Jean would resume their journey, returning home to Carrouges and their castle there, from which she had been away for most of the past year. But she may have known or suspected otherwise, given Jean's constant worries about money since his return from Scotland. As it turned out, her stay at Capomesnil would stretch out to a month or more, and during that time she would see more of her mother-in-law than of her husband.

Almost as soon as the couple arrived, Jean prepared to set out on yet another journey, despite the bad weather and his wretched health. Having spent a fortune on the disastrous foreign campaign, and failing to recoup his investment through plundered wealth, let alone make a profit, he desperately needed cash. His income scarcely covered his normal expenses, even if supplemented by rents from Marguerite's lands. He had unpaid debts for horses and supplies purchased for the expedition; and his own wages were still in arrears. So Jean decided that he must travel to Paris to collect the sizable sum owed him by the king's war treasurer, Jean le Flament. He might also call on some wealthy and influential friends in Paris who could help him secure royal patronage.

If Carrouges had not quarreled so often with Count Pierre, he might have had to travel no farther than Argentan to get the money he needed. Count Pierre was almost prodigal in showering gifts on his court favorites, especially Jacques Le Gris. But after the knight's many bitter disputes with his lord, and despite his reconciliation with the count's favorite before leaving for Scotland, he stood little chance of getting his lord's sympathy or help. And pride would never permit Carrouges to ask for help from Le Gris himself, despite the squire's wealth and their recent reconciliation.

But Carrouges still planned to stop at Argentan on his way to Paris. The town lay along the most direct route from Capomesnil to the city. Moreover, he had to report his return from Scotland to Count Pierre, who had released him from his regular military duty the previous spring. Carrouges, nearly bankrupt and in bad health, was hardly fit for battle or other official duties, and a winter campaign was not likely in any case. But he was still Count Pierre's sworn vassal, and duty demanded that he pay a visit to his lord.

Carrouges may have been drawn to Argentan by more than just duty. Perhaps he wanted to see if the court would welcome him back. Perhaps he wanted to boast to the other courtiers about his newly acquired knighthood, or surprise and confound those who had not expected him to return from his risky adventure abroad. He knew that some had hoped to profit by his death. Jean still had no heir, so much of his property would revert to Count Pierre, who could then bestow it on other vassals.

Carrouges also knew that at Argentan he might meet up with Jacques Le Gris, who had not volunteered for the Scottish expedition but stayed home to look after his own interests. The previous year, when the two men had reconciled at the home of Jean Crespin, had Le Gris's assessing eye lingered a little too long on Jean's beautiful young wife after their embrace? Perhaps. But Marguerite had spent much of the past year far away at her father's castle. And now, although much closer to Argentan, she was safely under Dame Nicole's watchful eye.

Still, Jean's estate was not the only thing that a courtier like Le Gris might covet. Before departing on his journey, which would take him away from his wife for several weeks, Jean called aside one of Marguerite's maidservants and instructed her never to leave her mistress's side, day or night, until he returned from Paris. In such matters, a husband could never be too careful.

Jean de Carrouges set out for Argentan during the first week of January 1386. He began the journey of about twenty-five miles—at least a half day's ride, especially on bad winter roads—by heading east along the south bank of the river Vie, past Saint-Julien-le-Faucon. Near Livarot he turned south and picked up an old Roman track that led up to high, hilly ground overlooking the Dives river valley and the vast Falaise plain. Much of the land he saw spread out before him belonged to Count Pierre.

Gradually descending from the heights, Carrouges crossed the Dives near Trun and headed up the other side of the river valley. A few miles on he passed through the Grande Gouffern forest, thick and dark with ancient pines. Emerging from the trees, he saw the walls and towers of Argentan rising ahead on a rocky height.

An ancient stronghold once held by the English, Argentan was where King Henry II got the news shortly after Christmas in 1170 that four of his knights had secretly crossed the Channel and murdered the archbishop of Canterbury, Thomas Becket. In the 1380s the town was girdled by a thick stone wall with sixteen great round towers.

Carrouges rode up to the town's well-guarded gate, where he was recognized as one of Count Pierre's men and allowed to pass. He headed for the palace, the grand four-story château with three great towers that Count Pierre had rebuilt after purchasing the town in 1372. There the weary knight dismounted, left his horse with a stable-hand, and went in.

After riding for many hours on harsh winter roads, Jean de Carrouges was a mud-spattered mess, and before presenting himself at court, he likely removed his soiled riding cloak and washed his hands and face in a basin of water offered by one of the palace servants. Then he climbed the steps to the great hall, where Count Pierre held court and dined with his friends and courtiers.

Jean's arrival took the court by surprise. By now some news of the ill-fated Scottish expedition had trickled back to Argentan, including the names of nobles killed in battle or felled by disease, and the plight of the impoverished survivors who had straggled back after losing their money, their horses, and their health. Having had no word of Carrouges so far, Count Pierre may have begun to think that his troublesome vassal had perished and that he was finally rid of him. Some of the count's men may have already been parceling up the knight's land. So when Jean de Carrouges, racked by fever and weak with fatigue but still very much alive and on his feet, suddenly entered the great hall, Count Pierre and many others were surprised—and even displeased—to see him.

What happened that day in the court is nearly a blank. But we know that while stopping at Argentan, Jean de Carrouges "encountered Jacques Le Gris and not a few of the Count of Alençon's other men, whom he told of his plans to visit Paris." When the knight divulged his plans to the court, he may also have revealed that his wife was staying nearby at Capomesnil with his mother. If he tried to conceal this fact, the courtiers could easily have guessed it, or learned it by other means.

The encounter between Carrouges and Le Gris may have begun amicably. After all, a little over a year before, the two men had publicly ended their quarrel and apparently made peace. But Jean de Carrouges, an impolitic and contentious man, was given to flashes of

THE COUNT'S PALACE.

*Count Pierre of Alençon held court at Argentan in his imposing palace. Here,
in January 1386, Jean de Carrouges met up again with Jacques Le Gris.*

Archives Photographiques, Coll. M.A.P.(c) CMN, Paris.

anger and sudden jealous rages. He had just spent six months abroad risking his life for France with very little to show for it. And a few miles beyond Argentan, the road to Paris would take him right past the lost fief of Aunou-le-Faucon, an old grievance that was perhaps gnawing at him again.

The knight's latest troubles, on top of his earlier misfortunes, may have pushed him to the brink, causing him to lash out at the most convenient target—the court favorite whom he had long suspected of plotting against him. Seeing Le Gris in the palace, Carrouges may have taunted him for staying at home, far from danger, while he had risked his life pursuing the manly art of war. Jean may also have boasted loudly of how he had left France a squire and returned a knight, after performing great feats of arms. Perhaps the newly dubbed knight even hinted that Le Gris, too, could improve his rank if he would only leave the safety and comfort of the court. With just a few angry or careless words flung at the squire in front of the other courtiers, Jean de Carrouges could easily have reopened old wounds and brought the dormant feud raging back to life.

Whatever happened at Count Pierre's palace that day, the encounter there between the knight and the squire apparently triggered something in Jacques Le Gris. For soon after the squire learned of the knight's plans to visit Paris, and the knight left Argentan to continue his journey, Le Gris secretly summoned one of his closest companions, a man by the name of Adam Louvel.

Louvel, a squire, allegedly served Jacques Le Gris as a procurer, introducing him to susceptible women. Apparently Louvel knew Carrouges quite well, having served under him in the Cotentin campaign of 1379–80. Louvel had a house in the small cluster of dwellings at Capomesnil, a stone's throw from the château where Marguerite was staying with her mother-in-law. Soon after the knight left Argentan for Paris, Adam Louvel galloped off in the opposite direction toward Capomesnil, under orders from his master to set a watch on Marguerite and to keep him supplied with fresh information about her.

Why Jacques Le Gris suddenly turned his attention to Marguerite is not clear. Jean de Carrouges later alleged that the squire simply coveted the beautiful young heiress and "began to consider how he might deceive and seduce her," as allegedly he had done with so many other women. A chronicler claims that "through a strange, perverse temptation, the devil entered the body of Jacques Le Gris, and his thoughts became fixed upon Sir Jean de Carrouges' wife, who he knew was living almost alone with her servants."

Perhaps Le Gris was one of the courtiers hoping to profit if Carrouges failed to return from Scotland. Le Gris was a widower by this time, and perhaps after meeting Jean's beautiful young wife, he began coveting more than just Jean's land and castles. Perhaps the squire, who possessed a valuable piece of land that nearly went to Marguerite's dowry, now wished to possess the woman herself.

Or it may have been less a desire for Marguerite than for revenge against her husband that tempted Le Gris to make a new conquest. Although the two men had publicly settled their quarrel, the squire had not forgotten—and perhaps he had not really forgiven—the knight's attempt to seize Aunou-le-Faucon from him, the quarrels with Count Pierre that had also entangled his favorite, and the hatred and suspicion that Carrouges had spread in the court. If Carrouges, during his latest visit to Argentan, hurled some scornful words in the squire's face, Le Gris, fed up with the knight's insults, may have decided to strike back at him in a way that would hurt the most.

The knight's extended absence and his wife's easy proximity may have given the squire a cunning idea. If he could secretly bed the knight's wife, what a splendid vengeance that would be, not to mention the pleasure of carrying out the conquest! Originally, thinking Marguerite susceptible, Le Gris may simply have planned to seduce the lady—a plan, as bad as it was, that turned into something far worse. With a motive, revenge against the knight, and a means, the seduction of his wife, all the squire needed now was an opportunity.

He soon got his chance. During the third week of January, about two weeks after the knight had left for Paris, Dame Nicole was unexpectedly called away to Saint-Pierre-sur-Dives, the abbey town about six miles away. The Viscount of Falaise summoned the widow to appear there before the bailiff of Caen, Guillaume de Mauvinet, as a witness in a legal case. The date set for the appearance was January 18, 1386. The journey to Saint-Pierre, the business there, and the return trip would take Dame Nicole away from Capomesnil for at least half a day.

When the summons arrived, Adam Louvel was already at Capomesnil, keeping an eye on the château from his house in the nearby hamlet, and keeping his master supplied with fresh news about Marguerite. Upon learning that Dame Nicole would be leaving Capomesnil a few days hence, Louvel immediately sent word to Jacques Le Gris.

Early on the morning of Thursday, January 18, Nicole left Capomesnil. Although it was only twelve miles to Saint-Pierre and back, and Nicole would be gone for only part of the day, she took with her an entourage that included nearly all the household servants. The widow, for reasons not clear, even took along the maidservant whom the knight had carefully instructed to stay with Marguerite at all times during his absence. Marguerite thus faced the prospect of spending much of the day virtually alone at the château. Only one maidservant reportedly stayed behind, and evidently she made herself scarce.

Shortly after Nicole left Capomesnil on Thursday morning, Marguerite heard a loud pounding on the château's heavy front door. Warming herself by the fire in an upstairs room, she wondered who it could be.

When the pounding continued, Marguerite threw a fur-lined mantle over her gown and went downstairs herself to see who it was. Entering the main hall, she cautiously slid back the panel behind the small barred window set in the thick wooden door.

She was startled to see there a man's face staring back at her. Then she recognized the face. It belonged to Adam Louvel.

When Marguerite asked what he wanted, Adam said he had come to ask a favor.

"What is it?" said Marguerite.

"It's cold out here, my lady," Adam replied. "May I warm myself inside while I tell you?"

Marguerite knew Adam, since he had a house nearby, and he had served under her husband on campaign. Now more annoyed than frightened by her unexpected visitor, Marguerite agreed. Raising the iron bar that locked and braced the door from within, she swung the heavy door open and let her visitor in. Then she pushed the door shut to keep out the winter air, without barring it again.

Standing inside the door, Adam looked around, as if seeking the fire. But when Marguerite made no move to invite him further into the house, he began to explain his errand.

He had come to see her about an outstanding loan, he said. He knew that the 100 gold francs he had borrowed from Sir Jean were long overdue, but he wondered if the knight might be willing to extend the term of the loan. Would Lady Marguerite be so kind as to ask Sir Jean, on Adam's behalf, to do so?

Marguerite knew nothing about the loan or the financial details, and she was puzzled that Adam had come to see her about this matter, especially now that her husband was away.

But before she could reply, Adam suddenly changed the subject. By the way, he said, he carried greetings for her from Jacques Le Gris, who had asked him to convey his compliments to the lady.

"The squire," Adam went on, "loves you passionately, he will do anything for you, and he greatly desires to speak to you."

Alarmed by this sudden turn in the conversation, Marguerite said she had no wish to see Jacques Le Gris or speak with him, and that Adam was to stop soliciting her affections for his master. Such talk greatly displeased her, as he could see.

At that moment the unbarred door was suddenly pushed open, and a blast of freezing air swept the hall. Marguerite turned in alarm to see Le Gris himself.

Stepping into the hall, the squire tossed his mud-spattered cape over a bench, exposing the dagger he wore at his belt, and approached the frightened lady. Seeing Marguerite back away in alarm, he stopped and smiled.

"My lady," he said, "as my servant has told you, I love you more than any other, and I will do anything for you. Everything I have is yours."

Marguerite was even more alarmed to hear these words from the squire himself. But she summoned the presence of mind to warn him, too, saying he must not speak to her in this way.

Once Marguerite made it clear she would not listen to any amorous flattery, the encounter became physical. Le Gris—a large and very strong man—stepped forward and seized her by the wrist, ordering her to sit down beside him on the bench. When Marguerite tried to pull away, he forced her down beside him, squeezing her hand in his fierce grip.

Seated unwillingly next to the squire, Marguerite could feel his hot breath on her face. Now in a great fright, she heard him say that he knew all about her husband's money troubles. Smiling suggestively in a way that sickened her, he promised to compensate her generously and help restore the Carrouges family fortune, if she would only let him have his way with her.

This frank offer of money for sex was rumored to be part of the squire's standard approach. It did not work with Marguerite.

Although held captive and nearly frightened out of her wits, she told Le Gris that she cared nothing for his money and would never submit herself to his will. And she began trying to wrest herself away, as best she could, from his powerful grasp.

Seeing he had no chance of gaining Marguerite's consent, the squire abandoned all attempts at persuasion. His smile vanished, his face turned savage.

"You'll go upstairs with me whether you want to or not," he threatened. Le Gris nodded to Louvel, who went over to bar the door.

Marguerite now realized the evil intentions of the two men. Terrified, and desperate to free herself from their violent hands, she began shouting for help.

*"Haro! Aidez-moi! Haro!"**

But no one heard Marguerite's cries of distress. Or at least no one came to her aid. Nicole had taken nearly all the servants with her to Saint-Pierre-sur-Dives. And the thick stone walls, and the barred door, muffled Marguerite's shouts beyond the château and in the nearby hamlet, where at this time of the year people kept indoors and out of the cold as much as possible.

Without bothering to stop their victim's screams, as if they knew that no one would come, the two men together began pulling Marguerite toward the stairs. Desperate, she grabbed hold of the heavy wooden bench, trying to anchor herself there. But each man seized her by an arm and pulled her loose.

As they dragged her thrashing to the stairs, Marguerite managed to shake free of their hold for a moment and threw herself down on the hard stone floor. Lying there, she swore aloud that she would tell her husband about their violence, and that he and his friends would avenge her.

Despite this further warning, Le Gris savagely seized her by the arms and tore her to her feet, while Louvel grabbed her around her waist from behind. Together the two men then forced her to climb the stone steps, as she continued shouting and struggling.

When they had finally dragged Marguerite to the top, Louvel helped his master shove her through the doorway of the nearest room. Louvel then shut the door, leaving the squire alone in the room with Marguerite.

Le Gris bent down to untie his boots. Marguerite, momentarily free, ran to the window, shouting for help as she frantically tried to open it. The squire jumped up and started after her.

Fleeing from the window, Marguerite ran for the door at the other end of the room, hoping to barricade herself on the other side.

---

* By law, shouting *"Haro!"*—or raising "the hue and cry"—warned the felon to stop his criminal act and obligated anyone within earshot to come to the victim's aid.

But Le Gris was across the room in a few bounds, running around the bed and blocking her escape.

Seizing Marguerite by the arms, Le Gris dragged her over to the bed and roughly threw her onto it. Pinning her there facedown, one huge hand gripping the back of her neck, he finished untying his boots, loosened his belt, and pulled down his leggings. Marguerite thrashed her arms and legs, but he tightened his grip around her neck until she thought it might break and she had to gasp for breath.

Leaning over the bed, Le Gris pushed aside her mantle and pulled up her gown. But as he released her neck and she felt him climb on top of her, she began thrashing around so violently beneath him that he could no longer restrain her.

Le Gris, shouting and swearing that he had never known a stronger woman, yelled for his accomplice.

"Louvel!"

The door flew open and Louvel ran in.

He seized Marguerite by one arm and one leg, while Le Gris took her by the other limbs, and together they spread her out facedown on the bed. Marguerite, greatly weakened by her terrific struggle, felt her strength begin to fade. With some rope or strips of cloth they either found in the room or had brought for the purpose, the two men tied down their struggling victim.

But even after she had been lashed to the bed, Marguerite kept crying out and shouting for help. So the squire took his leather cap and roughly stuffed it into her mouth to silence her.

Once Marguerite had been tied and gagged, she began to have trouble breathing. Exhausted from the lengthy struggle with her attackers, and with her air supply nearly cut off, her strength was draining away even faster than before, and she felt as though she might suffocate.

While Louvel stood by, and Marguerite continued to resist as best she could although tied and gagged, the squire now violated her—"having his desire of her against her will."

RAPE SCENE.

The man seizes the woman, his prominent sword suggesting what happens next.
The Romance of the Rose, *miniature.* The Bodleian Library, University of Oxford,
MS. Douce 195, fol. 61v.

After he had finished, Le Gris ordered his servant to free Marguerite. Louvel, who had been in the room the whole time, came over to the bed to untie her, carefully picking up the strips of rope or cloth used to bind her.

Once unbound, Marguerite remained on the bed, weeping and holding her disheveled clothing about herself.

When Le Gris had fastened his belt and tied his boots, he stood up and reached over to the bed to get his cap, which was still lying there, warm and wet from Marguerite's mouth.

The squire unwadded the cap and slapped it against his thigh as he stared down at her. "Lady, if you tell anyone what has happened here, you will be dishonored. If your husband hears of it, he may kill you. Say nothing, and I will keep quiet, too."

Marguerite, looking down, did not answer. Finally, after a long pause, she said in a choked voice, "I will keep quiet."

A faint look of relief crossed the squire's face.

Marguerite now looked up, staring angrily at Le Gris. "But not for as long as you need me to," she added bitterly.

The squire glared down at her. "Don't play with me, Marguerite. You are alone here, and I have witnesses who will swear I was elsewhere today. You may be sure I have covered my tracks!"

The squire took from his belt a small leather bag. It clinked softly in his palm. "Here," he said, tossing the sack of coins onto the bed beside Marguerite.

Marguerite stared back at him in amazement through her tears.

"I don't want your money!" she exclaimed. "I want justice! I will have justice!" Seizing the sack, she threw it back at him. It landed on the floor near his feet.

Le Gris said nothing. He picked up the sack, stuffed it back under his belt, and began pulling on his gauntlets.

Now Louvel spoke up. "Shall I slap her, sire, to help her remember what you said?"

Without warning, Le Gris turned and savagely struck him on the face with one of his heavy leather gloves. The blow drew blood, and the stunned Louvel stood there clutching his cheek.

"Don't you dare touch the lady," snarled Le Gris.

Then, without another word, he went to the door, hurled it open, and left the room. Louvel, without looking again at Marguerite, slunk out of the chamber after his master.

Marguerite heard their descending steps echo through the deserted château, and then the heavy door below being unbarred, thrown open, and slammed shut. Too weak to rise from the bed, completely overwhelmed by her ordeal, she listened to the crunch of boots on the gravel in the yard below. The sounds slowly faded away, until all was quiet, and she was once again alone.

People today often imagine a lawless Middle Ages where rape was rampant and scarcely considered a crime. It is true that medieval rape victims were sometimes forced to marry their attackers, who could save their own lives by agreeing to wed their victims. And marital rape was legal, since wives owed the marriage "debt" to their husbands, and girls as young as twelve were married off by their families to husbands several times their own age who were free to demand their sexual due. Rape was also a frequent fate of women in wartime, as with the French noblewomen raped by marauding peasants during the Jacquerie, a massive uprising in the late 1350s, and the Breton nuns captured and violated by English soldiers in 1380.

But medieval law codes and actual trial records show that rape was considered a felony and a capital offense. The law in France, including Normandy, usually followed Roman practice, according to which rape—defined as forcible sexual intercourse outside of wedlock—was punishable by death.* Philip de Beaumanoir, a thirteenth-century authority on French law, states that the punishment for rape is the same as that for murder or treason—namely, "to be dragged through the

---

* At this time, "rape" (*raptus*) could mean either forcible sexual intercourse or the related crime of abduction.

streets and hanged." And even in wartime, leaders often tried to restrain their men, as when the English soldiers who captured Caen in 1346 were ordered on pain of death not to harm any of the town's women, although many troops disregarded this warning.

Social attitudes toward rape varied widely. Courtly poets celebrated knights as champions of female honor, and the feudal aristocracy viewed the rape of a noblewoman as "the crime of crimes." But many poems and tales depict knights casually deflowering lowborn maidens who cross their path, and King Edward III allegedly raped the Countess of Salisbury in 1342—a now-disputed story but one widely believed at the time. Only a few medieval women had the means to raise their voices in protest against the idea that women even enjoyed being taken by force. Christine de Pisan, in her book *The City of Ladies* (1405), wrote that women "take absolutely no pleasure in being raped. Indeed, rape is the greatest possible sorrow for them."

The prosecution and punishment of rape often depended on the victim's social class and political clout. In France women convicted of lesser crimes like theft were often put to death, while many males guilty of rape escaped with a mere fine—compensation that was often paid not to the victim herself but to her father or husband, since rape counted less as sexual violence against a woman than as a property crime against her male guardian. Legal records show that clerics, men holding church office, numbered disproportionately among those accused of rape and that they often escaped serious punishment by claiming "benefit of clergy," which entitled them to have their cases tried by the church rather than by the secular courts.

The circumstances of the crime, including the frequent absence of any witnesses, often made a charge of rape hard to prove in a court of law. And in France the female victim, no matter what her social standing, high or low, could not bring charges in the first place without the cooperation of her husband, father, or male guardian. Many rape victims, threatened afterward by their attackers with shame and dishonor, chose to keep silent rather than risk ruining their reputation, or that of their family, by making the crime public. So if in theory rape was a serious crime for which the law provided heavy penalties, in practice it often went unpunished, unprosecuted, and even unreported.

Immediately after the savage attack, Marguerite had to suffer her pain and humiliation alone and in silence: "On the day when this miserable thing befell her, the lady of Carrouges stayed in the château half-dazed, bearing her sorrow as best she could." During those terrible hours alone, Marguerite must have heard echoing in her mind the squire's warning to keep silent. Her mother-in-law would soon return with the servants. What should Marguerite do?

Le Gris had threatened her with the worst sort of disgrace for a woman of her social rank. Among the nobility, honor was everything, and shame a fate worse than death. Female honor—a woman's reputation for loyalty and chastity—was especially prized. Le Gris's threat had a special sting for Marguerite, since her father's treason against the French king had left the Thibouville family under a cloud. The squire's threat may have been calculated to exploit her embarrassment about her family history. It is even possible that, in marking her as a victim in the first place, Le Gris counted on Marguerite's old family disgrace as a guarantee that she would remain silent about this fresh shame.

If Marguerite did publicly accuse Le Gris, her charge would be very difficult, if not impossible, to prove. Besides the knotty problem of proof, Le Gris was Count Pierre's favorite, and he could expect a friendly hearing in the court at Argentan, while Marguerite, as a traitor's daughter and the wife of one of the count's most troublesome vassals, would be instantly suspect. Le Gris was also well known and liked at the royal court in Paris as one of the king's personal squires. And if the knight and his wife pursued the case in the secular courts, Le Gris, as a cleric in minor orders, could always claim benefit of clergy and obtain a change of venue to a church court.

Le Gris had also warned Marguerite that if she told her husband of the rape, Carrouges might kill her. The knight—jealous, suspicious, and irascible—might not believe her and instead suspect her of covering up an adulterous affair with Le Gris or another man. Angry husbands sometimes killed their wives for suspected adultery and even got away with it as a crime of passion justified by the wife's illicit behavior. Le Gris knew Jean's jealous and suspicious nature from long personal experience in the court at Argentan, and he may have guessed that Carrouges did not fully trust even his own wife. Le Gris may also have assumed that Marguerite was afraid of her husband, playing on that fear as he warned her to keep silent.

But despite her attacker's threats, and the long odds against getting justice, Marguerite refused to be intimidated by the scandal and danger that might follow if she broke her silence. Soon after the attack, determined to divulge the crime to her husband when he returned and to be avenged upon the squire, "she fixed firmly in her memory the day and the time when Jacques Le Gris had come to the castle." By committing crucial details to memory, Marguerite prepared herself not only for her family's inevitable questions but also for the grueling public ordeal that surely awaited her once she told her terrible secret.*

The silence that Le Gris tried to coerce from Marguerite right after the assault lasted only a few days, until Jean de Carrouges returned from his business in Paris, probably on January 21 or 22. On the day of the crime, a few hours after Marguerite's two attackers left Capomesnil, Dame Nicole had returned from her own briefer journey to Saint-Pierre-sur-Dives. But Marguerite's mother-in-law was the last person in the world to whom she would have wanted to divulge her awful secret. And so, under what must have been a crushing strain and great anxiety, Marguerite kept quiet until her husband came back.

---

* Marguerite may have relied on memory because, even if she could read, she did not necessarily know how to write, a separately taught skill that many literate people never learned.

Upon his arrival at Capomesnil, Jean found his wife in a troubled and downcast state—"sad and tearful, always unhappy in expression and demeanor, and not at all her usual self." At first he suspected that there had been a falling-out between his wife and his mother. Marguerite had spent the entire three weeks or so of Jean's absence with Dame Nicole—except, of course, part of one crucial day—and so it was natural for him to think that the two women might have had a quarrel or disagreement while he was gone.

Marguerite refused to tell her husband what was wrong until they were finally alone together. "The day passed, night came, and Sir Jean went to bed. The lady would not come to bed, at which her husband was much surprised and kept asking her to do so. She put him off and walked up and down in the room deep in thought. Finally, when all of their people were asleep"—in a manor house or castle, the lord and his lady might not be truly alone, beyond the reach of eavesdropping servants, until they were together in bed—"she came to her husband and, kneeling beside him, told him in pitiful tones of the dreadful thing which had happened to her."

Marguerite put off joining her husband in bed—perhaps the very bed on which she had been tied down and violated—until she had a chance to tell him her story. Jean, after being gone for several weeks, was no doubt eager to be in bed again with his wife. But this was probably the last thing in the world that Marguerite wanted right now. Also, the violent attack by the two men may have left scars or bruises on her body. In the Middle Ages it was customary for people, including lords and ladies, to sleep naked, and before exposing herself to her husband's eyes, Marguerite would have wanted a chance to explain. Above all, Marguerite kept some control over the volatile situation by telling her story at a time, and under circumstances, of her own choosing.

Jean listened at first in amazement and then in outrage as Marguerite tearfully told him "the whole story of the foul, wicked, and criminal deed" that had been committed against her. As she finished, she pleaded with him to seek vengeance for the sake of his own honor.

Marguerite knew that Jean's honor and reputation would stand or fall with her own—a principle that from now on would join their fates even more closely than the usual shared fortunes of marriage. She also knew that under feudal law she had absolutely no legal standing in such a case without her husband's support and advocacy.

The next morning Jean de Carrouges called his family and friends together for a secret council. The knight had ample reason to hate Le Gris and suspect him of fresh wrong. Convinced of Le Gris's earlier treachery at court, he may have readily believed his wife's account of the squire's savage attack. But a premature or unpersuasive charge against Count Pierre's favorite, especially after Jean's many quarrels with the count over the past few years, could bring the knight even worse problems than he already had. A private council would enable him to get the valuable advice of his family and friends without turning the case into an embarrassing and possibly disastrous public affair.

The council, held at Capomesnil, no doubt included Nicole de Carrouges and perhaps Marguerite's cousin, Robert de Thibouville, who had recently returned with Jean from Scotland, as well as other relatives and friends, such as Bernard de La Tour, the knight married to Jean's sister. Thomin du Bois, another of Marguerite's cousins, may also have been there. When everyone arrived at the château, wondering why they had been called together in such secrecy and haste, Jean assembled them all in a room. "Explaining the reason which had caused him to send for them, he got his wife to relate the whole happening in every particular."

Again Marguerite had to describe her ordeal, this time to her gathered family and friends, reliving the terrible crime once more in all its painful and humiliating details. Completeness and accuracy were of the utmost importance, since her private account would lay the foundation for any later public testimony, which her original witnesses might be called upon to corroborate. In a sense, the family council was a preliminary legal hearing.

When the gathered council heard Marguerite's story of the brutal attack, "they were much amazed." If Marguerite's family believed her at once, some of Jean's relatives may have been initially skeptical. The Thibouvilles had a reputation for treachery, and the traitor's daughter had just told a most astounding tale—claiming that a few days earlier, she had been surprised at the lonely château and viciously assaulted by two men, and that one of them, none other than Jacques Le Gris, had raped her. Dame Nicole herself had heard nothing of the attack until now, although it had taken place right in her own home during her brief absence on the day in question. She and other members of the council probably asked Marguerite some probing questions. For example, exactly when and where had the crime taken place, how long were the two men at the château, and why had she opened the door to them in the first place?

But when Marguerite had answered all their questions and Jean finally asked his council's advice, they urged him "to go to his lord the Count of Alençon and tell him the whole story." Under feudal law, a lord was responsible for adjudicating quarrels between his vassals, so Count Pierre's court at Argentan was the only venue for the case. Of course, everyone knew that Count Pierre would hardly welcome a criminal accusation against his favorite squire. The count's reaction to the amazing story of Le Gris's assault on Marguerite might be sheer incredulity, followed by anger and perhaps serious reprisals. Carrouges and Le Gris had only recently patched up one quarrel; this fresh and even more dangerous dispute, if made public, was certain to make them mortal enemies. And Count Pierre would surely support his favorite squire against the knight.

Despite the odds against receiving a fair hearing in Count Pierre's court, however, the knight had another urgent reason to seek justice there for himself and his wife, and to pursue vengeance against the squire.

Not long after Jean returned from Paris and learned of the terrible attack on his wife, Marguerite revealed another secret she had been keeping to herself: she was pregnant.

The news must have struck Jean like a thunderbolt. The couple had been childless for their first five years of marriage, and the knight had waited a long time for an heir. Marguerite's pregnancy normally would have filled him with joy. But instead it gave him another vexing worry besides his health, his finances, his political misfortunes, and the terrible violation of his wife by a fellow courtier and former friend.

Whose child was it?

5

THE CHALLENGE

I n late January 1386, Count Pierre of Alençon heard a story that made his blood boil. Word reached him that Jean de Carrouges, one of his most troublesome vassals, was spreading a scandalous rumor about his favorite, Jacques Le Gris, claiming that Le Gris, with an accomplice, had surprised the Lady Carrouges at home during the knight's absence and violently attacked and raped her. The knight's charge incensed the count. Given the bad blood between the two men, how could Carrouges expect anyone to believe his preposterous story?

Once he learned of the rumor, Count Pierre immediately began to investigate. He ordered two respected nobles to come to his court and questioned them closely about the wild story concerning the lady and the squire. One of the men was Sir Bernard de La Tour, Jean's own brother-in-law. The other was Jean Crespin, the squire and royal forester at whose home, a little over a year earlier, Carrouges and Le Gris had supposedly reconciled and Le Gris had met Marguerite for the first time. Both men were presumably on good terms with Jean de Carrouges and knew something of his affairs.

Questioned by the count, the two men, according to later testimony, "affirmed that the said knight and Marguerite many times and in diverse places had said and made it to be known that the same Marguerite had been by the said Jacques violently and in the foresaid manner carnally known." Crespin and La Tour also reported that the knight and his wife wished to come to the count, place their complaint before him, and obtain justice.

Count Pierre replied that he was prepared to offer Jean and Marguerite a hearing, since he was responsible for settling quarrels between his vassals. Accordingly, he called his court together, assembling "prelates, knights, members of his council and other experienced men." Some of the prelates had legal expertise, and other clerics may have kept records of the proceedings (though none survive).

The hearing took place in the great hall of Count Pierre's palace, the ornate room adorned with tapestries and carpets, and furnished with heavy wooden benches, where the count held court. On the appointed day, the hall was crowded with nobles, clerics, and other courtiers. Word of the frightful attack on the lady, and of the knight's angry accusations against the squire, had spread from Argentan throughout the count's domain, and the great hall was filled with onlookers who had braved the bitter cold to see the parties in the quarrel and learn if there was any truth to the wild rumor sweeping the land.

It was no secret that Jacques Le Gris was Count Pierre's favorite. But many a feudal lord found himself having to pass judgment on disputes between his quarrelsome vassals, one of whom he often favored over the other. In this case, Count Pierre was hardly an impartial judge, although the law obliged him to be as fair as possible.

There was another problem as well. After the count had called witnesses to investigate the scandalous rumor, and after he had offered justice to Jean and Marguerite in their complaint against Jacques Le Gris, and after he had assembled his court to hear the case, the knight and his wife failed to appear on the appointed day.

Perhaps the couple's conspicuous absence, and the scant testimony about the alleged crime, prompted Count Pierre's next action. He ordered that Adam Louvel—the squire's alleged accomplice—be arrested and detained in prison for questioning. Then, with whatever new information he gained by this means, the count deliberated with his court over the charges against the squire and reached a verdict.

The court, with Count Pierre presiding, found "the said Jacques to be completely innocent and wholly without guilt." Annulling the criminal charge against the squire, the count struck it from the record, ordering that "no further questions ever be raised about it." Count Pierre also cast suspicion on Marguerite for having accused the squire in the first place. Insinuating that the lady had lied, he said of the alleged rape that "she must have *dreamt* it."

When news of the verdict reached Capomesnil, some twenty-five miles to the north of Argentan by muddy winter road, Marguerite may not have been surprised, but at first she may have despaired of ever getting justice. Still in seclusion after the terrible attack, she was no doubt furious to learn that Le Gris had been declared innocent, and that Count Pierre had virtually accused her of lying. But the news may have made her even more determined to get the vengeance she had vowed, right to Le Gris's face, after the attack.

As for the knight, the news may not have wholly surprised him either, but it must have enraged him. The count's verdict was not only a mockery of justice but also the worst insult Jean had suffered so far in his long series of public humiliations in Count Pierre's court. The news, even if received privately at home, must have struck him like a very public slap in the face.

But what else had the couple expected, given their signal absence from the count's tribunal on the crucial day and Jean's failure to make his charges there in person, backed up by Marguerite's sworn testimony? Had they failed to appear because Jean's illness had suddenly worsened? Or because Marguerite, after her ordeal, was in no condition to face the court? Had they intentionally stayed away because they were certain they would receive no real justice there? Or because they now feared for their lives from the squire's angry relatives and friends? Or was their absence part of a calculated plan to force an unfavorable verdict which they could now turn to their own advantage?

The law said that a vassal who felt that his lord had handed down an unfair verdict, a *faux jugement*, had the right to appeal the case to his overlord. Since Count Pierre was a vassal to the king of France, the knight could make his appeal directly to the royal court in Paris. Carrouges had lost in Count Pierre's court, but if the king agreed to hear his case, he might have another chance to get justice for his wife and himself.

Count Pierre seems to have anticipated the knight's next move. Hastening to squelch any possible appeal, he ordered that letters be rushed to Paris informing the king of his verdict exonerating the squire. Rumors of the quarrel between Carrouges and Le Gris may have already traveled from Normandy to Paris, several days' ride from Argentan, since both men had important friends there. But it was apparently the count himself who first made the case officially known to the royal court.

Jean de Carrouges had challenged Count Pierre's will in the royal court once before, during the dispute over Aunou-le-Faucon. But this new quarrel about Le Gris's alleged rape of his wife was a far more serious matter that raised the stakes much higher. Count Pierre already hated Carrouges for accusing his favorite, and he had tried to quash the case. The knight's defiance would greatly endanger him—and his wife. As the legal affair unfolded, the count became "so infuriated by the knight's obstinacy that there were many times when he would have had him killed."

In the late winter or early spring of 1386, Jean de Carrouges set off to Paris for the second time that year, very likely after he and Marguerite had returned home. By now Marguerite was two or three months pregnant, and if Jean left her behind again, planning to send for her later or to return for her himself, this time he left her well guarded—perhaps by a trusted relative such as her cousin Robert de Thibouville. The trip to Paris would become harder for the pregnant Marguerite as the year wore on, although as the roads dried out during the warmer months, she could travel more comfortably by carriage.

The journey of about 150 miles from Carrouges to Paris took the knight the better part of a week on the road heading eastward through Sées, Verneuil, and Dreux—one of the great routes from Normandy to Paris along which traders traveled from town to town and cattle were driven to slaughter in the capital.

The knight knew that his reception at the royal court would be influenced by many things: his past service to the king, his family connections, and the powerful web of friendships and personal alliances that shaped the politics of the court. To his credit, Jean's family had long and loyally served the kings of France. Jean himself had recently fought for King Charles in Britain, as well as in many other campaigns over the years. Some twenty years earlier, in 1364, he had also helped the royal family raise part of King Jean's ransom.

But Jacques Le Gris, although of much humbler birth, was better connected at the royal court, being a squire in the king's own service who had personally attended high councils of state in Paris. The wealthy squire enjoyed added status as the favorite of Count Pierre, a member of the royal family and a cousin to the king himself. The count's recent letters to the king about the results of the tribunal, a clear bid for royal support, were another stroke against the knight.

Then there was the problem of Marguerite. The royal court would certainly remember that Jean's wife, the woman at the center of the quarrel, was the daughter of the notorious traitor Robert de Thibouville. Sir Robert's treachery had forever tainted the Thibouville family name. And with Jean's marriage to Marguerite, just five years before, the taint had rubbed off on him as well.

Finally, there was the fact that when Carrouges arrived in Paris to present his case to the king, he planned to make a bold and unusual appeal.

Under French law, a nobleman appealing a case to the king had the right to challenge his opponent to a judicial duel, or trial by combat. The judicial duel, distinct from the duel of honor used to settle quarrels over perceived insults, was a formal legal procedure for determining which party had sworn a false oath. A combat's outcome was widely believed to reveal the truth in accord with God's will. Hence the duel was also known as the "judgment of God"—or *judicium Dei.*

Trial by combat was an ancient custom in France, especially Normandy, and both Jean and Marguerite had ancestors who had served as pledges, or sworn seconds, in judicial duels. In the earlier Middle Ages people of all social classes could resort to judicial combat, and public duels took place among peasants and townfolk as well as nobles. In parts of Europe even women were allowed to fight duels against men. The duel was used to adjudicate a wide range of felonies as well as civil cases such as property disputes.

In civil cases, the principals could hire proxies, or "champions," to fight in their place. But in criminal cases, the two parties had to fight in person, since the penalty for losing was usually death, and champions could stand in only for women, the elderly, or the infirm.

For centuries the duel was also a form of appeal, and a litigant dissatisfied with a verdict could challenge the witnesses who had sworn against him, offering to prove his claims in combat. Even the lords serving as judges in the local seigneurial courts had once risked being challenged to duels by their own aggrieved vassals.

In the later Middle Ages, however, judicial duels became more rare. Popes denounced the duel as a tempting of God, a thing forbidden by Scripture. And kings frowned on trial by combat because it infringed on their judicial authority, which they were trying to wrest away from their powerful barons and consolidate around their own thrones.

By 1200 the duel began disappearing from civil proceedings in France, while in criminal cases it was increasingly limited to males of the nobility. In 1258, Louis IX eliminated the duel from French civil law, substituting for it the *enquête,* a formal inquiry involving evidence and testimony. But this still left the duel in place as a last resort for a noble seeking to appeal his lord's verdict in a criminal case.

In 1296, King Philip IV completely outlawed the duel in times of war, because judicial combats among his nobles sapped the realm of manpower needed for military defense. In 1303, Philip outlawed the duel in peacetime as well. But Philip's nobles resented the abolition of their time-honored privilege, and three years later, in 1306, the king relented, restoring judicial combat as a form of appeal in certain criminal cases, including rape, but now only under the king's direct jurisdiction.

The 1306 decree was still in force eighty years later, when Jean de Carrouges went to Paris to appeal Count Pierre's verdict, but by now judicial duels were extremely rare. Four strict conditions had to be met for a case to qualify for a duel. First, the crime had to be a capital one, such as murder, treason, or rape. Second, it had to be certain that the crime really occurred. Third, all other legal remedies had to be exhausted, with combat—"proof by one's body"—the only means of conviction left. And fourth, the accused person had to be strongly suspected of the crime.

Besides the legal restrictions, calling for a duel was a very risky strategy that would greatly raise the stakes for the knight. Jean de Carrouges would put his own life in peril, as well as his estate and his family's reputation, and even the salvation of his soul, since he would have to swear a solemn oath damning himself should he be proved a liar by the combat's outcome.

Jean would also place his wife in jeopardy, since Marguerite was the chief witness in the case. She would have to swear her own oath about her charges against Jacques Le Gris, and if Jean lost the duel as Marguerite's champion, she, too, would be proved a liar. Since ancient times, false accusations were severely punished. If a judicial duel proved that a woman had perjured herself by swearing falsely about a rape charge, she would be put to death.

But despite the long odds against obtaining a trial by combat, and the grave risks of fighting one, Jean de Carrouges may have felt by this point that only a duel to the death would enable him to avenge the terrible crime against his wife, to prove his charges against Jacques Le Gris, and to vindicate the couple's honor. Perhaps he believed that God would favor him and that he could not fail in battle. Whatever the knight believed, as he made his way toward Paris along the rutted roads of Normandy, he was riding toward what would prove to be the most perilous adventure of his life.

In 1386, Paris was the largest city in Europe, with a population of over 100,000, although the city's walls then enclosed only about three square miles, a fraction of its more than twenty square miles today. Medieval Paris was a noisy, crowded, smelly, dangerous place. Walled and ditched against enemy armies—especially the invading English—the city was also threatened from within by riotous mobs, rebellious troops, unruly students, and a large criminal class that preyed on everyone else. Just north of the city walls stood the infamous hill of Montfaucon, where condemned felons were hanged by the dozens on a great stone gallows nearly forty feet high, their rotting corpses left to dangle for weeks as a warning to others.

Through the center of Paris ran the river Seine, the city's largest thoroughfare and also its main sewer. Its foul waters carried ceaseless river traffic around the Île de la Cité, the city's central island, adorned with some of the greatest shrines in Christendom. Near one end loomed the great cathedral of Notre-Dame, seat of the bishop of Paris, its two massive square towers completed only a century earlier, in 1285. Near the other end rose the graceful spire of the Sainte-Chapelle, the exquisite reliquary of gilded stone and colored glass built by Saint Louis in the 1240s to display precious relics brought back from the Holy Land, including Christ's Crown of Thorns and a piece of the True Cross. Nearby stood the Palais de Justice, which housed the Parlement of Paris, the king's high council.

South of the river lay the University of Paris, the most celebrated school in Europe. Here berobed doctors expounded Aristotle and Aquinas in Latin, the common tongue of the medieval lecture hall; and students, freeborn males from every nation, filled the streets and taverns and brothels with their polyglot jokes and arguments. From time to time, fed up with the local prices, they rioted against the shop-keepers or fought one another across national lines, the Germans

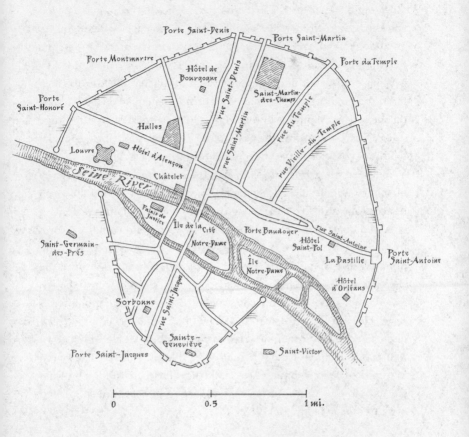

PARIS IN 1380.

Jean de Carrouges lodged near the Hôtel Saint-Pol (east), while Jacques Le Gris
lodged at the Hôtel d'Alençon (west), near the Louvre.

hurling horse dung from the streets at the Italians, or the English pelting the Scots with wood grabbed from piles of kindling stacked in the streets.

Along the main streets that crisscrossed the city, leading to a dozen gates that pierced its walls, sat the grand stone palaces belonging to great noble families, rich church prelates, and even a few of the city's wealthiest merchants. These private retreats, or *hôtels,* surrounded by gardens and set within their own walled and gated enclosures, sheltered the mighty from the masses and from the city's constant assault on the senses. Many *hôtels* were clustered near the Louvre, the huge square fortress guarding the city's western edge. One of these, the Hôtel d'Alençon, was owned by the family of Count Pierre.

Between the great routes through the city stretched a tangled web of smaller streets and alleys, thickly lined with narrow half-timbered houses four and five stories high where extended families lived in cramped quarters over their shops below. Waste and rubbish thrown from above littered the cobbles or was churned into the mud of still unpaved streets by the wheels of passing carts. Scattered around the city, one for every parish or guild, scores of churches and chapels raised their spires above the city's smoky pall. A few large monasteries stood clear of the city, surrounded by open fields or suburban gardens, like Saint-Germain-des-Prés to the south, encircled by its own wall for protection from brigands and thieves. Others, like Saint-Martin-des-Champs to the north, had been absorbed into the growing city and now lay within its newest wall, begun in 1356 and completed just three years before, in 1383.

When Jean de Carrouges arrived in Paris, one of the first things he did was consult a lawyer. Any nobleman involved in litigation at the royal court was well advised to retain legal counsel, especially if he planned to call for a judicial duel. Jean's chief counsel was a lawyer named Jean de Bethisy, who was assisted by a bailiff or court administrator employed by Pierre d'Orgement, the powerful bishop of Paris.

The lawyers doubtless told the knight that, under the restrictive laws governing judicial duels, he had only a slim chance of ever meeting Jacques Le Gris in battle, and they may have urged him to give up his risky quest.

When Carrouges remained undaunted, continuing to insist on a duel, his lawyers described the long, complicated legal process he would have to follow.

The first step was the initial appeal. This was a formal ceremony where the plaintiff, known as the *appelant,* accused the defendant, or *défendeur,* naming the cause that brought him to court and demanding his right to prove his charges in combat—or "the wager of battle," as it was also known. The *défendeur* did not have to be present in the court for the appeal, so that if he had fled or could not be found, the *appelant* was not deprived of legal recourse.

The second step was the formal challenge, a separate ceremony requiring the presence of both parties to the quarrel, where the *appelant* accused the *défendeur* to his face, offering to prove his charges in battle "with his body." At the challenge, each party in the suit had to be accompanied by a set number of noblemen serving as pledges. The pledges took oaths swearing to compel the presence of both parties whenever they were summoned to court again—and to the battlefield, should a duel be declared.

Whereas the appeal could be addressed to the king alone, the challenge had to be witnessed by the assembled Parlement of Paris, a body of thirty-two magistrates. The Parlement, also known as the *curia regis,* or king's court, had jurisdiction over all duels, deciding in any given case whether combat was warranted or not. The formal challenge before the Parlement of Paris could not take place on short notice but had to be arranged well in advance to ensure the presence of all necessary persons, including the king and his magistrates, both parties to the dispute, their legal counsel, and their pledges.

The royal decree of 1306 included a lengthy *formulaire*—an elaborate protocol governing all aspects of the judicial duel, including the initial appeal, the formal challenge, and the solemn oaths and other ceremonies that preceded the actual combat. From the moment that

Jean de Carrouges resolved to seek a trial by combat, he was bound by the strict rules and procedures of the royal decree.

The knight, accompanied by one or more of his lawyers, made his appeal at the Château de Vincennes, the royal retreat located in the vast hunting park several miles east of the city. The king had many dwellings in and around Paris, including the Louvre, the oldest royal residence; the Hôtel Saint-Pol, a palace on the city's eastern edge near the Bastille; and the royal apartments in the Palais de Justice on the Île de la Cité. But the king was often to be found at Vincennes. Charles V built this massive fortress after the citizens of Paris revolted in 1358, and here his son and successor, Charles VI, held court. Vincennes, with its huge moated keep, nine imposing guard towers, and double ring of high, thick walls, was a town unto itself, with its own shops, foundry, hospital, and chapel—everything needed by a king afraid to live in his own capital.

Carrouges was known at the royal court, having visited Paris as recently as January, but he could not just appear unannounced and see the king at will. Many protective layers of walls, guards, officials, and servants surrounded the royal person both day and night, since there were frequent attempts on the king's life. Only the previous summer an emissary from Charles the Bad, king of Navarre, had been discovered at the royal court with poison sewn into his clothing in order to assassinate the young ruler and his uncles.

Arriving at the royal château, Carrouges rode up to the massive gatehouse or *châtelet* guarding its northern wall. A great ditch, forty feet deep and eighty feet wide, fronted the wall, which rose seventy feet above the ditch and stretched for over half a mile around the fortress, studded with huge square guard towers at its corners and along its sides.

Carrouges and his party crossed the lowered drawbridge, dismounted, and announced themselves to the guards. Allowed to enter the gatehouse, they led their horses through a passageway that could

CHÂTEAU DE VINCENNES.

Jean de Carrouges appealed his case to the king at the massive royal fortress outside Paris, in the great keep or donjon. *Seeberger, Archives Photographiques, Coll. M.A.P.(c) CMN, Paris.*

be instantly cut off by a heavy iron grate or portcullis dropped from overhead.

Entering the great courtyard, which covered nearly fifteen acres, they saw to the left the old manor house of the Capetian kings, and to the right, halfway down the fort's western wall, the massive new keep built by Charles V as the main royal residence.

The great square keep or *donjon*, with its four round towers, rose nearly 170 feet into the air behind yet another heavily fortified wall and a stone-lined moat forty feet deep. Its single entrance, a drawbridge over the ditch, had its own *châtelet* manned by a separate garrison. Leaving their horses with a stablehand in the courtyard, Carrouges and his entourage presented themselves at the gatehouse and announced their errand. After a short wait, a page appeared from within the *donjon* and led them into its recesses.

The huge keep had eight floors and stone walls ten feet thick containing nearly a mile of iron rods to support its many chambers and arches, one of the first examples of reinforced masonry in Europe. The keep was the center of the king's household, with staterooms below, private apartments for the royal family above, and guardrooms at the very top. From a tower at its summit, far above the green canopy of the surrounding royal forest, the king could survey several hundred square miles of his realm, including the spires and towers of Paris three miles to the west, and the irregular hills bordering the valley of the Seine where it flowed in great loops beyond the city and toward the sea. One of the keep's upper floors had a plush private study built by Charles V to house his rich collection of illuminated manuscripts; one of the massive corner towers contained the royal treasury, a locked and guarded chamber with coffers full of gold coins. Each floor had its own latrine in a great stone spur jutting from the back of the keep. An internal well and amply provisioned storerooms equipped the château for a very long siege.

The page led Carrouges and his legal counsel through several stone chambers and up a spiral stairway in one of the towers to see Sir Bureau de La Rivière, who managed the royal household and of whom it was said, "To see him is to see the King." Once the knight explained his urgent business to Sir Bureau, he was granted a royal audience as soon as possible, unless the king were absent from Paris, or more urgent business delayed royal attention to the knight's suit.

In the spring of 1386, King Charles VI, ruler of all France, was still a youth of seventeen. Since 1380, when he had inherited the crown from his father at the age of eleven, the young king had been governed by his ambitious uncles, especially Duke Philip of Burgundy. Charles would soon shake off his uncles' control and declare himself sovereign in his own right. But for now, the inexperienced and pliable youth followed his elders' advice in most matters of state—raising or lowering taxes, waging war, making peace, forming alliances, and the myriad other duties of a monarch. The previous summer Charles had even married a girl his uncles had chosen for him, the fourteen-year-old Isabeau of Bavaria.

Charles V, the king's father, had received petitioners each morning in the courtyard at Vincennes after attending mass in the nearby chapel, or later in the day at rising from table. But Charles VI, still a youth and less at ease in his role as supreme judge of France, probably heard the knight's appeal in the Salle de Conseil, a richly decorated stateroom on the great keep's second floor.

The Salle de Conseil was about thirty feet square with a vaulted ceiling paneled in Baltic wood and supported by brightly colored stone arches—red, blue, and gold—all resting on a single pillar at the room's center. The capital was carved with fleurs-de-lis, and royal medallions adorned the vaulting overhead. Silk and wool tapestries woven with classical and religious scenes draped the walls. Dominating the chamber from a low dais on one side was the king's throne, sumptuously arrayed in blue and gold. Men-at-arms stood guard by several arched doorways, and nobles, clerics, and other courtiers stood in attendance.

Carrouges, ushered into the king's presence, first bowed and then knelt to make his plea, his lawyer kneeling beside him. The teenaged monarch, seated on his throne and flanked by his watchful uncles, gazed down upon his kneeling subject, who, at about fifty, was nearly three times his own age.

Still kneeling, Carrouges drew his sword—the sole weapon he had been allowed to bring into the royal presence—and raised it high, taking care not to brandish it at the king. His drawn sword, the traditional sign of an appeal for a duel, signaled his readiness to fight for his cause.

As he knelt before the king with raised sword, the knight said, "My gracious and sovereign lord, I, Jean de Carrouges, knight, and your loyal servant, present myself here to seek your justice."

The young king replied from his throne, "Sir Jean de Carrouges, I am prepared to hear your appeal."

In a clear voice, so that all those present could hear, the knight said, "Most excellent and sovereign lord, I do hereby charge that during the third week of this January past, one Jacques Le Gris, squire, did feloniously and carnally know my wife, the Lady Marguerite de Carrouges, against her will, in the place known as Capomesnil. And I stand ready to prove this charge by my body against his and to render him either dead or vanquished at an appointed time."

With these solemn and fateful words, the knight set in motion the slow wheels of royal justice, beginning a chain of events that would entangle himself, his wife, Jacques Le Gris, the families and friends of both men, and many other members of the French nobility by the time his appeal reached a resolution.

After presenting his appeal and thanking the king, Carrouges and his legal counsel were escorted from the Salle de Conseil and out of the keep. Now the knight would have to wait—quite possibly several weeks or even months—for the next step, the formal challenge. The king, following the law, immediately turned the case over to the Parlement of Paris, which had jurisdiction over all duels and would handle the details of the case. But Charles, as the nation's supreme judge, presided over the Parlement, and for the next several months he would avidly follow the Carrouges–Le Gris affair.

THE APPEAL.

The appelant, kneeling in the royal court with raised sword, appeals his case to the king. MS. fr. 2258, fol. 2r. Bibliothèque Nationale de France.

Arrangements now had to be made for the challenge. A courier was dispatched from the Château de Vincennes to the Palais de Justice in the city with a letter bearing the royal seal. Amid the Gothic splendor of the Palais, on the bank of the Seine, clerks employed by the Parlement prepared a formal summons to be sent to Jacques Le Gris, whom the knight had named as the *défendeur*. Then the summons was sent by another courier all the way to Argentan, or wherever the squire was to be found in Normandy.

When Jacques Le Gris received the summons to Paris, he may not have been all that surprised, but he must have been worried. Count Pierre had already written to the king to prevent Carrouges from appealing the case. But the determined knight had obtained a royal hearing, and the resulting summons, ordering Jacques Le Gris to appear before the Parlement of Paris, could not be ignored.

When Le Gris arrived in Paris, he, too, immediately sought legal counsel. Le Gris's chief lawyer was Jean Le Coq, a well-known and much-sought-after attorney. Le Coq kept some notes on the case in his professional diary, recording facts and observations in his careful legal Latin. The diary, one of the oldest surviving casebooks of its kind, offers a valuable glimpse into the legal affair and also the squire's character, since Le Coq wrote down there some of his private thoughts about his client and their confidential exchanges.

At the time of the quarrel, Jean Le Coq was about thirty-five years old. The son of an eminent lawyer likewise named Jean Le Coq, he had inherited along with his father's name and profession his intimate ties to the French royal family. The younger Le Coq's clients included Louis of Valois, the king's brother, and the king's powerful uncle, Duke Philip of Burgundy.

Le Coq may have been chosen by the Parlement to represent Le Gris, as sometimes happened with cases brought on appeal. Or Le Gris's family—or Count Pierre—may have specially selected him, because of his close ties to the crown, for the job of defending the imperiled squire.

Le Coq soon found that defending the squire accused of raping Marguerite de Carrouges was no easy task, especially since Le Gris did not always follow his lawyer's advice. Le Gris showed his obstinacy early on when his counsel urged him to exercise his right to "benefit of clergy."

Since Jacques Le Gris was not only a squire but also a cleric—a member of the clergy having some education—he could escape the jurisdiction of the Parlement of Paris altogether and have his case heard instead by a church court, where a duel was out of the question. Le Coq says that he strongly urged his client to do so in order to avoid any risk of fighting a duel.

But as the frustrated lawyer wrote in his diary, the squire "sharply disagreed," rejecting Le Coq's advice and "refusing to help himself." Le Gris may have stood firm on this issue because his vanity would not permit him to be thought a coward, especially now that the quarrel had been heard by the king in the royal court and was becoming known throughout France.

Once Carrouges appealed his case to the king, and Le Gris arrived in Paris to answer the Parlement's summons, both men had to secure their pledges in preparation for the challenge. Each also had to arrange for extended lodging in the city and see to many other details. The knight, of course, had to send for Marguerite, or return to retrieve her, if she had not already come to Paris. For the next several months, the lives of both men would be consumed by the case, which now took on an inexorable life of its own.

As is usual with legal matters, the case was not only time-consuming but costly as well. This posed a particular risk for the knight, with his shaky financial resources. It was not uncommon for the parties in protracted legal quarrels to borrow money from relatives or friends, or to take out loans, to cover the costs. While the squire's family was wealthy, and Count Pierre was probably more than willing to help out his favorite, the knight had fewer resources and may have had fewer friends to rely on. But by this point in the quarrel, with the question of a duel in the air, there was much more at stake for both men than just money.

I n the late spring or early summer of 1386, the knight and the squire received official letters summoning them to appear at the Palais de Justice before the king and his assembled Parlement. The date set for the appearance was July 9, a Monday. Nearly six months after the alleged crime, Jean de Carrouges finally would face his enemy before the high court of France, accuse him of the terrible crime against his wife, and offer to prove his charges in battle. The knight had waited a long time for this moment, but there was still no guarantee that once he issued his challenge he would actually get his chance to fight the squire. That decision would rest with the Parlement.

The setting for the challenge was one of the most exalted in Paris. The Palais de Justice, actually a cluster of buildings on the north side of the Île de la Cité, had been splendidly rebuilt in the early 1300s as an official royal residence, although now it was mainly home to the Parlement and visited by the king only on state occasions. At its northeast corner, on the riverbank, the royal clock tower built by Charles V chimed the hours. The Palais's three other towers—César, Argent, and Bonbec—lined the river to the west. Just south of the palace, connected to it by a covered passageway, stood the glittering splendor of the Sainte-Chapelle.

On the morning of July 9 the knight and the squire arrived separately at the Palais from opposite ends of the city. Jean de Carrouges came from the east, where he was lodging in the rue Saint-Antoine, near the bishop's palace and the Hôtel Saint-Pol. Jacques Le Gris approached from the west, where he was staying with Count Pierre at the Hôtel d'Alençon in an equally prestigious quarter amid the many other princely *hôtels* clustered in the shadow of the Louvre. Both men were accompanied by their lawyers, pledges, relatives, and friends.

Each man and his entourage crossed from the *rive droite* to the Île de la Cité via the Grand Pont—a wooden bridge built on pilings driven

Palais de Justice.

In July 1386 Jean de Carrouges challenged Jacques Le Gris to a duel, as the king and his Parlement watched, in a chamber adjacent to the two towers on the right. The royal clock tower stands at center. Archives Photographiques, Coll. M.A.P.(c) CMN, Paris.

into the river mud—passing the royal clock tower on the opposite bank and entering the palace precincts through a gate on the east side.

Here they had to wind through the noise and confusion of the Cour du Mai, a vast courtyard where all of Paris seemed to have congregated. Lawyers and litigants having business with the Parlement jostled against merchants tending their stalls, shoppers hunting for bargains, and beggars pleading for alms, while idlers stood about watching the endless spectacle of city life. Amid the chatter and gossip of the courtyard, the shouts of vendors mingled with the iron tread of soldiers and the laments of prisoners being led off in chains to execution.

Once the knight and the squire crossed the courtyard and entered the palace, the tumult faded behind them. Climbing a great stone staircase, they passed through a Gothic doorway guarded by a statue of the Virgin and Child and entered the Grande Salle, a vast and ornate room more than seventy-five yards long and thirty wide where the Parlement conducted much of its business.

The cavernous hall had a double-vaulted and gilded ceiling that rested on a row of eight columns dividing the room in two. Here lawyers met with clients, law clerks bustled about with documents, and ushers, scribes, and other officials kept the complex machinery of the law in motion. Leaded windows colored with the arms of France lighted the chamber's upper walls; below these, several huge fireplaces alternated with seating benches along the walls. Statues of fifty French kings ringed the room, and animal skins adorned the walls, including a crocodile hide brought back from Egypt by the famous crusader Sir Godfrey de Bouillon. At the hall's east end was an altar dedicated to Saint Nicholas, the patron saint of lawyers, where mass was said each morning. The altar was maintained by a tax on lawyers and alms paid by the accomplices in the murder of Evain Dol, a judge of the Parlement slain by his wife's lover in 1369.

In the Grande Salle the government of France met in times of crisis, as after the calamitous defeat at Poitiers and the capture of King Jean in the terrible autumn of 1356. Some eight hundred delegates from all over the kingdom had packed the hall to confront the shaken dauphin—the future Charles V—demanding that he purge the corrupt royal administration of the counselors who had led France into such a debacle. Two years later a mob of three thousand poured into the Grande Salle behind their leader, Étienne Marcel, the fiery provost of the Paris merchants' guild, to protest the scandalous terms of the peace treaty with England and the crushing royal ransom of three million gold *écus*. Marcel, backed by his angry followers, burst into the dauphin's chamber on the second floor, shouting, "We have business to do here!" The mob seized one of the royal counselors and hacked him to death on the spot. Another counselor fled the room, but the mob caught and killed him, too, dragging his bloody body out and throwing it with the other corpse to the yelling crowd in the courtyard below. The terrified dauphin was saved only when Marcel placed him under his personal protection, handing him a hood of blue and crimson—the rebel colors—to put over his head.

At the entrance to the Grande Salle, Carrouges and Le Gris were met by liveried ushers armed with sticks or *bâtons* for keeping order, who separately led each man and his retinue across the hall, over a black-and-white marble floor resembling a giant chessboard. At the hall's northwest corner they passed through a guarded door and entered a narrow passageway. This led to the Grand' Chambre, the inner sanctum of the Parlement, a much smaller but even more elegantly appointed room on the north side of the palace flanked by the Tour d'Argent and the Tour César. Here the king sat in state whenever visiting his council.

Entering the Grand' Chambre, the knight and the squire found themselves facing the plush and canopied royal throne, known as the *lit de justice*, which stood on a dais draped with blue cloth dotted by golden fleurs-de-lis. Cushioned benches for the council's magistrates flanked the throne, clerics to the king's left, laymen to his right, thirty-two in all. An altarpiece depicting the Crucifixion hung on one wall, while rich tapestries adorned the others. The room's single large fireplace sat silent in the July heat, and freshly cut grass was strewn over

The Challenge.

The appelant *(to the king's right) accuses the* défendeur *(king's left), offering to prove his charges in battle. Behind each litigant are his legal counsel and pledges.* MS. fr. 2258, fol. 4v. Bibliothèque Nationale de France.

the tiled floor for cleanliness and quiet. A low barrier divided the king's throne and the council seats from the rest of the room, where wooden benches were set up for lawyers and their clients.

When the ushers had shown everyone to their places, bidding all to remain standing in silence, the magistrates filed in and stood before their seats, the clerics first, followed by the laymen. At last the king appeared at a doorway behind the throne. As the bailiff announced his arrival, and everyone in the room bowed, Charles entered the chamber, followed by his brother, Louis of Valois, and his hovering retinue of watchful uncles. Seating himself on his throne, the young monarch surveyed the assembly as everyone else silently took their seats. One of the clerics remained standing to offer a prayer, solemnly asking for God's blessing on the proceedings. Then the first president of the Parlement, Arnold de Corbie, rapped his gavel. The high court of France was now in session.

The Parlement's register for July 9, 1386, describes the noble company gathered in the Grand' Chambre that day to witness the challenge: "On this day the King our Lord was in Parlement in his royal majesty, accompanied there by our lords the Dukes of Berry and Burgundy, his uncles, and by our lord the Count of Valois, brother to our lord the king, and many other great lords. And the pleading concerned a wager of battle between Jean de Carrouges, knight, the appellant on one side, and Jacques Le Gris on the other."

The register does not mention Marguerite, so we cannot be certain whether she was there that day, although she did appear before the Parlement later that summer. By now the Lady Carrouges was six months pregnant, making even worse the ordeal of appearing before a public tribunal where her husband was to accuse another man of having raped her.

For the ceremony of the challenge, the knight and the squire stood facing each other before the court, each flanked by his entourage. By tradition, the *appelant* stood to the king's right, and the *défendeur* to the king's left.

The knight, as the *appelant* in the case, spoke first, raising his voice so as to be heard by the entire court:

"Most excellent and powerful king and our sovereign lord, I present myself, Jean de Carrouges, knight, as an appellant in your court and do hereby accuse this squire, Jacques Le Gris, of a most foul crime against my wife, Lady Marguerite de Carrouges. I charge that during the third week of this January past, the same Jacques Le Gris did feloniously and carnally know my wife, against her will, in the place known as Capomesnil, with the aid of one Adam Louvel. Accordingly, I demand that he now confess his crime, submitting to the judgment of this court and to the penalty of death and the confiscation of all his goods, according to the law in such matters. And if the said Jacques Le Gris denies his crime, I do hereby offer to prove my charges with my body, on the enclosed field, as a gentleman and a man of honor shall do, before your royal presence, as judge and sovereign lord."

After having named, charged, and challenged the squire, the knight had to throw down his gage of battle, traditionally a gauntlet or a glove. As the court watched, he threw his gage to the floor in front of the squire, signifying his pledge to live up to his challenge and face the accused on the enclosed field—or *champ clos*—the traditional place of judicial battle. To throw down the gage (*jeter le gage*) was one of the ancient rituals of the duel.

Now it was the squire's turn, as *défendeur*, to reply. Facing his accuser, and also speaking loudly to make certain he was heard by all, the squire said:

"Most excellent and powerful king and our sovereign lord, I present myself, Jacques Le Gris, squire and defendant, and I do hereby deny all the aforesaid charges, and especially the accusation of Jean de Carrouges that I did unlawfully and carnally know his wife, the Lady Marguerite de Carrouges, in the third week of January last, or at any other time, in the place known as Capomesnil, or in any other place. And I further maintain, saving the honor of your majesty, that the said knight has falsely and wickedly lied, and that he is false and wicked to say this thing. And with the aid of God and of Our Lady, I pledge to defend myself from his charges with my body, without any excuse or plea for release, if your court judges that a wager of battle shall take place, at such a place and time as you shall ordain as sovereign lord and judge."

Jacques Le Gris then bent down and picked up the gage lying on the floor at his feet. This, too, was a time-honored part of the ritual. The *défendeur* was obliged to lift and hold *(lever et prendre)* the gage in order to signify that he accepted the other man's pledge to prove his charges in battle, and that he in turn agreed to defend his own claims against him by mortal combat in the *champ clos,* if the court should so decide.

Once the two men had exchanged words and the gage of battle, the magistrates deliberated and rendered an official decision *(arrêt)* concerning what would happen next—whether or not the challenge would go forward. The *rapporteur,* the magistrate placed in charge of the case, announced the Parlement's decision to the assembly in elaborate legalese:

"Between Sir Jean de Carrouges, knight, the appellant and plaintiff on one side in a case of the wager of battle, and on the other side Jacques Le Gris, defendant, it is ordered, now that the parties have been heard, that they present their facts and reasons in writing before the court, in the manner of an affidavit, which the court, having received, will consider and weigh in accordance with reason, so as to resolve the case."

The Parlement was ordering a formal inquiry, or *enquête,* into the facts of the case. Each party to the quarrel would submit written testimony, which the court would then examine in order to decide whether a duel was warranted.

The Parlement's ruling must have pleased the knight. So far, at least, his appeal had been successful. His challenge had initiated a formal inquiry that might eventually cause the high court to authorize a duel. Yet the Parlement rarely permitted duels, and not for over thirty years had it approved a judicial combat in a case of alleged rape.

Jacques Le Gris was probably not so pleased. His lawyer, Jean Le

Coq, had urged him to avoid any risk of a duel by claiming benefit of clergy, but Le Gris had refused, giving up his chance to escape the Parlement's jurisdiction. Now he would have to submit to the inquiry and accept its result.

The court took steps to ensure that the knight and the squire remained securely within its reach during the *enquête*. The Parlement could imprison both men but granted them their liberty within the city walls, demanding oaths and pledges instead. Each man had to "swear, promise, and obligate himself" to appear again, whenever summoned, "on the day, hour, and place assigned." If either man fled Paris or failed to appear when summoned, orders would be issued for his arrest. His absence or attempted escape would be taken as proof of his guilt, resulting in his summary conviction and execution.

To guarantee his presence when summoned again, each man had to name six pledges, respected noblemen sworn to make him appear—by force, if necessary. The record for July 9 lists the twelve men who undertook this solemn duty, all of them distinguished nobles, many renowned for their military service to France.

The knight's chief pledge, Count Waleran de Saint-Pol, of the House of Luxembourg, was close to the king and a celebrated veteran of many royal campaigns, including the French victory over the Flemings at the Battle of Roosebeke in 1382. One of the squire's leading pledges, Philip of Artois, the Count of Eu, had recently returned with the king's uncle, Duke Louis of Bourbon, from fighting the English in Gascony.

The small army of knights and lords serving as pledges shows how the quarrel, once it came before the king and his Parlement, rapidly entangled many other French nobles. The twelve pledges, each with his own following of family and friends, multiplied by many times the number of people directly involved in the Carrouges–Le Gris affair. By now the quarrel had become a subject of gossip and heated debate in the royal court, where the principals or their families were well known to many, some of whom had already taken sides before the official *enquête* even began. Soon the affair would attract great controversy all over France and even beyond the realm. What had started as a local dispute at a seigneurial court in Normandy was rapidly becoming a cause célèbre that would play itself out on the French national stage.

After Carrouges and Le Gris had stood face-to-face for the challenge, they turned their backs on each other and left the Palais with their retinues, returning to their lodgings on opposite sides of Paris. Now they would begin preparing the required testimony, so that the Parlement could proceed with its *enquête.* If, after examining the evidence, the court rejected the knight's appeal, Count Pierre's verdict would stand firm, and the squire would remain innocent of the charges. But if the high court decided to permit a duel, in effect voiding the count's verdict, Carrouges would have a chance to prove his charges by facing his enemy in battle, while Le Gris would have to earn his innocence all over again, this time with the sword.

6

THE INQUIRY

Once the Parlement of Paris announced the inquiry, Jean de Carrouges and Jacques Le Gris began preparing their testimony. As required by the court, all the evidence had to be put into writing. Although women were not allowed to bring charges themselves in criminal cases, Marguerite, as the chief witness in the case, clearly testified, since the official record states that "certain information was received by the deposition or oath of the aforesaid Marguerite before this our court." Indeed, the Lady Carrouges was "closely and repeatedly questioned and examined" about her accusations against the squire.

A remark made by Jacques Le Gris indicates that Marguerite appeared that summer at the Palais de Justice before the king and the assembled Parlement—like her father, Robert de Thibouville, summoned there forty years earlier to answer charges of high treason. Le Gris testified that he had "never seen or spoken with" the lady except one time in Normandy (at Jean Crespin's house two years earlier) and now in the king's presence, "as a party in these proceedings." Thus Le Gris must have seen Marguerite near the beginning of the inquiry when she stood to be sworn in before the high court, before being deposed in private by the court officers. By mid-July, when the inquiry began, Marguerite was already six months pregnant, which made her public appearance before the Parlement an even more trying ordeal.

The knight, the squire, and the lady all testified in their native Norman French. No transcript of any direct oral testimony survives, but the Parlement's official records contain a detailed summary of the case, rendered into Latin and recorded by one of the court's professional scribes or *greffiers*. This summary, which survives in a unique manuscript copy, runs to nearly ten densely written folio-sized pages in faded brown ink. It includes the knight's itemized charges against the squire, based on his wife's sworn testimony, followed by the squire's lengthy and formidable defense.

The knight begins by recounting how for many years he trusted and confided in Jacques Le Gris as one of his closest and most loyal friends, even honoring the squire by naming him godfather to his firstborn son. Jean de Carrouges stresses the intimacy and sanctity of this relationship, describing how Jacques Le Gris lifted up and held the child at the baptismal font to be dipped in the sacred water by the priest.

The knight then recounts the incident at the home of Jean Crespin, where Jacques Le Gris met Marguerite for the first time, and where Jean instructed Marguerite to kiss Le Gris as a sign of peace and friendship between the two men.

He passes over in silence the interval separating these two very public events—a period of five or more years during which he lost not only his first wife, his son, and his father but also his father's prestigious captaincy at Bellême, and several fiefs he had lawfully purchased, and during which his friendship with the squire soured amid their rivalry in Count Pierre's court.

Carrouges alleges that after the encounter at Crespin's home, where Le Gris first met Marguerite, the squire fell into a lustful desire for the lady. Painting the squire as a notorious libertine, the knight claims that Le Gris plotted to seduce Marguerite and add her to his long line of conquests.

Relying on his wife's sworn testimony, Carrouges next details the attack on Marguerite, alleging that Le Gris "carnally knew the same Marguerite, as said before, against her will and consent, foully committing rape, adultery, treachery, incest, and perjury"—five separate and very serious criminal counts. Besides rape, he accuses Le Gris of adultery for having unlawful intercourse with the lady; treachery for breaking his bond of trust and friendship with the knight; incest for violating the kinship bond established when Le Gris stood godfather to Jean's son; and finally perjury because the squire, in denying his guilt before two separate tribunals, bore false witness. Although the crime of rape leads the list, stressing Le Gris's violation of Marguerite's body, will, and legal rights, the other charges address the squire's alleged crimes against the knight as well.

The knight claims that he first learned of the crime from Marguerite herself when he returned from Paris, and that she begged him, for the sake of his own honor, to seek justice and avenge her against the squire. Marguerite, he says, swore to the truth of her story many times, steadfastly maintaining her testimony "on the peril of her own soul and under many oaths when questioned and examined about these things."

The knight—doubtless on the advice of his lawyer, Jean de Bethisy—concludes by stating that his case satisfies all the necessary conditions for a wager of battle: the crime definitely occurred; it involves a capital offense; conviction is possible only by battle, since the *défendeur* refused to confess; and Le Gris, the *défendeur*, "is widely and notoriously suspected and accused" of the crime.

Against the knight's accusations, Jacques Le Gris and his legal counsel mounted a vigorous defense that offered a very different picture of how the squire came to be accused of the crime, and of his actual whereabouts on the day in question.

The squire begins his account by reminding the court that he is of a noble family loyal to the kings of France and to Count Pierre of Alençon, and that he has always served his lords "wisely, lawfully, loyally, and praiseworthily," leading "a good and respectable life, and conducting himself honorably toward others." He adds that on account of his good conduct, King Charles retained him as his own personal squire.

Turning to his relationship with the knight, Le Gris describes how he and Carrouges once served the Count of Perche and together joined Count Pierre's service after their first lord's death. The squire also mentions that he stood godfather to Jean's son. But whereas Carrouges cites this fact to show Le Gris's later breach of trust, the squire uses it to illustrate the knight's headlong descent into enmity against himself.

Le Gris describes how he and the knight fell out at court, as Carrouges became progressively more hostile toward him and Count Pierre. When Jean's father died, vacating the captaincy of Bellême, Count Pierre refused to grant this post to the younger Carrouges, says Le Gris, because he knew him to be "gloomy and unpredictable." Le Gris also says that after Carrouges lost Cuigny, which he tried to purchase despite Count Pierre's prior claim to it, he began blaming Le Gris for his disappointments at court. Resenting the trust Count Pierre placed in Le Gris, the angry and suspicious Carrouges jumped to the conclusion that Le Gris "had behaved in such a way as to injure him," and "he began to hate and despise him."

According to Le Gris, if Carrouges was a bad sort around the court, he was even worse at home. He alleges that Carrouges, while married to his first wife, Jeanne de Tilly, fell into an "insane jealousy," forcing her to lead such an austere life that she died an early death. Even more damaging, Le Gris charges that Carrouges tried to get his first wife to say that Le Gris had slept with her—"which the said wife, wise and good, refused to do, since it was not in any way true." With these sensational attacks on Carrouges's character and credibility, Le Gris tries to show that the knight's charges against him were part of a long pattern of lies and enmity.

After painting a damning portrait of the knight's conduct in both public and private, Le Gris turns to his own relationship with Marguerite. He claims that he has seen or spoken with Marguerite on only two occasions—the present litigation before the Parlement of Paris, and the social gathering, "at least two years ago," at the home of Jean Crespin. Overtly, this piece of testimony is meant to show that Le Gris was not at Capomesmil on the date of the alleged crime and so could not be guilty of the rape. But indirectly it suggests a case of mistaken identity. Since Marguerite met Le Gris only once before, over a year before the alleged crime, perhaps she accused the wrong man of the attack—if there was any attack at all.

Le Gris also narrows the window of time during which he could have committed the crime. In his statement of charges, Carrouges does not specify the date of the crime, saying that it occurred "on a certain day during the third week of January." In reply, Le Gris attempts to show that the crime could have occurred *only* on Thursday, January 18, the one day when Nicole was absent from Capomesnil and during which Marguerite stayed behind at the château.

Le Gris cites Nicole's summons on Thursday to the nearby town of Saint-Pierre-sur-Dives. He stresses the relatively short distance she traveled, saying that Saint-Pierre lies "scarcely two leagues" from Capomesnil, making for a round trip of no more than twelve miles.* Le Gris also claims that Nicole returned from her errand "by the morning meal, or a little after," indicating the main daily meal often eaten around ten A.M. but sometimes as late as noon. If Le Gris is right—and Carrouges never contradicts him on this point—Nicole was gone from Capomesnil for five or six hours at most. Le Gris also notes that Carrouges, although failing to give the exact day of the crime, specifies the time of the alleged rape as "around the hour of prime"—or nine A.M., some two hours or so after Nicole's likely departure.

Surprisingly, Le Gris also claims that Marguerite was attended during the entire time of Nicole's brief absence from Capomesnil by "a seamstress and two other women." This is a very different picture from

* A league was a unit of measure varying between 2.75 and 3.0 miles.

the one presented by Carrouges, who claims that Nicole left Marguerite "virtually alone" and beyond anyone's earshot or assistance. Moreover, Le Gris says that when Nicole returned from her journey, she found her daughter-in-law in a cheerful mood—"happy and mirthful, showing no sign of any displeasure." The implication is obvious: does this sound like a woman who just a few hours before had been brutally attacked and raped?

Le Gris goes on to offer a damaging account of Jean's subsequent return from Paris three or four days later. Darkening his portrait of the knight as a jealous and violent man, Le Gris claims that when Carrouges learned that the maidservant he ordered to stay by Marguerite's side disobeyed his orders and instead went to Saint-Pierre with Nicole, he flew into a rage and "right then began to hit the said maidservant—and later Marguerite as well—on the head with his fists." This report of the knight's savagery doubtless had a certain shock value in the court. Whereas the knight portrays himself as a loyal and loving husband, the squire paints him as a cruel and violent man given to beating his own wife and other women. Denying that he ever attacked Marguerite, the squire instead shifts this notorious charge to the lady's own husband.

Le Gris claims that the knight's brutal beating of his wife was followed by another kind of violence, as Carrouges, "on the very next day," forced Marguerite falsely to accuse the squire of having raped her—"although the said Marguerite had never said anything about this before." The last clause is crucial, since it reduces the knight's entire set of charges to a vicious falsehood coerced out of his wife in a fit of rage to avenge himself on the innocent squire. It also paints a new picture of Marguerite, with fresh bruises from her husband's fists, now forced to collaborate in a further violence to herself, a violence to her mind and soul, by falsely accusing the squire of a heinous crime.

According to Le Gris, the knight made public his notorious charges against the squire "by himself and through Marguerite, by threats and fear, as well as through others whom he told."

H aving offered the court a completely different story from the knight's of how he came to be accused of the notorious crime, Le Gris began the second part of his defense—his alibi. If in fact he was not at Capomesnil on January 18, and he did not brutally attack and rape Marguerite, where was he, and what was he doing?

To answer these questions, the squire details his whereabouts and activities not only on the date of the alleged crime but during the entire third week of January. Since Carrouges was vague about dates, Le Gris tries to show that he could not have committed the crime on *any* day of that week.

Le Gris claims that on Monday, January 15, he traveled two leagues (about six miles) from Argentan to visit his friend Jean Beloteau, a squire, and to attend a mass for Beloteau's recently deceased wife. Le Gris says he remained with Beloteau until Wednesday, January 17, when he returned to Argentan, at Count Pierre's command. He dined that day with the count and attended him in his bedchamber that evening. Afterward, the squire claims, he "lay down and passed the night in a certain room of his in the same town," where the word *villa* (town) clearly refers to Argentan.

On the morning of Thursday, January 18, Le Gris says he was roused from sleep by Pierre Taillepie and Pierre Beloteau, brother of Jean Beloteau, who were then visiting Argentan. The squire went with his two friends to the palace for morning mass and was "continually" with them from that time on. After mass, the count invited the three men to join him for the late-morning meal, and Le Gris dined "openly and publicly" there in the palace. After dining and "taking spices and wine," the squire led his two friends to his nearby room and was continually in their company until the dinner hour, after which the squire again attended the count in his bedchamber, returning then "to his own room" to pass the night.

On Friday, January 19, the squire says he left Argentan with Pierre Taillepie and Pierre Beloteau and went to Aunou, a place about one league away, where they remained until Saturday, January 20, returning then to Argentan. "Aunou" clearly refers to the same estate, Aunou-le-Faucon, which Le Gris had acquired, through Count Pierre, from Marguerite's father. Le Gris's prominent mention of Aunou-le-Faucon in his alibi, and his claim that he spent the day after the alleged crime there, no doubt enraged the knight.

Having detailed his whereabouts from Monday, January 15, to Saturday, January 20, Le Gris concludes that it would have been "impossible for him to have committed a crime or offense of this sort," especially given that the distance from Argentan to Capomesnil is "nine leagues on bad and difficult roads, which would require at least a full day of travel in winter." Nine leagues (24½ to 27 miles) is over four times as far as the two leagues (5½ to 6 miles) that Nicole de Carrouges traveled on the day of the alleged crime in comparable weather and road conditions. In winter, the squire's round-trip journey from Argentan to Capomesnil and back, some fifty miles or more, would have taken many hours, if not quite the "full day" that he claimed, even with a strong and fast horse. With relays of fresh horses, a courier could cover eighty or even ninety miles a day under good road conditions.

Jacques Le Gris was a wealthy man with excellent horses at his disposal. If the squire posted Adam Louvel to spy on Marguerite at Capomesnil, as Jean de Carrouges alleged, he could easily have arranged for relays of fresh horses as well. Even so, it strained credulity that Le Gris had accomplished the round trip of fifty miles or more between Argentan and Capomesnil in the five or six hours during which Nicole de Carrouges made the round trip of eleven to twelve miles between Capomesnil and Saint-Pierre-sur-Dives.

Then again, perhaps Le Gris lied about his whereabouts on the night of Wednesday, January 17, when he claims to have slept "in his own room" at Argentan. Perhaps instead he was already lying in wait for his victim at the home of Adam Louvel in Capomesnil as dawn broke on the morning of January 18. If so, then after raping Marguerite, Le Gris had to travel only the twenty-five or twenty-seven miles back to Argentan, a little over twice the distance covered by the elderly

Nicole de Carrouges on the same morning—hardly an impossibility for a skilled rider on a strong horse, despite the winter roads.

After attacking Jean's character and motives and offering a detailed alibi, Jacques Le Gris declares that it was impossible for him to have committed the crime. He even raises doubts about whether a crime actually occurred—one of the four conditions necessary for a duel. First, he says, the charges seem to have arisen from the knight's jealousy and his wife's forced testimony. Second, it defies belief that he himself, "fiftyish and already entering old age," had within a few hours on the morning of January 18 galloped nonstop the nine leagues to Capomesnil, attacked Marguerite in a struggle so vigorous that he required the help of a second man, and then galloped the nine leagues back, "on bad roads and in freezing weather." Third, if the crime really occurred, the "noble, honest, strong, and virtuous Marguerite" certainly would have left scars or injuries on her assailant's face or other parts of his body "with her fingernails or other bodily members"—but no such scars or injuries were found on the squire, nor "was the said Marguerite evidently injured or scarred." Fourth, the supposedly isolated château at Capomesnil was actually adjacent to "ten or twelve houses" whose inhabitants surely would have heard Marguerite's cries for help but who knew or had heard nothing of the supposed attack.

Le Gris also cites some potentially damaging testimony relating to Nicole de Carrouges. According to the squire, Nicole herself looked into her son's charges, "diligently investigating" the matter, and concluded "that the said crime had never actually taken place." Le Gris earlier stated that Nicole returned from her errand on January 18 to find Marguerite "happy and mirthful." If true, the claim that the knight's own mother and the victim's mother-in-law did not believe the charges was even more damning. Le Gris further claimed that Nicole—who had died by the time of the Parlement's inquiry—was driven to her grave by her son's relentless prosecution of the case.

On the strength of all this testimony, Le Gris argues that the charges against him should be dropped, that he should be completely exonerated, and that the knight's demand for a trial by combat should be thrown out. The squire also submits his own counterclaim against Jean de Carrouges. He says that the knight has publicly and so gravely defamed his good name and reputation with his lies and accusations, "his injurious words," that he should be required to pay damages. As compensation, Le Gris demands the immense sum of 40,000 gold francs.

The squire's demand for a huge damage award, an amount that would bankrupt the financially strapped knight many times over, raised the stakes of the quarrel even higher. If the Parlement now failed to decide the case in the knight's favor, refusing his demand for a judicial duel, the squire would be free to begin a suit against Jean de Carrouges.

After Jacques Le Gris finished his defense, his accuser was given a chance to reply. Mounting a vigorous counterattack, Jean de Carrouges disputes the squire's claim that, out of jealousy and hatred over their rivalry in Count Pierre's court, he sought revenge against his enemy by fabricating the rape charge. Calling the squire's explanation "a flimsy invention without any truth or semblance of truth," the knight says it has no bearing on the case anyway, which is about such a grave matter, "so great and difficult and dangerous," that he has brought charges against Le Gris at the risk of his own "soul, body, wealth, and honor."

The knight next challenges Le Gris's allegation about wife abuse, trying to undo the squire's powerful attack on his character as a husband, especially the portrayal of himself as a jealous, cruel, and even deranged man who tried to force false accusations against Le Gris out of both of his wives. The knight rejects this damning portrait out of hand, insisting that he never mistreated Marguerite but always lived with her "respectably, peaceably, and chastely, without any sort of jealousy or spite whatsoever."

The knight then counters the squire's claim that the charges against him are somehow flawed or incomplete. Carrouges maintains that he has presented his charges according to the law and in good order, describing the crime in the correct form, without failing to specify the date. Jean stresses that the crime took place "just as it seemed from the testimony and assertions of the said Marguerite, for her testimony was true and sufficient."*

Jean de Carrouges also insists that his wife was telling the truth, and that the crime could not be more apparent, inasmuch as Marguerite, whom Le Gris himself describes as "chaste and honest," brought upon herself "perpetual blame" by revealing the crime in the first place. How could she have maintained her testimony "so firmly and constantly, without any change or variation, if the said crime had not really occurred"?

Jean's final point of rebuttal addresses the doubts raised by Le Gris about the improbable gallop north from Argentan to Capomesnil, on bad winter roads, to commit the crime. Jean answers this objection by saying that Jacques was "a rich man abundantly supplied with good horses," and that it was quite possible to travel from Argentan to Capomesnil and back again "in a short time." With this, the knight rests his case.

There is one issue that apparently neither man mentioned in court but that had a potential bearing on the case and that became more and more obvious as the inquiry progressed over the summer: Marguerite's pregnancy.

We cannot know for certain whose child Marguerite was carrying—the knight's, the squire's, or that of some third man. But since she was apparently childless for the first five or six years of her marriage and then became pregnant around January 1386, delivering a child later the same year, it is quite possible that it was Jacques Le Gris's.

---

* Since the alleged crime could have occurred *only* on Thursday, January 18, the one day when Nicole left Capomesnil to attend a legal proceeding whose date is certain, Le Gris's claim that Carrouges failed to specify the date of the crime may have seemed negligible to the court. But cases could be lost on technicalities. Indeed, the 1306 decree says that a nobleman calling for a duel must specify the date and time of the alleged crime, and Le Gris may have counted on this requirement to disqualify the knight's case.

However, the magistrates in the Parlement of Paris may have questioned whether Marguerite could have become pregnant at all as a result of the alleged rape. A widely credited theory of reproduction, based on the teachings of the physician Galen (ca. A.D. 200), held that the female "seed" necessary for conception along with that of the male was released only if the woman had an orgasm, meaning that "the woman could not possibly conceive if she did not participate fully in coitus." This belief was so firm in the Middle Ages that "it was recognized in law that rape could therefore not cause pregnancy."

This belief flies in the face of modern knowledge, but it was bolstered in the Middle Ages by the desire to protect family bloodlines from accidental or criminal contamination, especially among the propertied nobility. Inheritance depended on paternity, and paternity on the woman's word of honor or the trust between husband and wife. The risk of adultery was threat enough to the purity of noble bloodlines, so the idea that nonconsensual sex, or rape, could likewise produce illegitimate children, further contaminating the family lines, was too threatening to admit as a possibility. It was unthinkable that a man could rape another man's wife and by the same criminal act foist an unwanted and illegitimate child on the victim and her husband.

Given the beliefs of the time, the court might have found it more likely that the pregnant Marguerite had had consensual sex with a third man—i.e., had committed adultery—than that she had been raped. The squire could even have used Marguerite's pregnancy to argue his own innocence, claiming that she had accused him of rape in order to cover up an illicit affair with another man. But to this the knight would have had an irrefutable reply: his wife had become pregnant as a result of intercourse with *him*, after his return from abroad, when the couple had been apart for six months and were eager to renew their conjugal bond. The squire would have been unable to deny this, despite his allegation that the marriage was an unhappy, even brutal union in which fertile sex was unlikely, as the couple's five or six childless years might suggest. Le Gris never cited Marguerite's preg-

THE MYSTERIOUS LETTERS.

*An expense receipt for the courier who galloped from Caen to Paris
in July 1386 carrying letters containing information about
Jacques Le Gris and Marguerite de Carrouges.* MS. fr. 26021, no. 899.
Bibliothèque Nationale de France.

nancy in his own defense, perhaps because he—or his shrewd legal counsel—saw this strategy as too risky.

What Jean de Carrouges thought privately, or what Marguerite knew from the evidence of her own body, is another matter. Did the knight discount the received wisdom about rape and conception, suspecting that in fact Marguerite's child was not his own? Did Marguerite worry that she might be carrying the child of the man who had raped her? Or did the couple take comfort in the popular lore, assuring themselves that Le Gris, who had brutally attacked and raped Marguerite, could not in addition to this terrible violation have foisted on them his own illegitimate offspring?

As the *enquête* continued through July and into August, there were a number of surprising new developments. At the end of July a courier named Guillaume Berengier arrived in Paris carrying sealed letters for the Parlement "touching on the Lady Carrouges and Jacques Le Gris." Berengier was sent to Paris by the bailiff of Caen, Guillaume de Mauvinet, who also told him to report "by word of mouth certain other secret things not to be committed to writing." The courier's expense receipts still survive on slender strips of parchment, but the letters themselves have vanished, and the "other secret things" apparently too dangerous to be written down are also lost to us. But Guillaume de Mauvinet, who ordered these mysterious letters rushed to Paris, was the same official before whom Dame Nicole appeared at Saint-Pierre-sur-Dives on the day of the alleged crime. Count Pierre had earlier sent letters to Paris to stop the knight's appeal, and these new letters and reports seem to have been a further attempt to damage the knight's case by discrediting Marguerite's testimony.

Around this time the Parlement of Paris summoned Adam Louvel, Le Gris's alleged partner in crime. Louvel had been arrested and held for questioning several months earlier on the orders of Count Pierre, although the same verdict that exonerated Le Gris had absolved his accomplice as well. Now Louvel was wanted again in court. Letters from the Parlement dated July 20 demand guarantees for Louvel's appearance in Paris.

Two days later, on July 22, a Sunday, Louvel answered the summons, appearing before King Charles at the Château de Vincennes. Louvel had already been named in the knight's statement of charges on July 9 as Le Gris's accomplice. But he may have been very surprised by what happened now. When he arrived at the huge fortress outside the city, entered the great keep, and was ushered up the spiral stairway into the Salle de Conseil and before the royal throne, Louvel was confronted there by a squire named Thomin du Bois, a cousin to Marguerite. As the king, his uncles, and the courtiers watched, Thomin angrily accused Louvel of having attacked the Lady Carrouges. Then he threw down his gage of battle and challenged Louvel to a duel. Thomin also demanded that if Louvel denied the charge but refused to fight him, this must be taken as an admission of guilt, and that Louvel must accordingly be imprisoned until he confessed. This second challenge, issued less than two weeks after the first, suddenly raised the possibility of not just one duel but two.

Louvel asked the king for a deferral, known as a *jour d'avis*, in order to confer with his legal counsel, and he was given until the following Tuesday, July 24, although the Parlement records no further action in the case on that date. But an entry for nearly a month later indicates a widening circle of arrests, detainments, and interrogations in the case. On August 20, Adam Louvel's son, Guillaume Louvel, along with two other men—Estiene Gosselin and Thomas de Bellefons—were taken into custody in order to examine "certain matters touching the case of the wager of battle pending between Sir Jean de Carrouges, chevalier, and Thomin du Bois, the plaintiffs on one side, and Jacques Le Gris and Adam Louvel, defendants on the other." The entry suggests that the two wagers of battle had been combined into one.

Around this time the Parlement ordered that Adam Louvel, by now under arrest and confined to the Conciergerie, the grim prison attached to the Palais de Justice, be taken from his cell and "put to the question" about the crime—that is, examined under torture. Torture was often used to extort information from witnesses and confessions from defendants. As ordeals and duels gave way to confession as a proof of guilt, judicial torture was actually increasing in France. Standard techniques included the strappado, where the victim's hands were tied behind his back with a rope by which he was winched off the ground and then suddenly dropped, as well as the rack, "fire applied to the soles of the feet," prolonged sleep deprivation, immersion in cold water, and water forced down the throat to the point of suffocation.

The squire's lawyer, Jean Le Coq, says in his diary that those "put to the question" about the alleged crime included Adam Louvel and a maidservant "who was said to have been that day in the Carrouges residence." So common was judicial torture at the time that the lawyer does not say what methods were used on these two witnesses, but neither Adam Louvel nor the nameless maidservant confessed to anything.*

Besides Adam Louvel, another of Jacques Le Gris's friends ran

---

* Jeanne de Fontenay, Adam Louvel's wife (and sister to one of Jacques Le Gris's later pledges), followed her husband to Paris and was also "interrogated" in connection with the case, after which she lodged at the Hôtel d'Alençon with many others in Le Gris's party.

afoul of the law that summer. Jean Beloteau, the recently widowed squire who figured in Le Gris's alibi, was arrested by the bailiff of the bishop of Paris under suspicion of *"raptus,"* meaning either abduction or rape.

It is a curious thing that Beloteau, Jacques Le Gris's close friend and a key witness in his alibi, was accused of *raptus* during the same period that the squire was summoned to Paris for the Parlement's inquiry into whether he had raped Marguerite de Carrouges. Perhaps the charges against Beloteau were groundless. But it does seem that Jacques Le Gris traveled in some rather rough company.

Throughout July the king and the royal court avidly followed the quarrel between the knight and the squire. In August, however, as the *enquête* entered its second month, the king's attention turned from domestic affairs, including the prospect of an exciting duel to the death, to a far bigger conflict looming again on the international horizon. With summer at its height and the weather again friendly to war, hostilities were once more imminent between France and England.

The previous year the king had sent Admiral Vienne to Scotland with an army of French knights and squires, Jean de Carrouges among them. The French had burned and pillaged their way through the border counties, drawing King Richard II and his troops north and away from London. But a second and even larger French invasion from the south was never launched, and the original plan to attack the English on two fronts had been abandoned. Philip the Bold, Duke of Burgundy, now proposed that King Charles earn an immortal name for himself and strike a deathblow against England by undertaking a larger and more devastating invasion than ever before.

The young and impressionable king instantly approved the plan and prepared to leave Paris for Sluys, the Flemish port, to take his place at the head of the huge French invasion force and an armada of more than a thousand ships. Before leaving Paris, Charles attended a solemn mass at Notre-Dame cathedral, vowing not to reenter the city until he had first set his conquering foot on English soil.

After the king and his uncles departed, the business of the Parlement resumed, including the inquiry into the Carrouges–Le Gris affair. As August turned to September, the case would soon enter its third month. The knight and the squire were prisoners of Paris, free to move about the city but required to appear at the Palais de Justice whenever summoned, which could happen at any time.

Marguerite, by now at least eight months pregnant, was imprisoned not just by the city, and by the house where she and her husband were staying, but increasingly by her own body as well. Waiting for her pregnancy to reach its term, and for the Parlement to reach a decision in the case, must have been an agonizing ordeal in the unfamiliar surroundings.

As the inquiry continued into late summer and everyone waited for the Parlement's decision, Jean Le Coq was drawing his own conclusions about the controversial affair. In his diary, Jacques Le Gris's lawyer lists a number of considerations for and against his client, adding some of his own private thoughts about this thorniest of cases.

Among the points weighing against his client, Le Coq cites the fact that "the wife of Carrouges never relented in affirming that the deed had occurred." Marguerite's steadfast testimony, in the face of denials, alibis, and countercharges of all sorts, appears to have impressed the lawyer no less than everyone else.

Le Coq, clearly a close observer of people, also notes in his journal that the squire once asked him "whether I had doubts concerning him, because he saw me thinking."

Le Coq also reveals that Jacques Le Gris "told me that when he heard the news that Carrouges intended to prosecute him in this matter, he immediately went to a priest to make confession." If the Parlement authorized a duel, both combatants would have ample time to confess their sins before they met in battle. But Le Gris apparently took no chances with his immortal soul, making sure to confess what-

Nota de duello Iacobi le gris.

JEAN LE COQ'S NOTEBOOK.

This page contains some of the notes kept by Jacques Le Gris's lawyer about the legal case. MS. Latin 4645, fol. 47r. Bibliothèque Nationale de France.

ever was on his conscience long before he might have to face his day of doom.

The lawyer lists various points in his client's favor, recapitulating much of what Jacques Le Gris had said to the court in his own defense, adding "that many knights swore they saw him with the Count of Alençon throughout the entire day in question."

"But some said," the lawyer adds, that Jacques Le Gris refused to confess to anything because doing so would have led to scandal among his sons and his friends, since Count Pierre had already sworn that the squire was innocent of the crime. This raises the possibility that Jacques Le Gris may have stuck to his story because of pressure from others. And it hints that Le Coq had some doubts about his client's truthfulness.

Le Coq's final comment on the case is the most telling. Despite his privileged viewpoint on the legal proceedings, and his many opportunities to observe and question his client, the careful lawyer seems to have recognized the limits of his own knowledge, and the limits of human knowledge in general. For he concludes his commentary on the case by tersely remarking that "no one really knew the truth of the matter."

In mid-September, more than two months after the inquiry began and eight months after the date of the alleged crime, the Parlement finally reached a decision. The high court summoned the knight and the squire to the Palais de Justice to hear its decision on September 15, 1386, a Saturday.

Summer was now turning to autumn, and King Charles and his uncles were long gone from Paris. Presiding over the high court in the king's absence and serving as chief judge was the first president, Arnold de Corbie. As the venerable jurist called the session to order in the Grand' Chambre, the noise in the ornate room died away, leaving the usual background sounds of the great city: the clatter of iron cartwheels and horses' hooves, the shouts of drovers and boatmen passing along the Seine in front of the Palais.

Once again the knight and the squire faced each other before the assembled Parlement, each accompanied by his lawyers, friends, and supporters, including his six noble pledges. Marguerite herself may have been conspicuously absent, since she was very near the term of her pregnancy.

Not since 1354 had the Parlement authorized a duel in a case of alleged rape. And over the past half century the high court had refused many appeals for judicial combat—in 1330, 1341, 1342, 1343, 1372, 1377, and again in 1383. So things did not look especially promising for the knight as he anxiously awaited the Parlement's decision.

After the judges finished deliberating on the case, they had written their decision on parchment, in French, and sealed it in a cloth sack with the other documents pertaining to the case. When the chamber came to order, and the knight, the squire, and their supporters had risen, the *rapporteur,* the magistrate charged with handling the case, opened the sack. Taking out the parchment sheet containing the court's decision, he slowly began to read it aloud:

"In the case pending before the King our lord, the wager of battle between Sir Jean de Carrouges, knight, plaintiff and appellant on the one side, and Jacques Le Gris, squire, defendant on the other, the court has considered the matter and reached a decision in the said case—namely, the court orders a trial by combat between the two parties."

Given the rarity of duels by 1386, the Parlement's decision to authorize a trial by combat, especially in a case that hinged on uncorroborated testimony, was unusual. But the court's decision may have been based more on political considerations than on strictly legal ones. For many months the celebrated quarrel had divided the royal court. Both the knight and the squire were well known in Paris; both were loyal servants of the king; and powerful nobles had aligned themselves with one or the other, serving as pledges in the wager of battle. Jean Le Coq cites the controversy aroused by the case in Paris, where "many people" supported the squire's cause, while "many others" supported the knight's. With the young king and his uncles away in Flanders and occupied with planning the invasion of England, the high court may have feared taking sides and arousing even more controversy, deciding instead to grant the knight's request, authorize a duel, and leave the whole perplexing matter in the hands of God.

The date appointed for the duel—by law at least forty days later—was November 27, 1386. This was still more than two months off, well after Marguerite would deliver her child. But at last the couple would get their day of reckoning.

Jacques Le Gris's lawyer wrote in his diary that "after the wager of battle was ordered, the squire fell ill." One can easily imagine why. Had not Le Gris already been vindicated of all charges in Count Pierre's tribunal, months before? And had he not thrown away his chance to avoid a duel by refusing to claim benefit of clergy? Suddenly he had fallen under full suspicion of the crime again, and now he had to prove his innocence all over, this time in mortal combat.

As for Jean de Carrouges, surely he was gratified by the Parlement's favorable ruling on his appeal. Against very long odds, after months of waiting, and at huge financial risk, he finally had been granted his wish.

But there was a catch. In capital cases, perjury was punished by death. The two men would fight without quarter to prove their charges, and even if Jean yielded in battle before being killed by his enemy, he would be dragged off the field to be hanged at Montfaucon, a proven liar.

Marguerite, as the chief witness in the case, faced an even more horrible fate. According to an ancient custom that was still part of French law in the late fourteenth century, if the outcome of a judicial duel proved that a woman had committed perjury and sworn a false oath about a rape charge, she was to be burned alive.

PART TWO

7

THE JUDGMENT
OF GOD

T he duel was to be fought at Saint-Martin-des-Champs, a monastery in Paris whose grounds had a special field for combat and enough space to hold thousands of spectators. Saint-Martin's, founded by the Benedictine order in the eleventh century, stood on the Seine's right bank along the rue Saint-Martin, about a mile north of Notre-Dame. One of the wealthiest religious foundations in Paris, it was named for one of the most celebrated saints in France. Saint Martin, originally a Roman soldier who one winter day divided his cloak with his sword and gave half to a freezing beggar, later became a missionary to Gaul and the first bishop of Tours. He was also the patron saint of military men, including armorers, horsemen, and soldiers. Saint-Martin's field, dedicated to the soldier-saint of France, was thus an apt setting for judicial combat, or "the judgment of God."

When Saint-Martin's priory was founded by King Henri I in 1060, it stood well outside the city on drained and cultivated marshland, encircled by a sturdy wall for protection against enemy invaders and thieves. The wall, enclosing about twelve acres, was rebuilt in 1273 by Philip III, who fortified each corner with an imposing forty-foot tower. Shops and houses soon sprang up beyond the city walls along the rue Saint-Martin, clustering around the prosperous monastery,

SAINT-MARTIN-DES-CHAMPS.

Carrouges and Le Gris fought their famous duel in the field behind the priory (north is to the left). Detail from Plan de Paris, Truschet/Hoyau (ca. 1550). Basel, University Library, Map Collection AA 124.

and before long Saint-Martin's was surrounded by its own neighborhood or *bourg*.

In 1356, when the English defeated the French at Poitiers and captured King Jean, the frightened merchants of Paris commissioned a bigger wall around the northern part of their city. The new wall stretched for nearly five miles around the Seine's right bank, encircling the Hôtel Saint-Pol to the east, the Louvre to the west, and Saint-Martin's to the north. The newly enclosed land rapidly filled up with streets and buildings, and in 1360 the *bourg* Saint-Martin was incorporated into Paris. By the 1380s, Saint-Martin-des-Champs no longer lay "in the fields" at all, as its original name suggested, having been engulfed by the medieval equivalent of urban sprawl.

In 1386, Saint-Martin's was still entered through the old fortified gate set in its south wall, near the main conventual buildings—chapel, refectory, cloister, and hospital. The refectory, where the monks ate in silence while one of their brethren nourished their souls by reading aloud from Scripture, is still a marvel today—a high Gothic hall held aloft by a line of slender pillars along its center and awash with light from tall pointed windows along its sides. The nearby *dortoir*, where the monks slept, had a convenient stairway leading down into the chapel for early morning prayers. And the latrines, some of the best in Paris, were flushed by Saint-Martin's own aqueduct, which delivered cool, fresh water from the hills north of the city directly into the monastery *enceinte*.

Besides a chapel, cloister, and other religious buildings, Saint-Martin's also had a tribunal and a prison, since the priory was the criminal court for the surrounding *bourg*, whose streets fell under *"la justice de Saint-Martin."* The court records are filled with murders, thefts, rapes, assaults, and other crimes, and the punishments meted out range from flogging and the pillory to mutilation, hanging, burial alive, and burning at the stake. In 1355, Thassin Ausoz lost an ear for stealing some cloth; in 1352, Jehanne La Prevoste was buried alive for larceny, women often being punished more severely than men for equivalent crimes. Animals, too, were tried and condemned. A sow that killed and ate an infant in the rue Saint-Martin was dragged through the street and hanged, and another pig that mangled a child's face was sentenced to death by burning. A horse that killed a man and then escaped with its master's help was convicted of murder in absentia and hanged in effigy.

But the most spectacular arena of justice at Saint-Martin's was the battlefield, laid out on the priory's grounds in the large flat area to the east of the conventual buildings. Saint-Martin's was one of only two monasteries at Paris that maintained a field of combat, and many judicial duels had been fought there over the centuries. (The other field was at Saint-Germain-des-Prés, just south of the city walls.) But trial by combat had grown rare, and Saint-Martin's field was now used mainly for jousts of sport, or "tilts," competitions where mounted warriors fought with lances and other weapons, whose points were often blunted to prevent serious injury or death.

The standard field for judicial combat was a flat rectangular space measuring forty by eighty paces, or about one hundred by two hundred feet. But the field at Saint-Martin's had been modified for the jousts of sport staged there, being "only 24 paces wide and 96 paces long"—about 60 by 240 feet. The longer field allowed jousting warriors to spur their mounts to higher speeds and strike even harder blows with their lances. And the field's narrower width, only a quarter of its length, placed many of the spectators watching from the sidelines much closer to the action.

The field of combat—or the "lists"—and its equipment were permanent fixtures at Saint-Martin's, always ready for jousts. But in 1386, since judicial duels had become so rare, the field needed some refurbishing for the combat between the knight and the squire. One report refers to "the lists for Jean de Carrouges and Jacques Le Gris that were made *[qui sont faittes]* at Paris in the field at Saint-Martin's," suggesting that new barriers, viewing stands, and other fittings were built at the field for the occasion.

The law required that judicial duels be fought in an enclosed field, or *champ clos.* Accordingly, the entire field was surrounded by a high wooden wall. The wall, taller than a man and made of sturdy timber latticework through which spectators could watch the duel's progress, served several purposes. It kept the two combatants from fleeing the field during the fight, prevented spectators from being injured by flying weapons, and ensured that no one interfered with the duel once it began. A second, shorter wooden fence stood around the first, and the two walls were separated by a space of smoothly raked ground, creating a cordon sanitaire around the entire field.

Regulations specified that the taller, inner wall be "seven feet in height, if not higher; and that the wood on all sides be a half-foot thick and so heavily joined, barred, fitted and made that nothing from outside the said lists can enter and nothing from within can escape. And the reason that the lists shall be made so high and so strong is so that the walls not be breached by blows, buffets, the impact of horses, or anything else that may hit them."

At the center of each short side of the field stood a heavy gate, eight feet in height, which opened and closed with a great key and was equipped on the outside with a sliding barrier. On one of the long sides of the field, adjacent to the viewing stands, was a third gate, four feet in width, by which the officials could enter and leave the field. This gate could also be locked from the outside with sliding barriers and a thick iron bar.*

At each of the four corners of the field, outside the inner wall, stood a wooden tower on which officials would stand to supervise the combat. The towers placed the officials as near as possible to the action so they were able to see and hear everything that took place. From these towers the combatants could also be supplied with food and drink during the combat.

The outer wall around the field, although not as high as the inner one, likewise had two entrances barred by heavy sliding gates, and during the combat it would be surrounded by guards to keep the crowd

---

* Instead of a third gate, one of the corners was sometimes equipped with a removable ladder so that the officials could hastily exit the field once the combat began, pulling the ladder up after themselves.

away from the inner fence and quell any noise or disturbances that might interfere with the duel.

As the date of the duel approached, Saint-Martin's field was also prepared for the thousands of spectators who would witness the combat. The vast majority of these were commoners, people from the city or its suburbs who would sit or stand on the ground around the field. But some were high-ranking nobles, members of the royal court, or guests from distant parts of France or foreign courts, all of whom expected to watch the duel in comfort.

So along one side of the field "big stands were erected, from which the lords could see the fight between the two champions." Like the wall around the field, these viewing stands were also heavily timbered affairs with railings, stairways, and comfortable seats for the most privileged spectators. The central stand, set a few feet forward of the others, was reserved for the king, his uncles, and other high-ranking nobility. Another, set to the right, held other members of the king's court. A third stand, to the left, was reserved for foreign nobles, who were to be seated "according to their rank." These three stands were reserved exclusively for the male nobility, including church prelates such as the bishop of Paris.

Additional stands to either side were set up for the ladies, these being fashioned so that their occupants could withdraw "at their pleasure," perhaps if overcome by fatigue or the violence of the spectacle. And finally, descending the social hierarchy, there were stands for "the burghers, merchants and, beneath them, the commonfolk," although most of the latter would have to find places on the ground around the field, watching the duel through the gaps in the heavy timber fencing that surrounded the field to a height well above a man's head.

Special equipment was also brought to Saint-Martin's for the duel, or constructed on the site. At opposite ends of the field, lengthwise, carpenters built two raised platforms on which they placed heavy thronelike chairs where the combatants would sit while waiting to swear the oaths. Near each chair, space was reserved for a tent or pavilion to be erected there a day or two before the duel. The small military encampment on each side of the field was completed by a mounting bench *(escabeau),* which each combatant would use to climb onto his warhorse just prior to battle. Jean de Carrouges, as the *appelant,* was assigned the camp to the right of the royal viewing stand, and Jacques Le Gris, as the *défendeur,* had the one to the left.

Once the fixtures at the field had been repaired or rebuilt, the field itself got a final treatment. First the soil within the enclosure was carefully raked to get rid of any foreign objects or irregularities such as roots and stones. Then every inch of ground was covered with a layer of clean sand. The sand rendered the field smooth and flat for a fair fight. It would also soak up any blood spilled in battle, helping prevent the iron-shod combatants from slipping and losing their balance once they were unhorsed or had dismounted to fight on foot.

The walled field at Saint-Martin's harked back to much older arenas of combat, for the judicial duel had ancient origins. Homer's *Iliad,* set in the late Bronze Age (ca. 1200 B.C.), describes two warriors fighting a duel over Helen of Troy on a carefully laid-out field that is first consecrated with oaths, prayers, and animal sacrifice. The Romans built special arenas for the bloody gladiator fights that flourished in early Christian times. And although Roman law did not include the judicial duel per se, the ancient arenas dotting medieval Europe were sometimes used for trial by combat.

The Vikings, who brought the duel with them to Normandy in the ninth century, often held their combats on islands, where they set up a circle of stones to mark out a battlefield. Among the Norse, a man could dispute any other man's claim to a piece of land—or even his wife—simply by challenging him to a duel.

In the late fourteenth century even kings still proposed battle in a *champ clos* as a way of settling their territorial disputes. During the Hundred Years' War the kings of France and England regularly challenged each other to duels. In 1383, King Richard II, only sixteen years old at the time, offered to fight the fourteen-year-old Charles VI, along with three royal uncles on either side. But nothing came of the

QUI AVOIT TUÉ SON MAISTRE FAICT A MONTARGIS.
Soubs le regne de Charles V. en 1371.

DUEL BETWEEN MAN AND DOG.

Legend tells of a combat at Paris in which a greyhound "proved" the guilt of a suspected murderer and avenged his slain master. Collection Hennin, no. 88. Bibliothèque Nationale de France.

proposal, which was very likely a negotiating tactic rather than an honest wager of battle.

A walled field was once reportedly set up in the great square before Notre-Dame cathedral for a duel between a man and a dog. The story goes that in 1372 a nobleman, one of the king's favorites, was found murdered on his estate near Paris. The murder remained a mystery, until suspicion was aroused by the fact that the victim's dog, an enormous greyhound greatly devoted to his master, always growled and barked at the sight of a certain man. This man, Richard Macaire, was known to have been jealous of the victim's good standing with the king. When the king learned of the dog's behavior, he took it as an accusation and ordered that the dog and Macaire be set against each other in a judicial duel.

On the appointed day a great crowd gathered around the wooden enclosure set up in front of Notre-Dame. Macaire was armed with a club, while the dog was provided with a large barrel open at both ends where it could take refuge. According to one account, "As soon as the dog was released, it bounded towards its opponent without delay, knowing that it was up to the appellant to attack first. But the man's heavy club kept the dog at bay, and it ran here and there around Macaire, just beyond the weapon's reach. Biding its time, turning this way and that, the greyhound finally saw its chance and suddenly leaped at the man's throat, seizing him there with such force that he dragged him down to the ground, forcing Macaire to cry for mercy." After Macaire was released from the dog's jaws, he confessed to the crime and was hanged at Montfaucon.

This story appears in many histories of France and was even put into verse by poets, although it may be apocryphal. Yet even if it has little basis in fact, it illustrates the popular belief that a bloody combat between "equals" could yield a just verdict. The king, who reportedly witnessed the duel between the man and the dog, saw the outcome as "a sign of the miraculous judgment of God."

By the time of the Parlement's decision, in mid-September, King Charles and his uncles had already left Paris for the Flemish coast to assemble the great armada for the invasion of England. Earlier that summer Charles had witnessed the knight's challenge to the squire, avidly following the quarrel until his departure from Paris. The king was in Arras, en route to the port of Sluys, when he received word that the Parlement had ordered a duel and set it for late November. This was still more than two months off, well after Charles expected to return in triumph from England.

But bad weather delayed the invasion, as violent thunderstorms sank many ships, uprooted huge trees, and felled people and animals with lightning bolts. Strange portents were also seen in France. At Plaisance, along the river Marne, lightning struck a church and flashed through the sanctuary, burning up all the wooden furniture and even the sacred vessels of the mass; only some fragments of the sanctified host remained miraculously untouched. And near Laon there occurred "a strange and unheard of thing," as great flocks of crows flew here and there carrying lighted coals, which they set down on the roofs of farm buildings filled with grain that caught fire and burned to the ground. Eventually the king and his uncles called off the invasion until the following year.

As Charles prepared to depart for Paris in mid-November, he was eagerly anticipating the duel to be fought there on the twenty-seventh. A youth of only seventeen, he loved violent sport and was devoted to the joust in particular, often riding in tournaments himself. The year before, at a tournament hosted at Cambrai, the young king had enthusiastically jousted with a Flemish knight, Sir Nicholas d'Espinoit.* Charles was so avid for jousts that a few years later, when forty English knights fought three French challengers during a three-day tourna-

---

* It was customary for kings to joust, despite the risk to their royal persons. In 1559 one of Charles's successors, Henri II, would be injured in the eye by a splintered lance and finally die of his wound after ten days of agony.

ment at Saint-Inglevert, he attended the event in disguise, accompanied by only one noble, so as to blend into the crowd and get a better view of the action.

Eager to see the combat between Carrouges and Le Gris, and alarmed at the prospect of missing it if delayed by bad weather or for other reasons, Charles took up the matter with his uncles. The dukes of Berry, Burgundy, and Bourbon, who also wanted to see the duel, urged the king to intervene. So with less than a week to spare, Charles sent a courier galloping back to Paris with sealed letters ordering the combat to be postponed until he returned and indicating as a more suitable day the Saturday after Christmas—that is, December 29.

The Parlement, in a hastily called session on November 24—just three days before the duel was to be fought—bowed to the king's wish and set the new date, postponing the duel for more than a month, although the field at Saint-Martin's was nearly ready and the two combatants were making their final preparations for battle.

Jean de Carrouges and Jacques Le Gris learned of the postponement immediately, since they were summoned to the Parlement, where the king's letters were opened and read aloud in their presence. The deferral of the duel from late November until after Christmas granted the knight and the squire—as well as the lady—another thirty days or so of life and breath. But it was not a happy or comfortable wait for any of them, especially Marguerite, who lived under a pending sentence of death by burning at the stake.

On November 26 the king and his uncles left Sluys. The next day, originally appointed for the duel, Charles arrived in Arras. On December 5, two days after his eighteenth birthday, the king entered Paris.

Waiting in Paris to greet the young king was his even younger queen, the sixteen-year-old Isabeau of Bavaria, whom he had married the previous year. Like most royal marriages, the match had been arranged by the families, who were more concerned with dynastic alliances than with the happiness of the prospective couple. The king's ambitious uncles had sought a military ally in Isabeau's father, Duke Stephen of Bavaria. And Duke Stephen equally welcomed an alliance with the French royal house. But to everyone's surprise and delight, a romantic rose sprang from the stony ground of realpolitik, as Charles and Isabeau fell passionately in love.*

During the marriage negotiations between the two royal houses, Isabeau bowed to all the customs of the French, even the requirement that any lady proposed as a bride for the king of France had to be undressed by ladies of the French court and examined completely naked—"*toute nue.*" This royal inspection, which took place before Isabeau ever met Charles, and even before Charles knew she was his prospective bride, was meant to ensure that the lady was "fit and properly formed to bear children." Isabeau accepted this test, conducted by three French duchesses, with good grace, and she apparently passed it with ease.

Shortly afterward, now clothed and bejeweled most resplendently, Isabeau was presented to Charles, as the French court eagerly watched the king's reaction. Charles spoke no German, and Isabeau knew scarcely a word of French. As Isabeau curtsied, "the King went towards her and, taking her by the hand, raised her up and looked at her long and hard. With that look love and delight entered his heart. He saw that she was very beautiful and was filled with a great desire to see her and have her." Isabeau's effect on Charles delighted the court, and the constable of France, who was there, remarked to another noble: "This lady is going to stay with us. The King cannot take his eyes off her."

Charles insisted on an immediate wedding, which took place on July 17, 1385, just four days after the couple met. Isabeau arrived in "a carriage of indescribable magnificence, wearing on her head the crown, worth a king's ransom, which the king had sent to her." The

---

* Charles sent artists to courts throughout Europe to paint pictures of the prettiest princesses for him to consider. Before he met Isabeau, he saw the image of another princess and fell in love with her, but by the time the picture reached him, she had been betrothed to another suitor.

high mass and the marriage vows, solemnized by the bishop of Amiens and witnessed by a multitude of noble guests, were followed by a great wedding feast, where counts and barons served the king and his bride at table from golden platters heaped with delicacies. Finally that evening the ladies of the court put the bride to bed, and the king, "who so much desired to find her in his bed, came too." Drawing down the curtain on the royal nuptials, the chronicler adds that "they spent the night together in great delight, as you can well believe."

By January 1386, Isabeau was pregnant, and the court buzzed with the news that a royal heir was on the way. On September 25, 1386, she gave birth to a son. All the bells of Paris rang to announce the birth of the prince, and the news was rushed to the king by courier. On October 17 the boy was christened Charles as the archbishop of Rouen performed the sacrament.

But the little dauphin was sickly, and he languished in his royal *lit d'enfant*, while his young mother fretted over him in the king's absence and the court physicians wrung their hands. By the time the king returned to Paris in early December, the infant's health had deteriorated further. All feared for his life, and the doctors watched helplessly as their future king grew weaker and weaker.

On December 28, 1386—the Feast of the Holy Innocents, just one day before Jean de Carrouges and Jacques Le Gris were to fight their long-awaited duel—the dauphin died. The court, the city, and the nation all mourned the loss of the little prince. That night his richly clothed body was carried by torchlight in a cortège of great lords to the royal sepulchre at Saint-Denis. The dauphin's death seemed to some a bad omen, since it fell on the day commemorating King Herod's slaughter of the infants.

But the royal heir's untimely death did not prevent Charles or his court from celebrating the holidays as planned. New Year's Day was a feast almost equal to Christmas, and the king threw himself and his court into a frenzy of parties, banquets, dances, and other entertainments. "The New Year was celebrated that year with unprecedented *éclat* in the court of France. . . . And without question the highlight of the festivities was the judicial duel between Jacques Le Gris and Jean de Carrouges."

In a remarkable coincidence, the lady whose fate was at stake in the duel gave birth to her child around the same time as the queen. The child, a boy christened Robert, must have arrived after July 9, when the Parlement's inquiry began, and well before November 27, the date originally set for the duel, since the high court never would have risked executing a pregnant woman. Most likely he was born between early September, nine months after Jean de Carrouges returned from Scotland, and the middle of October, nine months after the alleged rape. These dates bracket the birth of the dauphin on September 25, so the two infants may have been very nearly the same age.

But whereas the son born to the king and queen of France was lost on the eve of the duel, the son born to Jean and Marguerite, likewise their firstborn, was at risk of losing both his parents, of being suddenly orphaned, if the duel fought on the next day went badly for the knight.

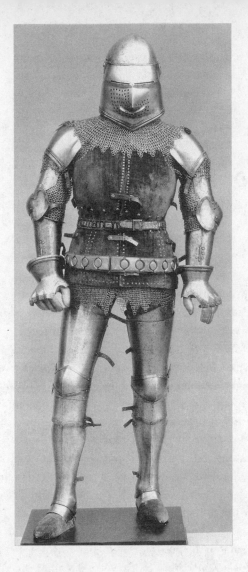

ARMOR.

Carrouges and Le Gris wore armor similar to this suit (ca. 1400), which combines mail (linked iron rings) with steel plates, and a helmet equipped with a beaked visor.

8

Oaths
and Last Words

Early on the morning of Saturday, December 29, the knight and the squire rose from bed at their separate lodgings on opposite sides of Paris. They first bathed and then heard mass, afterward breaking the fast they had kept since the night before. It was customary for combatants to fast and even keep a vigil at the altar before fighting a duel the next day. On the eve of the duel both Jean de Carrouges and Jacques Le Gris reportedly had prayers said for them in churches throughout Paris, each calling upon God to give him the victory.

After washing, praying, and eating, each man was carefully prepared for battle by his attendants. Next to his skin each put on a light linen tunic or *chemise,* and over this a heavier linen garment with padding for the ribs, groin, and other vulnerable areas. Then his armor was buckled on piece by piece, proceeding from the feet upward to reduce strain on the body during the lengthy process.

First the feet were covered with cloth or leather shoes, over which were fitted metal *sabatons* made of mail or jointed plates. Mail leggings or *chausses* followed, and over these plate armor for the fronts of the shins, knees, and thighs. A skirt of mail hung from the waist over the loins and upper legs. A sleeveless mail coat or *haubergeon* protected the torso, cinched at the waist by a leather belt. Over this went either a quilted coat covered with metal plates overlapped like scales, or a solid steel breastplate. More plates protected the shoulders and upper arms, and additional pieces the elbows and forearms. Gloves of mail and cleverly jointed plates covered the hands, with the cloth or leather lining exposed inside the hand for a better grip. A steel collar circled the neck. Finally, the head was covered by a padded leather cap, over which fitted the *bacinet*, a type of helmet with a hinged visor that lifted to expose the face and chin, and a *camail*, a curtain of mail that hung down over the neck and shoulders. A beaked visor, pierced by narrow eye-slits and breathing holes, concealed the wearer's identity when secured in place. For this reason each man wore over his suit of armor a *cotte d'armure*, a sleeveless coat embroidered with his family crest. The complete battle harness weighed about sixty pounds, not including weapons and other equipment.*

While the combatants were arming, their warhorses were also being readied for battle. The medieval warhorse was a breed apart from those produced for hunting, riding, farming, and other purposes. It was always a stallion—a knight never rode a mare into battle—and by the fourteenth century it was often a "great horse" *(equus magnus)*, standing as tall as sixteen hands and weighing up to fourteen hundred pounds. It was strong enough to carry three hundred pounds of man, armor, saddle, and weapons, with the stamina and special training needed for rapid charges, sudden turns, jumps, and other combat maneuvers. Some warhorses were even trained to attack and kill by kicking with their iron-shod hooves.

Good warhorses were expensive and could cost several hundred times the price of a workhorse or even a modest riding horse. Normandy, a region long devoted to horse-breeding, was dotted with stud farms or *haras*, producing stallions renowned throughout Europe.

---

* During the 1300s suits of mail (woven iron rings) were increasingly supplemented by riveted steel plates designed to fend off new armor-piercing weapons, from deadly crossbow bolts to spiked battle hammers. The first suits made entirely of plates appeared around 1380. But many men-at-arms still wore mail coats and leggings in combination with plate, and mail often covered the backs of arms, legs, and joints.

Carrouges had claimed during the trial that Le Gris was "a rich man abundantly supplied with good horses." As for the knight himself, despite his desperate financial straits, he hardly would have skimped on a good mount when his own life, his wife's life, and everything else depended on it. Whether each man brought to Paris a favorite mount or purchased one specially for the duel, his warhorse was reserved for combat alone.

The standard war harness for a horse included a steel bridle and bit with leather reins; four iron shoes fastened with nails; a saddle with a high pommel and cantle to keep the warrior firmly seated, girth straps to fasten it firmly to the horse, and various rings and chains for holding weapons; quilted blankets for the horse's body; a fitted headpiece of jointed metal plates known as a *chanfrain,* with holes for the eyes, ears, and nostrils; and padding to be worn beneath. Plates or curtains of mail often protected the horse's neck and flanks as well, sometimes sewn directly to the blankets. Metal stirrups hung from the saddle, and the combatants wore spurs with rowels (spiked wheels) to control their mounts, since they often dropped the reins in the thick of combat.

After putting on their armor, and while their warhorses were being readied, Jean de Carrouges and Jacques Le Gris carefully checked over their weapons. Each would carry into battle a lance, two swords, an ax, and a dagger.

The lance—a longer, heavier weapon than the ancient and early medieval throwing spear—had revolutionized warfare during the First Crusade (1095–99), when mounted French knights charging in coordinated sallies sowed panic among the Saracens. The weapon and the technique rapidly spread throughout Europe to the battlefield, tournament, and judicial duel alike. Lances measured from twelve to eighteen feet long and could weigh thirty pounds or more. The steel blade fitted to the lance tip was leaf- or lozenge-shaped and razor sharp. A rounded guard, or *vamplate,* protected the grip. The mounted warrior carried his heavy lance upright in its own stirrup, known as a fewter, until the instant he charged. Then he lowered or "couched" it (from French *coucher)* beneath his right arm, fixing the shaft in a notched rest on his shield, which in turn he braced against his chest and the saddle's raised front. A leather stop on the shaft in front of the shield kept the lance from sliding through the rest on impact. With the lance lowered and locked in place, and the knight standing astride his mount in his stirrups and his high war-saddle, the entire weight of the horse and rider lay behind the heavy wooden shaft and its sharp steel point, so that the galloping warrior became "a human projectile."

The sword was the nobleman's quintessential weapon, and a swordfight, either in the saddle or on foot, typically followed the opening joust with lances. A French royal tapestry (now lost) showed both Jean de Carrouges and Jacques Le Gris armed with "a strong short sword fashioned like a large dagger which hung along each man's thigh." A weapons inventory for a duel fought in Brittany just a few days before the Carrouges–Le Gris combat itemizes two swords, one with a blade "two and a half feet long" and a two-handed grip measuring thirteen inches; the other slightly shorter in the blade and with a one-handed grip of seven inches.* The longer, two-handed sword was for delivering terrific blows with the edge *(coups de taille)*. The shorter one-handed sword, or *estoc,* had a thicker but more pointed blade for delivering stabs or thrusts, known as blows with the point *(coups de pointe)*. Since multiple weapons were allowed, Jean de Carrouges and Jacques Le Gris probably carried at least two swords each. The two-handed long sword usually hung from the saddle in a leather sheath, while the shorter *estoc* was slung from the waist on the left, as most warriors were right-handed, so it could be drawn quickly and easily.

The ax—also shown in the lost tapestry of the Carrouges–Le Gris duel—was a popular weapon in the mid- to late fourteenth century, since it could cut through mail and plate alike and even cleave through a helmet and brain a man. Some knights favored the ax over all other weapons. The typical ax *(hache)* of this period had a flaring

---

* This duel, fought by two noblemen over a murder case on December 19, 1386, at Nantes, was not authorized by the French king or his Parlement but by the nearly independent Duke of Brittany.

blade on one side balanced on the other by a heavy spiked hammer or "raven's beak" *(bec de corbin),* and a sharp lance-blade mounted in between on the end of the stave. Men-at-arms reverenced this versatile three-in-one weapon as "the Trinity." For foot combat, the stave was five feet long or more, enabling great side-to-side swings that could clear a swath through enemy troops. But it was shortened to three or four feet for use in the saddle, where it hung within easy reach on a metal ring attached to the saddle-bow.

The dagger was for close hand-to-hand combat, and for dispatching a wounded or dying enemy in the final stages of battle. It could also be thrown through the air as a missile. A newer weapon than the ancient sword or centuries-old lance, the dagger was adopted by the nobility around the end of the thirteenth century. By the late 1300s, the typical dagger had a sturdy blade six to twelve inches in length with a sharp point for finding the crevices in plate armor or stabbing through the ear-holes or eye-slits of a helmet. The dagger listed in the inventory of dueling weapons from Brittany was "made of iron or steel or both together" with a blade "about nine inches in length from the grip."

Besides his lance, swords, ax, and dagger, each man bore a shield emblazoned with his family arms. Shields were made of tough wood such as oak or ash covered by boiled leather *(cuir-boulli)* dried and hardened to an armorlike finish and reinforced with horn plating or metal bands. As plate armor increasingly replaced mail and became the warrior's main defense, shields shrank in size, covering just the mounted warrior's neck and torso and forming a target for his opponent's lance. After drawing his sword in the saddle or dismounting to fight on foot, the warrior slung his shield around his neck by its strap to keep both hands free, or wore it on his left arm to fend off swings or thrusts from his opponent's weapons.

On the day of the duel Carrouges and Le Gris also carried to the field with their weapons a leather bottle filled with wine, some bread wrapped up in a strip of cloth, and a purse of silver coins to pay for the use of the field. Each carried fodder for his horse as well, in case the quarrel was not settled by nightfall and the combat had to continue into a second day.

As the two combatants dressed for battle at their lodgings in the early morning hours, spectators were already thronging the field at Saint-Martin's to see the duel. News of the combat had spread throughout France "as far as the most distant parts of the kingdom, and it caused such a stir that people came to Paris to see it from many different places," including Normandy, where the two men and their families were well known, as was the lady.

The duel fell not only during Christmas week but also on the feast day of the martyred saint Thomas Becket. Many shops in Paris were closed for the holy day, and people were in a festive mood. Spectators began arriving soon after first light, and by sunrise—between 7:30 and 8:00 A.M. in late December—they were streaming along the rue Saint-Martin and through the priory gate. By mid-morning an immense crowd of many thousands packed the monastery grounds. Guards armed with spears and maces were posted around the walled field to keep the crowd away from the fence and clear of the gates.

The winter of 1386–87 was bitterly cold and snowy in northern France. The sun threw little warmth onto the field, and the stone walls enclosing the priory grounds offered scant shelter from the freezing winds that gusted through the city. So the earliest spectators that morning had to endure a long, bone-chilling wait to secure good places. Nobles, prelates, and even some city officials and merchants had assured seats in the viewing stands and could arrive at their leisure. But most of the people pouring in to fill the space around the field—shopkeepers and artisans, laborers, apprentices, university students, and fishwives, as well as beggars and cutpurses—had to scramble for places, elbowing one another for choice spots. As the clock bells of Paris tolled each hour and space grew scarcer around the field, some people even sat on the monastery walls or perched in the few available trees for a better view.

The chief spectators in attendance that day were King Charles and his uncles—the dukes of Burgundy, Berry, and Bourbon. The royal party arrived several hours after the first spectators, although still well before noon, when the combatants were legally required to appear at the field, ready for combat. As the young king with his colorful entourage of courtiers rode through the gate and onto the monastery grounds, trumpets blared to announce his arrival. The huge crowd around the field turned eagerly to watch the royal procession, knowing that the official ceremonies of the duel would soon begin.

Almost every public event in the Middle Ages, whether a marriage or a funeral, a coronation or an execution, involved a procession. The trumpeters announcing the king were followed by the marshal, who would act as the master of ceremonies at the field. Then came the *roi d'armes,* an official who would supervise all matters relating to armor and weapons, followed by several heralds, "persons of loud voice" who would serve as the public address system. Next came a squire in royal livery bearing on a pillow the unsheathed Sword of Justice—a long, gleaming silver blade with a jeweled hilt symbolizing the king's authority over the field of battle. Then on a horse draped in the royal colors came young King Charles himself, escorted by four knights serving as official witnesses *(escoutes)* to the combat, and finally the king's uncles and other high-ranking nobility who would attend Charles in the royal viewing stand. Guards armed with spears also rode in the royal entourage or followed on foot.

The king was not just the most exalted spectator at the duel but also by law the presiding judge. The Parlement had authorized the duel in the king's name, and Charles, as God's anointed, acted in the name of the ultimate King and Judge, who was about to reveal his verdict on the case at hand. Charles, who had ordered the duel postponed for a full month so that he could see it after returning from Flanders, also insisted that on the day of the duel nothing begin until his arrival at the field. Once the king took his seat in the royal viewing stand, on a coal-warmed and cushioned throne draped in royal blue and embroidered with golden fleurs-de-lis, the ceremonies of the combat officially began.

Jean de Carrouges, the *appelant,* arrived at the field first, riding at the head of his own colorful procession of pledges and relatives, followed by squires and attendants carrying his combat necessaries. In accord with the rules, he rode to the field on a palfrey—a riding horse—"with visor open, sword and dagger on his belt, and in all respects ready to do combat." A page led the knight's saddled and armored warhorse, while other attendants carried his lance and shield.

Besides his weapons, the knight bore a three-foot pole painted blue and surmounted with a silver crucifix, frequently making the sign of the cross as he rode. His shield, like the embroidered coat worn over his armor, was emblazoned with the Carrouges family arms: a crimson field sown with silver fleurs-de-lis. The knight's retinue included the Count Waleran de Saint-Pol and Marguerite's cousin, Robert de Thibouville, also serving as one of his pledges.

Next came the Lady Carrouges, dressed in a long black robe and riding in a carriage draped in black. The carriage may have been customary for a lady, or a concession to Marguerite's having recently risen from childbed. Marguerite's entourage included her father, Sir Robert de Thibouville, and her cousin, Thomin du Bois, who earlier that year had challenged Adam Louvel to a separate duel that the Parlement of Paris had disallowed.

The excited crowd strained to catch sight of the infamous Lady Carrouges as she rode into view. Marguerite's youth and beauty, her stark black clothing, and her role as the accuser in the celebrated affair now made her the chief object of everyone's attention. People momentarily forgot the king and his splendidly attired uncles, and even the warlike knight, all turning to watch as the notorious cause of the quarrel arrived at the field.

Although Marguerite had not yet been legally condemned, she would witness the duel under a sentence of death, to be carried out immediately if her husband were slain. Black, the traditional color of mourning and death, was often worn by the executioner and his victims, including witches and heretics condemned to be burned. Marguerite's robe marked her as a woman whose fate hung in the balance that day.

The lady's relatives and friends, and probably many others in the crowd, pitied her plight. Her husband's friends included powerful and respected nobles who had welcomed the couple in Paris and offered themselves as pledges to guarantee the knight's appearance at the field. Many people, according to Jean Le Coq, the squire's lawyer, believed in the knight's cause and felt sympathy for the lady.

But many others, the lawyer says, supported Jacques Le Gris, including influential members of the royal court and perhaps the king himself, since Le Gris was the favorite of Count Pierre, the king's cousin. Le Gris's family and friends fiercely hated Marguerite for having sullied the squire's name and imperiled his life by accusing him of the infamous crime. They dearly hoped to see the knight slain and his lady burned by day's end.

Feelings were not as sharply divided among those in the crowd who had no personal stake in the quarrel, many of whom were not even familiar with the details of the case. To the more casual onlookers at the field that day, the duel, a rare event that most had never witnessed, was mainly an entertaining spectacle to brighten up Christmas week with its pageantry and violence. Some no doubt pitied Marguerite, but others sent wild rumors and evil gossip flying through the chilly air, warming themselves to a fever pitch for the imminent duel and the even more spectacular burning of the lady that might follow.

Was she a witch? A sorceress? A seductress? As Marguerite arrived at the field, the winter breeze slapping at her face and tugging at her sable garments, she must have felt the mixture of sympathy, hostility, and curiosity in the thousands of faces that turned to stare at her from all sides. Even her public appearance before the Parlement of Paris several months earlier could not have prepared her for this ordeal.

Last in the procession rode Jacques Le Gris with his entourage of family and friends, including the nobles from Count Pierre's court who served as his pledges. As the man accused of the infamous crime, Jacques Le Gris likewise drew curious stares from the crowd. Behind him came his retinue of assistants carrying his shield and other equipment, and a page leading his warhorse. In an ironic symbol of the quarrel, Le Gris's coat-of-arms shared its colors with the knight's, but in reverse—a silver field slashed with a bloodred stripe.

At the edge of the walled field, the knight and his party rode to the king's right, while the squire and his entourage rode to the left. Each halted at the gate on his side of the field by his own pavilion, chair, and mounting bench. The marshal then rode from his place before the king's throne to the right-hand gate, followed on horseback by a herald and two of the four knights serving as official witnesses. Another herald and the other two witnesses rode to the left-hand gate.

At the right-hand gate the marshal reined his horse around to face the mounted *appelant* and demanded to know who he was, why he appeared here armed for battle, and the nature of his cause.

In a loud voice, so as to be heard by the huge crowd, the knight replied: "My very honored lord and marshal of the field, I am Jean de Carrouges, knight, who have come before you as commanded by our lord the king, armed and mounted as a gentleman who must enter the lists to do battle against Jacques Le Gris, squire, in the quarrel concerning his foul crime against my lady-wife, Marguerite de Carrouges. And I hereby call upon Our Lord, Our Lady, and the good knight Saint George as witnesses to my cause on this day.* And I hereby present myself in person to do my duty, asking that you give to me my just portion of the field and of the wind and the sun, and all those things profitable, necessary, and appropriate in such a case. And I hereby swear that I will carry out my duty with the help of Our Lord, Our Lady, and the good knight Saint George. And I declare that I will fight on either horseback or on foot as seems best to me, and that I will arm myself with my own armor, or disarm myself, and carry such weapons as I please, either for the attack or defense, both before the fight and during it, as God gives me leave and the might to do so."

---

* Saint George, the renowned dragon-slayer, was the patron saint of knights.

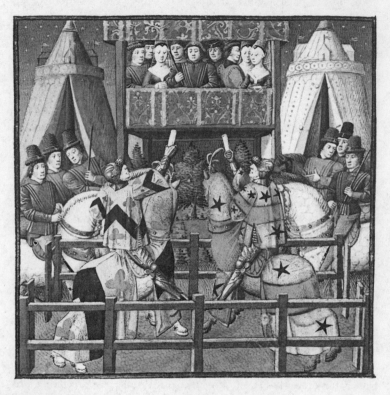

THE SCROLLS.

Prior to the duel, the combatants present scrolls containing statements of their charges. MS. fr. 2258, fol. 14v. Bibliothèque Nationale de France.

After the *appelant* had spoken, the *défendeur* was formally summoned to the field. At the marshal's signal, a herald cried out: "Monsieur Jacques Le Gris, come to do your duty against Monsieur Jean de Carrouges."

The marshal rode across the field until he was face-to-face with Jacques Le Gris, and he likewise demanded to know who he was, why he appeared here armed for battle, and the nature of his cause.

Le Gris answered loudly, "My very honored lord and marshal of the field, I am Jacques Le Gris, squire, who have come before you as commanded by our lord the king, armed and mounted as a gentleman who must enter the lists to do battle against Jean de Carrouges, knight, in the quarrel concerning the infamous accusation that he has falsely and most unjustly laid against my honor and good name. And I hereby call upon Our Lord, Our Lady, and the good knight Saint George as witnesses to my cause on this day. And I hereby present myself in person to do my duty, asking that you give to me my just portion of the field and of the wind and the sun, and all those things profitable, necessary, and appropriate in such a case. And I hereby swear that I will carry out my duty with the help of Our Lord, Our Lady, and the good knight Saint George."

After both men had spoken, they presented their charges in writing, each holding up a parchment scroll containing a summary of his case. The scrolls had been prepared in advance by their lawyers. Carrouges and Le Gris, still mounted and facing each other across the field, brandished their furled scrolls in the air like weapons. The verbal jousting of the law court was about to give way to actual battle on the field, and the marshal now asked the king to declare the field open for combat.

At the king's command, the marshal signaled for the combatants to dismount and take possession of their camps. Each man sat down on the large raised chair in front of his pavilion, facing his opponent across the length of the field. Their pledges were released, having ensured that each combatant had appeared at the field of battle on the appointed day. All mounts except for the two warhorses reserved for combat were led away from the field.

As Carrouges and Le Gris took their seats and the officials began preparing for the duel, Marguerite remained by the side of the field in her carriage, waiting for the formal oaths to take place and for the combat to begin. But she had not been there long when King Charles ordered her down from her seat.

Marguerite was then made to mount a scaffold of her own, all covered in black and within clear view of the entire field, "there to await God's mercy and a favorable outcome in the battle."

Once the two combatants and the lady were in their places, the *roi d'armes*, aided by the two *escoutes* assigned to each combatant, began examining each man's weapons, making sure that no illegal devices had been brought to the field and that the lances, swords, axes, and daggers were all the same length.

While the weapons were being examined, one of the heralds stepped onto the field to proclaim the rules and regulations to the crowd:

"Hear ye, hear ye, hear ye, lords, knights, squires, and all other manner of people, that by the command of our lord the King of France it is strictly prohibited, on pain of death and the loss of property, for anyone here to be armed or to carry a sword or dagger or any other weapon whatsoever, unless he be one of the official guardians of the field or one who has the express permission of our lord the king.

"Furthermore, by the command of our lord the king, it is strictly prohibited for any person of whatsoever degree to remain on horseback during the combat, except for the combatants themselves, and that any nobleman who so does shall lose his horse; and that any servant who so does shall lose an ear.

"Furthermore, by the command of our lord the king, it is strictly prohibited for any person, of whatsoever degree, to enter the field of battle or to be present in the lists, except for those expressly authorized to do so; and that any person who so does shall lose his life and his property.

"Furthermore, by the command of our lord the king, it is strictly prohibited for any person of whatsoever degree not to remain seated on his bench or on the ground and to obstruct the view of any other person, on pain of losing a hand.

"Furthermore, by the command of our lord the king, it is strictly prohibited for any person of whatsoever degree, to speak, gesture, cough, spit, cry out, or do any such thing whatever it may be during the battle, under pain of losing his life and his property."

Clearly, judicial duels were not raucous entertainments interrupted by cheers and catcalls from the crowd. Any interference, even an involuntary outburst, would be severely punished. Chroniclers describe enthralled spectators watching duels in complete silence, scarcely daring to breathe.

From this point on, a fearful symmetry marked all the ceremonies of the duel. The elaborate rules and rituals were meant to ensure a fair fight, leaving nothing to chance—or Providence—"except, of course, the outcome itself." Just as their weapons were checked for equal length, the two men themselves had to be placed on an equal footing. Jean de Carrouges was a knight, but Jacques Le Gris was only a squire. So Le Gris now stepped onto the field and knelt before the marshal to be knighted.

Knighting—or "dubbing"—was not always an elaborate ritual involving a vigil, the presentation of arms, and the like. Nor was it always conferred for valor on the field after the fact; men were sometimes knighted on the eve of battle in order to motivate them. All it took to make the squire a knight in name was three taps on the shoulder with the flat of the marshal's sword, and the ceremonial words "In the name of God, of Saint Michael, and Saint George, I make thee a knight; be valiant, courteous, and loyal!"

To be a knight in deed was a different thing entirely. This required constant practice with the sword, as well as sharpening one's skills on horseback in the joust or tournament, and the unequaled training of actual combat. Over the years Jean de Carrouges had fought in numerous battles. Since youth he had taken part in—and survived—many campaigns, most recently in Scotland. Jacques Le Gris, although one of the king's personal squires and captain of the fort at Exmes, had seen less military service than his opponent.

But Jacques Le Gris was the bigger and stronger man, which gave him a different advantage in battle. The much wealthier squire was also able to equip himself with a better horse, armor, and weapons. And Le Gris, despite having fallen ill in September after learning that a duel had been ordered, was now in excellent health, "appearing to be strong," while "Carrouges was weak from a fever that he had suffered from for a long time." The knight, says one report, "had been seized by a fresh onset of the fever that very day."

Any of these factors—physical size and strength, health, wealth, military training, and experience—could prove decisive in battle, and calculating how they would play out on the field was impossible. The duel could also turn on any of a thousand chance events that there was no predicting, from slippery footing or a broken armor-strap to the sudden glare of sunlight on the enemy's armor or a whirling blade.

After Jacques Le Gris was knighted and had returned to his chair, the herald stepped onto the field again, this time to proclaim the rules governing the combatants themselves:

"Item, if either combatant shall carry onto the field of battle any sort of arms forbidden by the laws of France, these arms shall be confiscated, and in place of them he shall have no others.

"Item, if either combatant shall carry onto the field of battle any arms that have been forged with spells, charms, enchantments, or any other evil arts whereby the strength or skill of his opponent is impeded either before, during, or after the combat, so that his rights and honor are put into jeopardy, then shall the malefactor be punished as an enemy of God, or as a traitor or a murderer, as the case may be.

"Item, each combatant must carry with him to the field enough bread, wine, and other food and drink to sustain him for the space of a day if he should have need of it, as well as anything else convenient or necessary for himself as well as his horse.

"Item, each man is to fight on horseback and on foot armed in the manner that pleases him, with any weapon or device of attack or defense, except for weapons or devices of evil design, or made with charms or spells, or any other thing that is forbidden by God and Holy Church to all good Christians.

"Item, each combatant must swear and declare that if it does not please God for him to have defeated his enemy or thrown him from the field by sunset, he will accept this as the will of God and agree to present himself again on the following day to continue the combat."

A duel might last all day and still not reach a resolution by sunset—or "by the time the stars appear in the sky." If so, the combat would resume the next day. As for occult influence on the outcome of a duel, this was a genuine concern in the Middle Ages, since combatants sometimes resorted to charms, spells, and even special weapons forged with magic in order to ensure a favorable result. Men engaged to fight a judicial duel were therefore strictly forbidden, on pain of death, to use any magical arts to thwart its divinely ordered verdict.

After hearing the rules, each combatant had to swear three formal oaths. The religious element of the duel now came to the fore, as priests brought onto the field and placed at its center an altar—a table "five feet long, three feet wide, and two feet high, richly covered with a gold cloth"—on which they set a silver crucifix and a prayer book opened to an image of Christ's Passion.

The priests, the altar, and the sacred objects on display were meant to sanctify the combat as a divine judgment, or *judicium Dei*. The crucifix and prayer book also called to mind the trial, judgment, and execution that Christ had innocently suffered for the sins of mankind. Here, on a field blessed by the symbols of Christ's Passion, God would reveal the guilty party, who this day would shed his blood for his own sins.

THE OATHS.

The combatants kneel face-to-face, touching a prayer book and a crucifix, as they swear solemn oaths witnessed by priests.

MS. fr. 2258, fol. 18v. Bibliothèque Nationale de France.

The first oath was sworn by each party separately, the marshal offi-ciating as the priests stood witness. First the *appellant,* Jean de Car-rouges, left his chair and approached the altar, where he knelt with open visor and right hand bared to touch the cross, saying "I swear upon this remembrance of the Passion of our Lord God Jesus Christ, and upon the Holy Gospel which is here, and on the faith of the true Christian and Holy Baptism, that I firmly believe my cause to be holy, good, and just, and that I lawfully defend myself in this wager of bat-tle." Then he again called on God, the Virgin Mary, and Saint George as his witnesses.

After the knight had returned to his chair, Jacques Le Gris ap-proached the altar, knelt, and similarly swore to his own innocence.

For the second oath, both combatants knelt facing each other across the altar, their bared hands again placed on the crucifix and nearly touching. Each man swore that his cause was just, that he spoke the truth on peril of his soul, and that he would give up the joys of heaven for the pains of hell if he swore untruthfully. Each also swore that he carried no magical charms on his own person or his horse, "and that he placed his sole reliance on the justice of his cause, his body, his horse, and his arms." Each man then kissed the crucifix.

The third and last oath was the most binding. The two men re-mained kneeling face-to-face across the altar, their visors open and their right hands touching the crucifix, but this time also clasping each other by the bared left hand (*"la main sinistre"*) as the marshal held their joined hands in his open palm. Thus locked together, the two combatants now swore an oath to each other, beginning again with Carrouges:

"O thou, Jacques Le Gris, whom I hold by the hand, I swear on the Holy Gospels and by the faith and baptism that I hold from God that the deeds and words that I have attributed and made others attribute to you are true, and I have a good and true cause to summon you, while yours is evil."

As his opponent still grasped him by the left hand, Jacques Le Gris replied: "O thou, Jean de Carrouges, whom I hold by the hand, I swear on the Holy Gospels and by the faith and baptism that I hold from God that you have an evil cause to summon me. And I have a good and loyal cause to defend myself."

After swearing, each man kissed the crucifix again.

The third and final oath was like those that marked many medieval rituals, from marriage to vassalage. But in swearing these other mutual oaths, the parties always held each other by the *right* hand, whereas for the duel they joined *left* hands, signifying that in this case their bond was a hostile one.

In swearing the oaths, the combatants put at hazard not only their lives, fortunes, and word of honor but also their immortal souls. One of the priests now pointed to the sacred objects on the altar and solemnly reminded both men, and all those present, that the duel's outcome would decide "the damnation of the one who is in the wrong, in both soul and body, as a result of the great oaths they have sworn, whence they will be judged by the sentence of God."

After the priest's warning, the two combatants rose together and returned to their chairs on opposite sides of the field.

Once both men had identified themselves, stated their charges, presented their scrolls, handed their weapons over to be examined, heard all the rules of combat, and solemnly sworn the three great oaths, one final ceremony remained.

Duels to the death had become rare in France, and rarer still were duels in which a lady's fate also hung in the balance. As the chief witness in the case, Marguerite had to swear her own oath after the two combatants had sworn theirs.

Jean de Carrouges approached his wife and stood before her, his visor raised, and spoke the following words:

"Lady, on your evidence I am about to hazard my life in combat with Jacques Le Gris. You know whether my cause is just and true."

As the huge crowd listened in silence, all eyes upon her, Marguerite replied: "My lord, it is so, and you can fight with confidence, for the cause is just."

Last Words.

Marguerite, shown here in her carriage,
saying good-bye to Jean just before the duel
begins. Jean de Wavrin, Chronique
d'Angleterre. *MS. Royal 14 E. IV, fol. 267v.*
By permission of the British Library.

To which the knight said simply: "Let it be in God's hands."

These were the last words that Jean and Marguerite spoke to each other before the duel. Both knew that these might be the last words they would ever speak to each other in this life.

The knight then "kissed his wife, pressed her hand, and made the sign of the cross." After this final embrace he turned and went back to his place on the right side of the field.

A chronicler describes how Marguerite anxiously watched her husband prepare to enter the lists to fight for their lives:

"The lady remained on the side of the field, praying fervently to God and the Virgin Mary, entreating them humbly to grant her victory on that day in accordance with her right. You will understand that she was in great anxiety and far from certain that her own life was safe, for if her husband got the worst of it, the sentence was that she should be burned without appeal. I do not know—for I never spoke with her—whether she had not often regretted having gone so far with the matter that she and her husband were in such grave danger—and then finally there was nothing for it but to await the outcome."

Marguerite was indeed in grave danger. The grisly death of a royal official executed on trumped-up charges of heresy during the reign of Charles VI suggests the horrible fate that awaited her if her husband should lose the duel: "They hustled him on. The fire was ready. A gibbet had been set up in the square, and at the foot of it a stake with a heavy iron chain. Another chain hung from the top of the gibbet with an iron collar attached. This collar, which opened on a hinge, was put round his neck, then fastened and hauled upwards so that he should last longer. The first chain was wound round him to bind him more tightly to the stake. He was screaming and shouting. As soon as he was secured to the stake, great heaps of wood were piled against it and set on fire. They flamed up immediately. So was he hanged and burned, and the King of France could have seen him from his window if he had wanted to."

If Marguerite was to be burned, the king of France would be able to watch her death, too. From the king down to the lowest peasant, medieval people thronged enthusiastically to gruesome spectacles of torture and death, and even children regularly witnessed burnings, beheadings, hangings, drownings, live burials, and other cruel punishments. Reports suggest that victims of burning at the stake could take half an hour or more to die in the flames.

The chronicler can hardly be exaggerating when he says that Marguerite was in great anxiety as she looked upon the field where her fate would soon be decided. He even imagines that by now she regretted taking her accusations so far as to put her own life, and her husband's, in such jeopardy. But he admits that he could not know what she was thinking, since he never spoke with her, drawing a curtain over her private thoughts and feelings at this agonizing moment.

9

MORTAL COMBAT

A fter all the ceremonies were performed and all the necessary words spoken, the time had come for battle. Jean de
Carrouges and Jacques Le Gris disappeared into their pavilions, where each man's attendants carefully checked over his armor
and weapons one last time. The priests hurriedly removed the altar,
crucifix, and prayer book from the field, taking care to leave no sacred
objects behind. Two attendants swept the sand smooth where the altar
had stood, turning the field again into a blank white sheet. The king,
his court, and the immense crowd all watched in anticipation, eagerly
awaiting the start of the combat.

When both combatants had signaled their readiness, and everyone
had exited through the gates, a herald again stepped to the center of
the field. He stood facing the king, waiting for complete silence. As a
hush fell over the crowd, the only sounds to be heard were the snap-
ping of the pennants above the red and silver pavilions and the snort-
ing warhorses held at the ready near the mounting benches.

Suddenly, in a loud voice that could be heard from one end of the
field to the other, the herald shouted:

"Faites vos devoirs!" (Do your duty!)

Before he could shout this command a third time, as required by
law, the two combatants sallied forth from their pavilions, weapons at

their side, their visors now locked down, each followed by a crowd of anxious attendants. Carrouges and Le Gris strode in their clinking armor toward their horses, held at the ready just outside the gates on opposite sides of the field. Each man placed one iron-shod foot firmly on the mounting bench next to his horse, poised for action.

The herald now left the field, and the marshal took his place. The four noble witnesses or *escoutes* also took up their posts, one pair of knights standing on each side of the field, before the open gates, barring the way with a lance held horizontally between them. The marshal stood at the center of the field, holding up a single white glove. All eyes were on him. As the two warriors stood at the ready beside their steeds, watching and listening intently, the marshal slowly raised the glove high over his head. Suddenly he threw it forward through the air, shouting the customary command:

"Laissez-les aller!" (Let them go!)

Before the glove touched the ground, or the marshal had shouted the command a third time, the combatants seized their pommels and hoisted themselves into their saddles, helped along by their attendants. Squires posted alongside the horses thrust toward each man his lance and shield. The combatants already wore swords and daggers on their belts, and each had slung his second, longer sword from a saddle-ring, along with his ax. The unwieldy lance, left for last, was seized from the saddle and rammed upright into its fewter. As soon as each man was mounted and fully armed, his attendants jumped back. The mounting was the last allowable contact with human hands prior to combat. From now on each man was on his own.

Jean de Carrouges and Jacques Le Gris at once spurred their horses forward. The four *escoutes* barring the field dropped their lances and leaped aside as the combatants charged through the gates on each side of the field. Guards instantly slammed the heavy doors shut and locked them, standing by with their weapons at the ready. The marshal had hurriedly left the field through the small central gate in front of the royal box, carefully locking it behind himself.

Carrouges and Le Gris were now imprisoned together on the field, all escape blocked by a double timber wall and a hedge of sharp steel thrown up by the guards. Just inside the gates they halted their horses to size each other up across the field through their lowered visors, their mounts stamping impatiently beneath them. "They sat their horses very prettily, for both were skilled in arms. And the lords of France delighted to see it, for they had come to watch the two men fight."

As the huge crowd seethed with pent-up excitement, the two deadly enemies studied each other intently, their breath hot behind their visors, and the inside of their armor already damp with sweat. Each sought the other's death as fire and water seek each other's annihilation.

The *champ clos,* at first a prison, now became a crucible where one man would be destroyed and the other purged in the name of justice. Carrouges and Le Gris would fight without quarter until one of three things happened. Either one man killed the other, thus proving the truth of his charges and his enemy's guilt; or one man forced the other to confess he had sworn falsely, resulting in the convicted man's summary execution by hanging; or one man ejected his opponent from the field, which likewise proved his guilt and thus condemned him.

They would fight not only without quarter but also without rules. In mortal combat, unlike a friendly tournament, nothing prevented a man from stabbing his opponent in the back or through the eye-slits of his helmet, or blinding him with sand, or tripping him, or kicking him, or jumping on him if he should slip and fall. In a duel fought in Flanders in 1127 the two exhausted combatants finally threw down their weapons and fell to wrestling on the ground and punching each other with their iron gauntlets, until one reached under the other's armor and tore away his testicles, killing him on the spot. Chivalry might have been alive and well in jousts of sport, and even in the preliminary ceremonies of the judicial duel, but once the actual combat began, chivalry was dead.

KNIGHTS JOUSTING.

Two mounted warriors charge with lowered lances on a field surrounded by a heavy timber fence. Jean de Wavrin, Chronique d'Angleterre. *MS. Royal 14 E. IV, fol. 81. By permission of the British Library.*

Jean de Carrouges, as the accuser, began the combat by charging first. The knight lowered his lance into its rest, couching it tightly under his right arm, and took careful aim at his enemy. Then he clapped spurs to his horse and began advancing down the field. Jacques Le Gris, seeing his enemy on the move, instantly lowered his lance as well and spurred his horse forward, running directly at his opponent.

At the moment they started toward each other down the field, the two mounted men were more than seventy yards apart. But a strong warhorse could go from a dead stop to a gallop in a few seconds. Even at a modest trot of ten to fifteen miles per hour, the combined speed of the two horses racing toward each other closed the distance between them in a little over five seconds.

For Marguerite, watching from her scaffold alongside the field, those few seconds must have seemed an eternity. She saw her husband lower his lance and spur his horse forward, its flank muscles flexing as it kicked back a white plume of sand. Jacques Le Gris began his charge an instant later at the other end of the field, and suddenly the air was filled with the rumble of pounding hooves. Every eye at the field was riveted on the two charging warriors and their leveled lances.

Since this was not a joust of sport, the field had no tilt-fence down its center to guide the combatants and keep their horses from colliding, but they "advanced on as straight a line as if it had been drawn with a cord." The two warriors sped toward each other, the sharp steel points of their lances flying through the air before them like deadly missiles. The combined weight of horse, man, armor, and lance put nearly a ton of galloping momentum behind each tip. A blow with the speeding lance could penetrate shield and armor and flesh to the bone, or snag a metal joint and dislocate a shoulder, or lift a knight clear out of the saddle, dashing him to the ground in his heavy battle harness with broken or twisted limbs.

The pennons fluttered on the warriors' lances as they flew along, and their horses' caparisons rippled above the spraying sand. Sunlight glittered on their polished steel helms and armor plates, throwing beams of light around the field as the stallions raced toward each other. At the center of the field the marshal's white glove still lay where it had fallen on the sand.

Near that spot the two charging warriors met with a terrific crash, "hitting each other clean and hard on their shields, so that both were nearly knocked to the ground." As the spectators all winced at the concussion, each man "was bent almost backward on the crupper of his horse." But both were skilled riders, and "they gripped their horses with their legs and stayed on." By striking each other at the same instant with their measured lances, they had perfectly balanced their blows on either side. Neither man was injured or thrown, and neither lost his lance or shield. Recovering from their blows, "each went back to his own end of the field to rest a little and get his breath back."

For the second course, each man pointed his lance a little higher than before, taking aim at the other's head. Sir Jean lowered and braced his lance, "gripped his shield tight and spurred his horse on. When his opponent saw him coming, he did not hold back but rode at him in the straightest possible line." Advancing toward each other furiously, the two knights met again with another terrific crash, "hitting each other with their war lances on the steel helms, and striking them so clean and hard that sparks of fire flew from them." But as their blades struck the tops of their helmets, "their lances slipped over them, and they passed each other without hurt."

The combatants, having "grown warm," rested again before their third charge. Then, "after bracing their shields and examining each other through the visors of their helmets," they again clapped spurs to their mounts and charged with "lances lowered and braced." This time they aimed again for each other's shields. Thundering down the field, they struck each other "with great violence," each driving his steel lance-tip into the other's shield with a tremendous crash that echoed from the stone walls around the field.

The force of the blow shattered their lances, and the pieces "flew to a greater height than they could have been thrown." Each lance broke off at the stump, and the steel tip, with a length of splintered shaft, stuck fast in each shield. The shock of the blow "staggered their horses," knocking the riders back in their saddles and nearly throwing them off. But the splintering of the lances absorbed much of the blow, and both combatants managed to stay in the saddle. "Had the lances not broken, one or both must have fallen to the ground."

As Carrouges recovered, cantering to his end of the field and wheeling about, he threw down his useless lance butt and wrenched the shattered tip from his shield. Then he drew his ax from its saddle-ring. Le Gris, at his end of the field, did the same.

Their axes at the ready, the two men rode toward each other again, but this time more slowly, jockeying and maneuvering for position. As they met in midfield, they closed in an ever tightening circle, until their horses were nearly nose to tail, and the two men could grapple with their weapons across the narrowing space between them.

As their horses circled, kicking sand to all sides, the two men fought nearly "body to body, chest to chest," their ax-blades flashing above their heads. During this chivalric dance of death, they locked axes several times. Pulling each other back and forth in their saddles, each tried "to unbalance his adversary and to make him fall from the saddle by hooking him in the curved part of his *hache*."

Several times they broke apart, wheeled away, and came at each other again with axes raised as if to cleave each other in half. Back and forth they traded ferocious blows, their horses rocking beneath them, so close together that the warriors kicked each other with their stir-ruped feet, their metal shoes clanging, as they maneuvered their mounts.

At times they fought one-handed, raising their shields with their free arms to fend off each other's blows. But they could not strike full blows this way, and often they let their shields hang loose to swing their axes with both hands, using them for both attack and defense. The steel blades rang against each other, and wooden stave thudded against stave.

The ax battle raged on without either combatant gaining the advantage, until both men grew tired from their efforts. "Several times they broke apart to rest and catch their breath, afterwards resuming in vain their struggle."

Finally Jacques Le Gris spurred his horse away again, as if to rest once more, only to wheel suddenly about and ride straight back at the knight. Carrouges raised his shield to fend off Le Gris's attack. As Le Gris swerved into striking position, gripping his ax with both hands, he swung with all his strength. The blade struck the knight's upraised shield at an angle, glanced off, and came down on his horse's neck just below the overlapping plates that hung from the *chanfrain* along its mane.

The blade sliced through the horse's spine, and the animal screamed and shuddered beneath Carrouges. Its legs folded, and it sank to the sand, blood pouring from its nostrils and neck. As his horse crashed to the ground, the knight leaped clear of his stricken mount, having the presence of mind to hang on to his ax.

Without pausing, Le Gris wheeled and charged again, his ax raised menacingly at the unhorsed knight. As he bore down on Carrouges, Le Gris flipped the bloody blade to the back and led with the weapon's spiked hammer. The sharp metal prong could punch a hole through a helmet and brain a man, especially when swung from high in the saddle against an enemy on foot.

Carrouges, seeing Le Gris riding down on him with raised ax, and hearing his horse's death throes behind him, jumped away from its thrashing hooves and stood to face the charge, his own *hache* at the ready. As Le Gris began another two-handed swing, Carrouges suddenly leaped out of the way, throwing Le Gris off balance as he twisted in the saddle to follow his moving target, and causing him to check his blow.

As Le Gris's horse swept past him, Carrouges lunged forward and drove the lance-point of his ax into the horse's belly just behind the girth strap. The weapon's entire head sank into the horse's entrails— lance, blade, and spike—catching in its guts like a harpoon, and the galloping animal tore the stave from the knight's grip as it charged

SWORD BATTLE ON FOOT.

Two combatants fight with swords, as officials and spectators watch from outside the enclosure. MS. fr. 2258, fol. 22r. Bibliothèque Nationale de France.

past. The horse crumpled to the ground with a terrific groan, plowing into the knight's fallen and thrashing steed. The surprised Le Gris stopped short, thrown forward in the saddle but still astride and holding his ax, perched precariously atop the two dying horses.

Carrouges, his ax gone, drew his sword. This was the shorter, one-handed blade—or *estoc*—worn on his belt. His longer, two-handed sword was still in its sheath under his dying horse.

Le Gris sprang free from his saddle, leaving his ax behind in his haste to escape his horse's agonized thrashing. As he ran, he drew his own *estoc,* then turned to face Carrouges across the pile of expiring horseflesh.

Both men were out of breath, and they paused to rest for a minute and get their footing. All this time not a sound was heard from the crowd, who watched everything in silence, mute with fear and fascination. Marguerite leaned forward, gripping the wooden rail of the scaffold, her body rigid, her face drained of color.

Carrouges made the first move, striding around the horses to confront his enemy with his drawn sword. Le Gris hesitated, as if calculating his chances of retrieving his ax or one of the two long swords still pinned in the pile-up. Besides their *estocs,* each man also wore a dagger on his belt.

As Carrouges came closer, Le Gris retreated a few steps in the direction of the royal viewing stand and then planted himself firmly on a stretch of smooth and level sand, awaiting Carrouges with raised sword.

Wearied by the strenuous joust and the ax fight, and now out of the saddle and on their feet, both men felt the full weight of their sixty pounds of armor. With sword and shield in hand, they had to be poised at every instant to lunge forward for the attack, jump back out of harm's way, or turn suddenly to parry a hostile blow. They were hot and sweaty inside their armor, despite the winter cold. And they had little chance of stopping to quench their thirst with the wine on hand, or to wipe the perspiration off their visored faces with their iron gloves.

Facing off before the royal box, they circled each other warily, swords raised, each looking for the advantage. Suddenly they closed, "advancing toward each other and attacking with fury and intrepidity." Slowly at first and then faster and faster, they began to swing, thrust, and parry with their weapons, both fighting "very courageously."

Their sharp steel blades clashed in the air, rang off their armor plates, and smashed down on the wooden shields, filling the air with a brutal song that echoed off the monastery walls. The pale winter sun cast almost no shadow, but its light glanced from the flashing steel swords and polished armor, making it even harder to follow the rapidly unfolding battle through the gaps in the thick wooden fence.

Soon the crowd could hardly see the whirling action as it moved this way and that amid the clouds of dust and sand kicked up by the warriors' heavy iron shoes. Everyone was rapt with awe, some with a personal stake in the battle's outcome, all breathless with wonder at how the combat would end.

Jean de Carrouges, now fighting on foot and feeling the weight of his armor, also felt weak from the fresh attack of fever that had struck him that day. Perhaps the fever slowed his reflexes; or perhaps he was blinded for a second by a flash of sunlight from his adversary's sword. Or perhaps Jean stole a glance at Marguerite, and Le Gris caught the knight off guard for a fateful second.

Whatever the cause, as the two panting men circled each other, "thrusting and striking and slashing," Le Gris suddenly found an opening and lunged forward, driving his sword into the knight's leg and wounding him in the thigh. As the squire's swordpoint pierced his flesh, Jean de Carrouges felt the sharp pain. Blood shot from the wound and began streaming down his leg.

"The sight of flowing blood sent a shiver through the spectators," and the crowd made a low, murmuring sound. Leg wounds in general, and thigh wounds in particular, were very dangerous, since they could cause a rapid loss of blood and also immobilize a combatant, preventing him from maneuvering for self-defense, let alone for attack.

Jean de Carrouges was now at great risk of losing the battle, and "all who loved him were in a great fright." Marguerite, seeing her husband wounded and bleeding on the field, sank against the wooden railing. In a few seconds it might all be over. "A feeling of great fear seized all those witnessing the battle. All mouths were stopped; people hardly breathed."

Le Gris then made a critical error. Rather than pressing his advantage, he pulled his blade from the knight's wounded thigh and stepped back. "The wound could have been fatal to Carrouges, if his enemy had kept his blade in the wound. But the squire withdrew his sword immediately."

Did Le Gris think he had mortally wounded the knight, who would simply bleed to death in a few minutes? Or was Le Gris wary of remaining in close quarters with his stricken but still formidable enemy, withdrawing to safety beyond sword range until Carrouges weakened enough from his injury and loss of blood for the squire to finish him off?

The instant the squire retreated, Jean de Carrouges saw his own chance. Despite his painful wound, "the knight, far from being vanquished, only showed more ardor for the fight. He mustered all of his strength and all of his courage and strode toward his enemy."

Now on the attack against the astonished squire, Carrouges cried out so that all could hear: "This day shall decide our quarrel!"

What happened next surprised and amazed all who saw it. "With his left hand Jean de Carrouges seized Jacques Le Gris by the top of his helmet, pulled his enemy toward himself, and taking several sudden steps backward, hurled his opponent down to the ground, where he lay stretched out at full length and was prevented from rising to his feet again by the weight of his own armor."

With this sudden improvised move, Carrouges turned the tables and seized the advantage. Stunned by his sudden fall and immobilized by his armor, Le Gris could not swing or thrust with his weapon from the ground below. The knight now stood directly over him, brandishing his sword, easily able to parry whatever awkward blows the squire might attempt while lying stretched out on the sand.

A strong man—and the squire was reputedly very strong—could move rapidly on his feet in well-made armor. But for a heavily armored man to get up again after tripping or falling was another matter, especially with an opponent looming over him, ready to knock him back down with his sword or with a well-aimed kick from his iron shoe. Fallen knights were often butchered like lobsters in their own shells.

But as the panting knight stood over his fallen opponent, his sword at the ready, looking for the kill, this was hardly the end of Jacques Le Gris. Although the squire lay stretched out on his back, scarcely able to defend himself, the wounded and bleeding knight now found to his consternation that he could not pierce Le Gris's armor. "He searched a long time for a crack or crevice in his enemy's armor, but the squire was covered from head to foot in steel."*

Carrouges had felled his enemy and virtually disarmed him, but he was exhausted and seriously injured, with no time to lose. His life and strength were draining away with the blood still oozing from his dangerous thigh wound. And as long as the squire remained sheathed in his sturdy defenses, the balance was slowly tipping back in his favor. If Le Gris could hold out long enough, Carrouges might lose too much blood to carry on the fight. He might even bleed to death.

Carrouges, desperate to exploit his hard-won but fleeting advantage while Le Gris still lay stunned before him, knocked Le Gris's sword from his grasp with a deft blow of his own blade and leaped upon his fallen enemy.

Now began a deadly struggle on the ground, as Carrouges straddled Le Gris, one knee to each side of his chest, and began stabbing at his helmet with the point of his sword. As Le Gris bucked and

---

* The wealthy Le Gris could afford the latest military fashion, a full suit of plate armor, although heavy armor could make its wearer a prisoner of his own defenses.

kicked under the knight, sand flew in all directions. The knight's sword point kept glancing off the pointed beak of Le Gris's heavy visor and sticking in the ground.

Finally Carrouges stopped and began fumbling instead with the lock that held the visor shut. Le Gris, realizing the knight's aim, struggled all the harder. He rocked from side to side and wrenched his head around to thwart the attempt on the lock, all the while grasping uselessly in the sand for his sword. Le Gris still wore his dagger but could not unsheathe it as long as the knight sat astride him.

As the two men struggled, and the huge crowd watched the spectacle in fascinated horror, Carrouges began shouting at Le Gris. His voice was muffled by his visor, but the nearest spectators could make out the words:

"Confess! Confess your crime!"

Le Gris shook his head even more violently, as if refusing to admit his guilt even as he resisted the knight's efforts to unlock his visor.

Carrouges, fumbling desperately at the lock with his clumsy iron gauntlet, began using his sword again, but now held it upside down by the guard and slammed its heavy steel hilt against the lock. The hammering of metal on metal could be heard to the corners of the field, and the din inside the helmet must have been terrific. As Le Gris twisted his head this way and that, Carrouges grasped the helmet with his other hand to steady it under his blows.

The knight was still losing blood, and his strength was draining away. He slowed his efforts, pausing longer after each blow to take more careful aim. Finally, after yet another sharp blow with the sword hilt, he knocked the steel pin loose from the lock. The visor sprang open, exposing Le Gris's face from his forehead down to below his chin.

Le Gris blinked at the light and at his enemy's visored face, which hovered just a few inches away.

Carrouges drew his dagger, again shouting: "Confess!"

Le Gris, pinned down by the relentless knight, shouted back, trying to make himself heard by all at the field:

"In the name of God, and on the peril and damnation of my soul, I am innocent of the crime!"

"Then be you damned!" cried the knight.

With that, Carrouges put the point of his dagger to the squire's underjaw, while bracing the helmet with his free hand, and with all of his remaining strength drove the sharp thin blade into the exposed white flesh, sinking the weapon into his enemy's throat up to the hilt.

A spasm shook the squire's body, and blood spurted from the wound. Le Gris's eyes fluttered rapidly open and shut, and his throat gurgled with his final choking breaths. His body shuddered again under the knight, and then his limbs relaxed and he lay still.

Carrouges remained astride his enemy for another minute or two, until he was sure Le Gris was dead. Then he got slowly to his feet, leaving the dagger stuck in the lifeless body stretched out on the blood-soaked sand.

Weak with exhaustion and loss of blood, Carrouges loosened his visor and turned to look at his wife. Marguerite now clung to the rail, wiping away her tears. As the crowd quietly watched, the couple exchanged a very long look, both seeming to gain strength as they locked eyes.

Turning around to face the royal stand, Carrouges bowed to the king. Then, nodding to each side, he acknowledged the huge crowd, who gaped in awe at the bloody scene before them. The knight, hoarse with thirst and fatigue, then tilted back his head and shouted into the air as loudly as he could:

"*Ai-je fait mon devoir?*" (Have I done my duty?)

Ten thousand voices—silent since the beginning of the duel, on pain of the severest penalties—now answered as one:

"*Oui! Oui!*"

The crowd's roaring affirmation of the knight's victory rose into the air above the battlefield and carried beyond the monastery walls, where a deathly silence had reigned until now. Throughout the *bourg* Saint-Martin and in the streets of Paris beyond, people heard the great shout and paused for a moment in what they were doing, perhaps guessing that the celebrated quarrel had been resolved but not yet knowing which man had won the duel.

As the crowd's tremendous shout echoed off the stone walls of the old priory, the guards threw open the right-hand gate, and Jean de Carrouges limped painfully off the field. At the gate he was met by an attendant, who quickly unbuckled the knight's thigh piece and bandaged his wound with a strip of clean cloth. Then the knight continued toward the royal box. Before he could embrace his lady again and celebrate their triumph, he had to pay his respects to the king, who still presided as judge.

The crowd fell silent again, as the victor slowly made his way around the field until he faced the royal stand. King Charles, his uncles, and their courtiers gazed down in wonder upon the battered but victorious knight standing before them in his dusty and blood-stained armor. The knight's hard-fought and narrow victory over the stronger, healthier squire seemed to one witness "like a miracle."

Jean de Carrouges fell to his knees before his sovereign, but "the king made him rise and presented him with a thousand francs, making him also a member of his chamber with a pension of two hundred francs a year for life." King Charles then ordered one of his personal physicians to accompany the knight to his lodgings and tend his wound.

The knight, back on his feet with some difficulty, thanked the king for his generous gifts and bowed once more. Then he backed away from the royal box, turned, and still limping but with a quickening step went around the field to see his wife.

The guards had released Marguerite by now, and she was waiting at the foot of the scaffold, where "the knight went to his wife and embraced her." The couple stood locked together, he in his filthy armor, she in her long black gown, their arms thrown around each other, before the staring crowd. Just before the duel, the two had kissed and embraced for what could very well have been the last time. Their reunion after the duel must have felt very different. God had answered their prayers. Their long ordeal was over, and they were free.

After Jean and Marguerite were reunited, joined by their jubilant families and friends at the edge of the field, the victorious couple "went together to the Cathedral of Notre-Dame to make their thank-offerings before returning to their house" in the city. As with their journey to the field of battle earlier that day, the couple departed from the field in a stately procession, but now one of triumph, as their joyful relatives, friends, and attendants fell in behind them.

Etiquette required the victor to leave the field "on horseback and in his armor," displaying the weapons he had used to slay his enemy. So as Jean de Carrouges rode forth in victory from Saint-Martin's, mounted on the palfrey he had ridden to the field, he held aloft, for all to see, the sword and the still-bloody dagger that he had thrust into Jacques Le Gris's throat.

Leaving the priory grounds and turning into the rue Saint-Martin, the couple traveled the mile or so south to the river and the Île de la Cité. All along the way, as their horses passed along the cobbled streets, the couple and their retinue drew curious and admiring stares from the city folk streaming back from Saint-Martin's field. People who had not attended the duel now came out of their houses to watch the passing procession. The battle was over, but the spectacle was not.

Notre-Dame stood at the other end of the island from the Palais de Justice, where the challenge and the inquiry had taken place that summer. The cathedral had been completed a century earlier, in 1285, and when Jean and Marguerite went there to give thanks to God for their deliverance, its two great towers loomed over the square where friars preached, traders hawked their wares, beggars pleaded for alms, prostitutes plied their trade, traitors were drawn and quartered, and heretics were burned.

There, too, during the reign of Charles V, the famous duel between the man and the dog supposedly took place. And there, in the late afternoon on the feast day of the martyred saint Thomas Becket, the knight and his lady, having survived their long and harrowing ordeal, made their way across the darkening square toward the tall bronze doors of the church and went inside to pray. Before the high altar, amid the candlelit gloom of the immense sanctuary and the sweet clouds of incense, they together raised prayers of thanksgiving for their victory at the field that day.

It is said that at Notre-Dame the knight offered up with his prayers some of the spoils of his victory. The victor of a judicial duel customarily received the armor of his slain opponent, and one report says that Jean de Carrouges placed on the altar the still-bloody armor of his dead enemy. With this donation to the church, the knight acknowledged his debt and his gratitude to God.

And what of the slain squire? As Jean and Marguerite left the field of battle at Saint-Martin's to offer prayers of thanksgiving at Notre-Dame, a very different destination awaited the remains of Jacques Le Gris. While the family and friends of the triumphant couple rejoiced with them over their victory, the squire's relatives and friends had nothing to celebrate but instead bore the shame now heaped on the body of their dead kinsman.

After the squire was killed in battle, his body was "condemned to be dragged to the gibbet, following the established customs of the duel." Le Gris's corpse, stripped of armor, was carried from the field feet first and then "delivered to the executioner of Paris." The executioner threw the bloody corpse onto a horse-drawn sled or hurdle and dragged it through the streets along the accustomed route to the Porte Saint-Denis and beyond the city walls to Montfaucon.

Had the outcome of the duel been otherwise, the executioner of Paris, the fearsome black-capped *bourreau,* would have taken charge of Marguerite's still-living body and fastened her to the stake amid a great pile of wood, consigning her to the flames after the priests had shriven her. Now instead this burly figure strode onto the field to drag away the squire's lifeless body, the corpse of a proven criminal and an object of scorn and shame.

In the 1380s, Montfaucon still lay well over half a mile to the north of Paris, a city of the dead unto itself. This notorious destination of

MONTFAUCON.

*The bodies of those slain in judicial duels were dragged outside the walls of Paris
and hung from the great stone gallows seen here behind heretics being burned.*

MS. fr. 6465, fol. 236. Bibliothèque Nationale de France.

murderers, thieves, and other condemned felons was a low hill topped by a great stone gallows nearly forty feet high with heavy timber cross-bars that could accommodate sixty or eighty bodies at once. Here live criminals with ropes already around their necks were forced up a ladder and hanged, while the remains of those drawn and quartered, beheaded, or otherwise executed in the city were suspended in chains. The bodies of those slain in judicial combat, and thus proven guilty, were also displayed here, joining the vast "crowd of skeletons swinging aloft, making mournful music with their chains at every blast of wind." The infamous hill was the haunt of rats, crows, magpies, and other scavengers, which found food aplenty amid the rotting corpses, attracted by the stench of death that kept living humans away—an odor of decay that could be smelled a half-mile away in the city when the wind blew from Montfaucon.

The bodies of executed felons were supposed to hang from the gallows until their bones were picked clean by scavengers and bleached white by the wind and sun. A high stone wall with a locked iron gate prevented relatives or friends from retrieving the bodies—and doctors from stealing them for dissection. But the continuous demand for space on the gallows often necessitated removing the bodies sooner and throwing them into a charnel house below, where the criminal dead found no Christian burial or peaceful rest but only the grisly anonymity of a common grave.

Jean Froissart, one of the chroniclers who left an account of the duel, wastes little pity on the squire's shameful end at Montfaucon, viewing the gibbet and the charnel house as Le Gris's just reward for his notorious crime. Froissart portrays the squire as "a man of humble birth who had risen in the world, favored by Fortune as many people are. But when they are right on top and think themselves secure, Fortune flings them back into the mud and they end up lower than they began."

In Froissart's scale of values, the mud where Lady Fortune flings down the squire is the moral equivalent of the ground where the avenging knight threw down and killed Le Gris during the combat, and the floor to which Le Gris himself had hurled down the defenseless lady to violate and shame her. The squire's ultimate fall thus embodies a justice both poetic and real. The chronicler even hints that the one Lady punished the squire for his terrible crime against the other lady. Although Fortune rules the world blindly, and her inexorable wheel overturns the lives of the good and the bad alike, sometimes the humble grown proud are humbled once again, and there is a rough justice in the great scheme of things.

10

CONVENT
AND CRUSADE

The royal pension awarded to Jean de Carrouges after defeating and killing Jacques Le Gris on the field of battle, and his appointment as royal chamberlain, were not the only fruits of his victory. Within two months of the duel, the Parlement of Paris awarded the knight an additional sum of 6,000 livres in gold. According to an *arrêt* of February 9, 1387, this sum compensated Carrouges for the "expenses and injuries" caused by the squire during the prosecution of the legal case. The 6,000 livres, charged against the dead squire's estate, further increased the knight's spoils of battle. But after slaying his enemy, vindicating his cause, saving his wife from the stake, and receiving royal gifts and public acclaim along with a sizable damage award, the knight still was not satisfied.

At Le Gris's death, much of his land reverted to Count Pierre of Alençon, including Aunou-le-Faucon. This was the fief that Marguerite's father had sold to Count Pierre in 1377, and that the count in turn gave to Le Gris in 1378. When Jean de Carrouges married Marguerite two years later and realized that the valuable estate of Aunou-le-Faucon had slipped from his own grasp into the hands of his rival, he had started a lawsuit to recover it. But Count Pierre obtained the king's approval for his gift to the squire, quashing his vassal's protest. Now, after killing the squire in the duel, Jean de Carrouges tried once more to get this coveted piece of land, as though his revenge would not be complete until he possessed it.

Carrouges even attempted to use part of his 6,000 livres from the squire's estate to purchase Aunou-le-Faucon. The new dispute over the fief went on for nearly two years. But in the end the knight again failed to get his way, and for the same reason that he had earlier been denied two other estates—namely, Count Pierre's prior legal claim to the land. On January 14, 1389, the Parlement of Paris ruled that Aunou-le-Faucon rightfully belonged to Count Pierre, permanently putting it out of the knight's grasp. Years later the fief would end up in the hands of Count Pierre's bastard son.

Jean de Carrouges had first quarreled with Jacques Le Gris over this fief. Did he now feel that his revenge against the squire had fallen short because he had not succeeded in recovering it? As for Marguerite, what did Aunou-le-Faucon mean to her? She had been Jacques Le Gris's chief victim, suffering far more than her husband from the crime and its consequences. After enduring the terrible attack, the agonizing trial, and the ordeal of the duel, how much did she really care about recovering a piece of her patrimony whose very name—indelibly associated with these events—would forever remind her of things she would spend the rest of her life trying to forget?

In the months following the duel, Marguerite may have had a welcome distraction from her own traumatic experiences, and her husband's seigneurial concerns with land and money, in caring for the child born shortly before the duel. The boy, Robert, named after Marguerite's father, Robert de Thibouville, was Marguerite's first child, or at least her first known child. Eventually two brothers followed him into the world.

As he grew up, Robert must have become aware that he belonged to one of the most famous—or infamous—families in Normandy. His grandfather had twice betrayed the king of France and nearly lost his head for high treason. His father had fought a celebrated duel in Paris against a man accused of raping his mother. And despite the beliefs of the time about the impossibility of conception after rape, it may have been rumored that Robert, born to his parents after many childless years of marriage, was actually the bastard son of Jacques Le Gris. Nonetheless, as Jean and Marguerite's firstborn son and principal heir, Robert stood to inherit the lion's share of the family lands and wealth.

Although Jean de Carrouges had lost Aunou-le-Faucon once again, his victory on the field of battle brought him recognition and rewards that had eluded him for years at Count Pierre's court in Argentan, as he found a new and higher sphere for his ambitions at the royal court in Paris. Within a few years of the duel Jean was named one of the king's own knights. On November 23, 1390, King Charles awarded 400 gold francs to Carrouges as one of his *chevaliers d'honneur*. This was an even more exalted post than Jacques Le Gris had once enjoyed as a royal squire. After removing his hated rival by killing him in a duel, Carrouges seems to have taken Le Gris's place at the royal court.

Upon joining the privileged circle around the king, Jean began receiving important commissions. In 1391 he accompanied other French nobles to eastern Europe to gather information about Ottoman incursions there. The sultan had recently invaded Hungary with a large army, raising new fears of a Muslim threat to Christendom. This military intelligence from Turkey and Greece "was brought by the elder lord Boucicaut, marshal of France, and Sir Jean de Carrouges." The fact that Carrouges is named in the same breath with Marshal Boucicaut shows the prestige that the knight now enjoyed in the French royal court.

Before returning to eastern Europe five years later on a crusade launched to check the Ottoman threat, the knight helped deal with another peril closer to home. In 1392, France was thrown into an uproar when Pierre de Craon, a disgraced noble who had been banished from the royal court the year before, tried to assassinate Olivier de Clisson, the constable of France, whom he blamed for his exile. Craon surprised Clisson one night with a troop of mounted men-at-arms in the darkened streets of Paris, knocking him from his horse with a terrific sword blow to the head and leaving him for dead. But Clisson survived the attack to name his assailant. When Craon fled to the protection of the Duke of Brittany, who refused to yield him up, King Charles raised an army and set out to subdue the rebellious duke and bring Craon to justice.

It was for this reason that Jean de Carrouges, newly raised to the rank of *chevalier d'honneur,* found himself riding in the king's retinue toward Brittany in the summer of 1392, with ten squires in his own entourage. King Charles, now twenty-three, had lately thrown off the yoke of his uncles, declaring himself sole ruler of France. But the campaign led by the young king was to have a surprising conclusion.

On August 8 the king's army was passing through a large forest near Le Mans. It was very hot, dry weather. Suddenly a bare-headed man in a smock ran into the road and seized the king's horse by the bridle, shouting, "King, ride no further! Turn back, for you are betrayed!" Thinking him a madman, the king's attendants began to beat him, and when he released the reins, the royal procession rode on.

Around noon they left the forest and began crossing a broad sandy plain under a fiercely hot sun. The great lords rode apart, each in his own company, the king to one side of the army to avoid the dust, and his uncles, the dukes of Berry and Burgundy, a hundred yards or so to his left. As a chronicler paints the scene, "The sand was hot underfoot and the horses were sweating." The king was ill-dressed for the season, wearing "a black velvet jerkin, which made him very hot, and a plain scarlet hat." Behind the king rode a page wearing a polished steel helmet, and behind the first page another who bore a lance with a broad steel head.

At some point the second page accidentally dropped his lance, which fell and struck the helmet of the page riding in front of him. "There was a loud clang of steel, and the King, who was so close that they were riding on his horse's heels, gave a sudden start. His mind reeled, for his thoughts were still running on the words which the madman or the wise man had said to him in the forest, and he imagined that a great host of his enemies were coming to kill him. Under this delusion, his weakened mind caused him to run amok. He spurred his horse forward, then drew his sword and wheeled round on to his pages, no longer recognizing them or anyone else. He thought he was in a battle surrounded by the enemy and, raising his sword to bring it down on anyone who was in his way, he shouted 'Attack! Attack the traitors!' "

The frightened pages reined their horses aside to escape the king's whirling blade, and in the ensuing confusion the delusional king struck and killed several men in his entourage. Then he spied his brother, Louis of Valois, and made for him. Louis spurred his horse and galloped off in a great fright. The dukes of Burgundy and Berry, hearing the commotion, looked over and saw the king chasing his brother with raised sword. Burgundy shouted, "Ho! Disaster has overtaken us. The king's gone out of his mind! After him, in God's name! Catch him!"

At the duke's cry of alarm, many knights and squires charged off in pursuit of Charles. Jean de Carrouges, who was in the king's entourage, may well have joined the chase. Soon a long ragged line of galloping horsemen, with the king's terrified brother in the lead and the king close behind him, was pounding across the sand under the blazing sun, trailing a cloud of dust.

Eventually Louis managed to outride the king, and the men-at-arms caught up with Charles and surrounded him. They formed a circle, as he continued swinging his sword at his imagined enemies, then let him tire himself out as they parried his blows, taking great care not to hurt him. Finally the exhausted king collapsed in his saddle.

A knight quietly came up behind Charles and pinioned him. The others took away his sword and lifted him from his horse, laying him gently on the ground. "His eyes were rolling very strangely," and he did not speak, failing to recognize even his uncles or his brother. The king was carried back to Le Mans in a litter, and the military expedition was immediately called off.

This was the first public display of the madness that would afflict the king for the rest of his very long reign. For the next thirty years, until his death in 1422, Charles alternated between periods of lucidity, when he seemed quite normal, and bouts of debilitating insanity. Abnormally sensitive to bright light and loud noises, he at times complained of being so brittle that he might break like glass. Charles, who only recently had shaken off his uncles' control and declared himself sole ruler of France, was now unable to govern himself, let alone his nation, and his powers passed back to his uncles and his brother, Louis of Valois, who had nearly fallen victim to the king's sword.

Within a year Charles had another narrow escape when he and five young nobles sprang into a crowded ballroom chained together and disguised as savages in linen costumes covered with pitch and flax. The nobles, friends to Charles, imagined that this ill-conceived prank would distract the king from his melancholia and raise his spirits. An excited guest trying to identify the savages held a candle too near and ignited the costumes, which flamed up like torches. The nobles were burned to death—except for one who plunged into a nearby tub of water, and Charles himself, who had stepped away to show himself to the ladies and who was saved when the quick-thinking Duchess of Berry threw her skirts around the king to detain him as the other burning revelers writhed in agony on the floor. The infernal evening, which became known as the Bal des Ardents, shattered what was left of the king's nerves and only seemed to worsen his dementia.

All this time France and England were engaged in peace talks, urged on by an unusual ambassador—Robert the Hermit, a Norman squire who had had a vision during a storm at sea on his way back from Palestine, and who visited both royal courts to tell the two kings that God wanted them to end their lengthy war and heal the schism in the church. France and England were also being driven closer by the growing Ottoman threat, and in 1396 the two nations cemented a twenty-eight-year peace with a royal marriage between Richard II and Charles's daughter, Isabelle. The mismatched partners—Richard was twenty-nine, and Isabelle only six—would never consummate their marriage, as Richard would be deposed just three years later. But by

NICOPOLIS.

European crusaders, including many Norman knights, fought the Ottoman Turks
and their allies at their stronghold on the Danube in 1396. Froissart, Chroniques.

MS. fr. 2646, fol. 220. Bibliothèque Nationale de France.

the time of the betrothal, in March 1396, the two nations had also allied themselves in a great crusade to save Christendom from the
Turks.

Jean de Carrouges, apparently eager for another military adventure, joined the crusade, which attracted nobles and knights from all
over Europe. The Burgundians took the lead, under Jean of Nevers,
son of Duke Philip. The French commanders included Marshal Boucicaut, with whom Carrouges had visited Turkey and Greece; Philip of
Artois, the Count of Eu, who had served as one of Jacques Le Gris's
pledges; and Admiral Jean de Vienne. Carrouges had fought with
Vienne in Normandy against the English nearly twenty years earlier,
and in 1385 he had joined Vienne on the ill-fated Scottish expedition.
This was the knight's third campaign with the famous admiral.

Some leaders spoke of marching all the way to Jerusalem, but the
loose coalition of armies never agreed on a clear plan. The French
and Burgundians gathered at Dijon in late April 1396, where they
were paid four months' wages in advance. From there they marched
east through Switzerland, Bavaria, Austria, and Hungary, joining up at
Budapest with the other crusaders, including King Sigismund of Ger-
many and Hungary. From Budapest, some crusaders continued south
into the Balkans along the Danube, a fleet of supply ships following
them on the river, while others took a more direct overland route to
the north, past Belgrade and Orsova.

The crusaders met again in early September at Vidin, which they
besieged and captured, putting its entire garrison to the sword. As
they continued east along the Danube, the crusaders, running short
on supplies, attacked and plundered several more towns. On September 12 they arrived at Nicopolis, in present-day Bulgaria. The well-
fortified city stood on a high bluff overlooking the river and was
strongly defended by the Ottomans. An initial attack, with mines and
scaling ladders, failed for want of siege engines.

Sultan Bayezid, the Ottoman leader, had for the past year been be-
sieging Constantinople, three hundred miles away. Learning of the
Christian attack on Nicopolis, he abandoned his siege and ordered a

rapid march north. The sultan's army joined with its Serbian allies at Kazanlak around September 20 and, thus reinforced, proceeded toward Nicopolis. Arriving on September 24, they encamped nearby, sending messengers by night to encourage the city to hold out, as help was at hand.

Rather than attack, the sultan chose the battlefield and set up his defenses—on a ridge behind a narrow wooded ravine a few miles south of the city, where he ordered his troops to plant thick rows of sharp wooden stakes. The crusaders saw that they were pinned between the city and the sultan's army. Having taken thousands of prisoners while raiding nearby cities and now fearing a rescue attempt from Nicopolis, the crusaders massacred them all, leaving the bodies unburied in their haste.

On the morning of Monday, September 25, the crusaders rode out to meet the sultan's army. The French and Burgundians refused to march behind King Sigismund's forces, whom they regarded as peasants, and insisted on taking the lead. Sigismund yielded, warning his allies not to get too far ahead or give up a good defensive position in their haste to attack.

As the crusader lines were forming up, the headstrong Count of Eu seized a banner and shouted, "Forward in the name of God and Saint George!" Jean de Vienne and the other French commanders were horrified, but when they begged the count to hold back until all the troops were ready, he accused them of cowardice, and so the premature attack began.

The heavy French cavalry charged but soon found itself heading downhill into the wooded ravine, as mounted Ottoman archers poured down a hail of arrows on them from the ridge above. After reaching the dry streambed at the bottom, the crusaders then had to ride up the opposite slope. Some climbed it on foot, unhorsed by the enemy arrows; others dismounted because the slope was so steep in places.

Many crusaders made it to the top, since their plate armor deflected most of the arrows. But as the enemy archers retreated, they exposed a forest of sharp stakes protecting the massed Ottoman infantry. The crusaders began wrenching up stakes to get to the enemy, and as they poured through the broken defenses the knights managed to kill or rout most of the lightly armed infantry.

The crusaders were about to give chase, but suddenly the Ottoman cavalry swept in. During the ensuing *mêlée*, the French knights fought on foot, attacking enemy horses with their daggers. Many fell on both sides, but the Turkish cavalry finally withdrew. The crusaders, thinking they had won the day, rested, exhausted from climbing a hill in the blazing sun under enemy fire, breaking through a thicket of wooden stakes, and fighting separate waves of infantry and horse.

But to their surprise, a hidden cavalry force held in reserve by the sultan now charged out from behind some trees and fell upon them. Some crusaders were killed in the initial charge, while others retreated down the slope they had just climbed and fled back to the city, some scrambling across the Danube to safety. The rest stood their ground, continuing to fight as their dead comrades piled up around them. Jean de Vienne was one of the many who fell that day, the banner of the Virgin still clutched in his hand. Sigismund's forces, which followed the Franco-Burgundian charge, were cut to pieces.

Faced with overwhelming odds, many crusaders who had stood their ground finally surrendered, including Boucicaut and the Count of Eu, who had led the overhasty French charge. The Turks took as many as three thousand prisoners. Some wealthy and high-ranking captives were eventually ransomed, including Boucicaut and Jean of Nevers, Duke Philip's son. But many paid with their lives for the Christian butchery the day before, as the sultan now took his revenge. On the day after the battle the Turks beheaded several hundred crusaders, until the sultan, sickened by the slaughter, ordered an end to it.

What fate befell Jean de Carrouges at Nicopolis is not known. In all likelihood he died fighting the Turks not far from where Jean de Vienne, his old commander, fell, and was buried with him in a mass grave. Or perhaps he was one of the prisoners executed by the Ottomans the next day in vengeance for the Christian massacre of their own captives. Given his bravery and ferocity, and his loyalty to his comrades-in-arms, it is unlikely that Carrouges was one of those who fled the field. Nicopolis, one of the greatest military debacles of all time, ended three centuries of European military adventures in the East. Jean de Carrouges thus died in what came to be known as the Last Crusade.

If Jean's departure on crusade had deprived Marguerite of her defender, the news of his death at Nicopolis left her permanently bereft of a champion. Her son, Robert de Carrouges, was just a ten-year-old boy at the time of his father's death and would not come of age for another decade; eventually he would take up arms for France when Henry V landed in Normandy with his army in 1415. Perhaps Marguerite could count on her cousin, Thomin du Bois, who had once challenged Adam Louvel to a duel on her behalf; or on her other cousin, Robert de Thibouville, who had been one of her husband's sworn pledges at Saint-Martin's field. But after Marguerite said good-bye to Jean for the last time in the spring of 1396, and he failed to return from abroad, she may have felt very much abandoned and alone.

The duel between Jean de Carrouges and Jacques Le Gris ten years earlier had officially ended the legal quarrel, but not the gossip, the rumors, or the second-guessing. Two chronicles report that some years after the duel another man—in one version of the story, a condemned felon about to be executed for a different crime, in the other version a sick man on his deathbed—confessed to the rape. Neither source gives any further details of this supposed confession, and neither version of the story has ever been substantiated, but many chroniclers and historians since then have repeated this hazy legend as fact.

Some have alleged that the "true" felon's confession was what prompted Jean de Carrouges to depart on crusade, either to escape the resulting scandal or to do penance for his sins. And some have claimed that news of the belated confession drove Marguerite into a convent, consumed by guilt and remorse for having accused the wrong man and unjustly caused his death. One account says that Marguerite took the veil and made a vow of perpetual chastity, another that she became a religious recluse and ended her days performing pious exercises while walled up in a cell. But no evidence has been offered for these implausible tales.* Wealthy noble widows sometimes did retreat to nunneries as paying "guests," and some even became nuns themselves. But Marguerite clearly kept possession of her worldly estates, for in later years she bequeathed them to her son Robert. So the idea that she ended her life in guilt-stricken seclusion is unlikely.

Ironically, fewer written traces of Marguerite survive than of the man who was accused of raping her and who died for that crime in the famous duel. A contract dated March 15, 1396, around the time of Jean's departure on crusade, records that the monks at Saint-Martin's abbey in Sées, near Argentan, were paid 200 gold francs by the slain squire's son, Guillaume, to sing masses in perpetuity for Jacques Le Gris's soul. In dying on the field without confessing to the crime, the squire, if truly guilty, had damned himself with his own oaths. But many people, including his family, believed him to have been innocent. And the masses they paid for may have been part of their continuing protest against what they saw as his unjust death and undeserved shame. The family's contract with Saint-Martin's defiantly names the squire killed for the infamous crime a decade earlier as "a man of noble memory." Five centuries later the squire's descendants were still protesting the duel's outcome as a miscarriage of justice.

We will never know for certain what happened to the lady at the lonely château. Although the squire's own lawyer seems to have suspected his client's guilt, some chroniclers doubted Marguerite's word, and many historians down the centuries have agreed with them, raising a cloud of questions about the famous crime, trial, and duel. But many others, then and now, have believed the lady and credited her

---

* Another erroneous legend about Marguerite claims that, as a rape victim, she committed suicide.

story, the truth of which, however astounding, she repeatedly and un-waveringly maintained under oath at great risk to herself in the high-est court of France.

As for the famous fight to the death between Jean de Carrouges and Jacques Le Gris, this was the last judicial duel sanctioned by the Parlement of Paris. The controversial outcome of that duel has even been credited with hastening the demise of an institution that some people at the time, and many people in later centuries, regarded as one of the most barbarous judicial practices of the Middle Ages. Several appeals for trial by combat came before the Parlement of Paris in later years, but none of these cases resulted in an *arrêt* authorizing a duel.

For the next century, however, judicial duels continued to take place in parts of France lying beyond the Parlement's jurisdiction such as Brittany, as well as in parts of Flanders under Burgundian control. Two nobles fought a duel in 1430 at Arras; in 1455 two burghers fought with clubs before a large crowd at Valenciennes; and in 1482 a duel took place at Nancy. Trial by combat also persisted elsewhere in Europe, especially Britain, where both nobles and commoners availed themselves of this privilege until it eventually fell into disuse. As late as 1583 a duel to the death was fought in Ireland with Queen Elizabeth's approval. And trial by combat was not actually outlawed in England until 1819, after a murder case provoked a challenge to a duel, caus-ing the English Parliament to abolish the custom for good.

By this time, in most European countries as well as in the newly in-dependent United States, the duel had evolved into a strictly private and illegal affair, fought in secret, usually with pistols, over fine points of gentlemanly honor rather than over formal criminal complaints. The victor who killed his opponent in a private duel even risked being charged with murder, clearly showing that the duel was no longer part of the legal system but a vestige of a bygone era.

An ancient ritual that was devised to settle quarrels before they es-calated into bloody feuds, the duel had been refined during the Middle Ages into a legal procedure of elaborate religious ceremony and chivalric display, staged in cities and towns before noble courts and enormous crowds. But in modern times—as pistols replaced swords, and the parties retreated from hand-to-hand combat—the duel dwindled into a furtive and outlawed custom confined to forest clearings or empty fields on the literal margins of civilization.

In its private and illegal form, the duel only dimly reflected the solemn grandeur of its medieval golden age, when angry nobles challenged each other and threw down the gauntlet, then sheathed themselves in armor, swore heavy oaths before priests, and spurred their warhorses onto a walled field to fight it out before thousands of witnesses with lance and sword and dagger, putting at risk their word and their honor, their fortunes and their lives, and even the salvation of their immortal souls. The world was not to see the like of such spectacles ever again.

EPILOGUE

Capomesnil, the scene of the alleged crime, is today a quiet, peaceful hamlet in the Normandy countryside. The river Vie is still the lifeblood of the fertile little valley where the family Carrouges once held a fief, and most of the year its course, well known to local trout fishermen, winds placidly through the fields and orchards, past the site of the medieval mill, and along the low bluff where the old château once stood. After the land passed out of the hands of the Carrouges family, the château was occupied by others, until it fell into ruin and was finally torn down around the time of the French Revolution. Not a stone of it remains today, except for bits of masonry reclaimed for the later houses and farm buildings that now dot the bluff along the river.

About a mile to the north, across the river valley and on higher ground, stands the village of Saint-Crespin, its church spire still jutting above the skyline, a sight that Jean and Marguerite must have seen many times while visiting Capomesnil. To the east is a line of low hills, and about ten miles beyond that the city of Lisieux, which lies along the road from Fontaine-le-Sorel that Jean and Marguerite followed to Capomesnil during the winter of 1385–86, as the most turbulent chapter in their lives was about to unfold.

Another road approaches Capomesnil from the south, in the direction of Saint-Pierre-sur-Dives, the town to which Nicole de Carrouges was called away, leaving Marguerite behind on the fateful

morning of the crime. The modern visitor can reach Capomesnil by
following the D16 highway north from Saint-Pierre and turning off on
the smaller country road that runs east along the river Vie to the non-
descript hamlet, a cluster of about a dozen buildings, that occupies
the site today.

On a morning in early March, the fields are still soggy from the late
winter rains, and the river is high behind the dam near the old mill
site. A floodgate opened by an official from the Bureau des Eaux has
submerged the road dipping north through the river valley, isolating
Capomesnil from Saint-Crespin behind a temporary moat, as peasants
once flooded ditches to protect their grain and livestock during the
Hundred Years' War. But the loosened floodwaters are already reced-
ing, the sun falling on the fertile soil carries the promise of spring,
and the crows perched noisily in the apple trees along the riverbank
are the only parties at quarrel today.

Near the sign identifying the place by its modern name as "Ca-
parmesnil," I spot a man in rubber boots at work with a shovel in his
muddy yard not far from where the old château once stood. I brake to
a stop by the roadside and get out of my rented Citroën. After several
days of talking with Normandy natives, including a local historian who
has generously given me a number of new leads, I am eager to find out
what the man with the shovel knows about the château that once stood
nearby and the history of its famous medieval inhabitants. Perhaps he
has even unearthed some relics of the past on his land.

Approaching the barbed-wire fence behind which he is working,
and hailing him in my best French, I introduce myself and ask him if
he happens to know anything about the old château or the family Carrouges. Pausing amid his excavations in the mud, the man studies me
warily, clearly startled by this unannounced visit to his quiet fiefdom
and suspicious of my probing interest in his land.

Perhaps it is my accented French, or my lack of a proper local in-
troduction, or my obvious Americanness, or simply the old Norman
distrust—after a thousand years of war, pillage, betrayal, and tax col-
lectors—of any stranger who suddenly appears on the scene asking im-

pertinent questions. Whatever the reason, the man tells me tersely that I should take my inquiry to the *mairie,* the local town hall. He raises his muddy shovel in the air to point over my shoulder toward Mesnil-Mauger, a couple of miles back in the direction from which I have just come. A large and ferocious-sounding dog begins to bark inside a ramshackle stockade behind him, jumping up and battering the top of the fence with its huge paws.

I stay on my side of the wire fence stretched between us. Obviously the man is not going to invite me in to tramp over his historic property and look for old foundation stones, or to sip some Calvados, the native apple brandy, while I savor his colorful stories about local medieval legends. Here, near where the lonely old château once stood, and where terrible things were done to a most unfortunate woman, this man now dwells, perhaps with his own wife and children, guarding the buried secrets of the land, either unwilling to tell what he knows or too busy to be troubled by the ghosts of the past. But I can hardly blame him for waving me off with his shovel. Normandy has a long, cruel, and bloody history, and still today strangers are potential enemies until they are proven friends. The dog still barking fiercely, the man still brandishing his muddy shovel, I thank him for his time and his helpful suggestion, go back to my car, and drive away.

APPENDIX:
THE QUARREL'S
AFTERMATH

The notorious crime against Marguerite, the inquiry by the Parlement of Paris, and the sensational combat between Jean de Carrouges and Jacques Le Gris at Saint-Martin's field were famous in their own time and enjoyed a long afterlife in history and legend. The celebrated affair continued to arouse controversy for centuries, with later commentators dividing as sharply over the quarrel as people did at the time of the events. The chronicler Jean Froissart, writing within a few years of the duel (ca. 1390), claimed that the king, his court, and the huge crowd of spectators rejoiced at the battle's outcome. But Jean Le Coq, the accused squire's lawyer, reports that reactions were mixed at the time of the duel, some people viewing Carrouges as vindicated, while others thought Le Gris unjustly slain. And the Saint-Denis Chronicle, a Latin record compiled ten or fifteen years after the events, claimed that Marguerite had mistakenly—though in good faith—accused Le Gris, and that a condemned felon later confessed to the crime. In the 1430s, Jean Juvénal des Ursins repeated this tale in his more popular French chronicle, substituting a sick man on his deathbed for the condemned felon but showing that the basic story had stuck. The legend of false accusation, unjust punishment, and tardy revelation is still current among historians today.

The question of what really happened to the Lady Carrouges at

Capomesnil on January 18, 1386, will probably never be resolved to anyone's complete satisfaction. As Jean Le Coq said in his notes on the legal case, even as he seems to have suspected his own client's guilt: "No one really knew the truth of the matter." Still, it seems highly unlikely that Marguerite accused Le Gris, and his alleged accomplice Louvel, wrongly *but in good faith.* She swore in court that she saw both men in the clear light of day, that Louvel specifically mentioned Le Gris by name to her before the latter appeared a few minutes later, and that she spoke with both at some length before they attacked her. All of this makes the case for mistaken identity very unlikely, and the actual guilt of another man improbable, even if Marguerite had seen Jacques Le Gris only once before in her life. Besides, Marguerite accused *two* men of the crime, yet the story about the "true culprit" who later confessed involves only *one* man, which seems odd.

The other main theory about the case that has circulated since the time of the quarrel—that Marguerite knowingly lied in accusing Le Gris—is also heavily flawed. According to this view, either Marguerite concocted the rape story herself, perhaps to cover an adultery, or it was forced out of her by her husband in order to avenge himself on his rival—the explanation put forward by Le Gris in his own defense. The fly in this ointment is the inclusion of Adam Louvel in the charges. Given the absence of any witnesses in her own favor, Marguerite's accusations against Louvel were a gratuitous and risky addition to her testimony *if* her story of the attack and rape was indeed a deliberate lie. The more complicated her story, the more vulnerable it was to challenge. The inclusion of Adam Louvel in the charges simply added to her burden of proof. Only Le Gris's alibi survives in the court records, but if Louvel had separate witnesses who placed him elsewhere at the time of the crime, their testimony would have exonerated Le Gris as well, just as Le Gris's alibi would have helped exonerate Louvel. Two alibis are harder to disprove than one. And two suspects are harder to convict than one—unless they can be turned against each other. But Adam Louvel reportedly confessed to nothing, not even under torture.

So the idea that Marguerite accused the wrong man "in good faith," only to realize her horrible mistake much later upon learning that another man confessed to the crime, seems to be a myth devised by a chivalrous age to save the lady's honor while at the same time explaining what many people at the time believed to have been a terrible miscarriage of justice. The other and even more troubling theory, that Marguerite fabricated the charges against Le Gris, either on her own initiative or under her husband's coercion—that she merely "dreamt" the rape, to echo Count Pierre's reported verdict—also seems very dubious. Nonetheless, the legend that Jacques Le Gris was wrongly accused of the crime and unjustly slain in combat, and that the true culprit was revealed only long after it was too late, took root early on and flourished over time.

The legend of false accusation and belated confession was seized upon in the eighteenth century by Enlightenment leaders who used it to indict the barbarous and superstitious Middle Ages. The *philosophes* denounced the judicial duel in general and pointed to the Carrouges–Le Gris affair as a prime example of its folly. The affair earned a brief mention in Diderot and d'Alembert's *Encyclopédie* (1767), which repeated the story that the squire was wrongly accused and the true felon later revealed. And Voltaire cited the case to show that judicial combat itself was "an irrevocable crime" that inexplicably enjoyed the sanction of the law.

The legend of Le Gris's unjust conviction and death was also given new life by popular historians such as Louis Du Bois, who devoted several pages to the affair in a popular review of Normandy history (1824). In Du Bois's account, adapted from the Saint-Denis Chronicle, the Lady Carrouges accused Le Gris mistakenly and realized her error only much later when "the true author of the crime" was revealed—"a squire who doubtless *[sans doute]* bore a certain *[quelque]* resemblance to the unfortunate Le Gris." Du Bois concludes with an embellished version of the by-now-familiar denouement: "Stricken with despair and determined to do penance for the audacity of her accusation, the lady became a nun. She died in regret and sadness, inconsolable for the cruel injustice of which she was the cause, and which she would have paid for at the stake had Carrouges been defeated."

Controversy over the famous affair flared up anew as regional historians and family genealogists, sometimes with a personal stake in the quarrel, weighed in on one side or the other. In 1848, Auguste Le Prevost published a history of Saint-Martin-du-Tilleul, a fief once owned by Marguerite's father. Le Prevost, a prolific historian of Normandy and also a native of Tilleul, devotes several pages to the case, maintaining that Marguerite was indeed attacked by Jacques Le Gris and that the squire was justly slain for his crime. Le Prevost admits that from the time of the affair down to his own, many doubts have been raised about Le Gris's actual guilt. But he stresses that the politics of King Charles's court, favorable to the squire and highly prejudicial toward Marguerite, shaped how contemporary and later historians told the story, generally to the lady's discredit.

Le Prevost censures those responsible for transmitting the story, stating that Le Gris, as Count Pierre's favorite and protégé, was welcomed in Paris by the king and his uncles "with a benevolence shared by most historians of the time, and continued by their successors, who never took the trouble to give the matter even a superficial examination, as has happened with so many other received truths of history." He also claims that in the decadent court of King Charles VI, few "would have been moved by the cry of indignation raised by a provincial woman who had no other claim on the court's good will than to be the daughter of that old traitor Robert de Thibouville." Le Prevost concludes by faulting historians for carelessly reproducing the opinions of the Saint-Denis chronicler, who claimed the lady was in error. And he urges a fresh reading of the primary sources (presenting excerpts), including the notes of Jean Le Coq, the squire's lawyer, "who after having listed with great force the arguments on both sides of the case, tilts the balance against his own client."

An opposite view was offered in the 1880s by F. Le Grix White, who claimed to be an actual descendant of Jacques Le Gris and indignantly protested his ancestor's shameful demise—completely undeserved, as he saw it. Le Grix defends his forebear mainly by disputing erroneous details in Froissart's account, but apparently without having consulted the court record or the casebook kept by the squire's lawyer (both of which had long been in print). Le Grix doubts that the squire could have traveled to and from the crime scene within the available time (although his figures, from Froissart, are faulty). And while he reasonably says that "no Trial by Battle could throw any more light upon that which, from the nature of the case, was dark and uncertain," Le Grix treats the old legend that another man later confessed to the crime as "incontestable evidence" of Le Gris's innocence. Le Grix, a chivalrous Victorian, views Marguerite as a woman wronged, but as one who herself wronged a man by mistakenly accusing him of the heinous crime. None of this amounts to a plausible brief for the squire's innocence, but it shows the affair's lasting power to arouse sharply divided debate and even passionate personal feelings some five centuries after the duel.

Despite Le Prevost's urging to read the primary sources afresh, twentieth-century authorities continued retailing the myths and errors that began collecting around the famous affair almost from the start. The highly regarded eleventh edition of the *Encyclopaedia Britannica* (1910) gave a few lines to the Carrouges–Le Gris affair in its article on the "Duel," getting many details wrong and turning the alleged rape into a kind of bed trick:

> In 1385 a duel was fought, the result of which was so preposterous that even the most superstitious began to lose faith in the efficacy of such a judgment of God. A certain Jacques Legris was accused by the wife of Jean Carrouge of having introduced himself by night in the guise of her husband whom she was expecting on his return from the Crusades. A duel was ordained by the parlement of Paris, which

was fought in the presence of Charles VI. Legris was defeated and hanged on the spot. Not long after, a criminal arrested for some other offence confessed himself to be the author of the outrage. No institution could long survive so open a confutation, and it was annulled by the parlement.

Here Marguerite is fooled by an imposter husband while her actual husband is off on the Crusades, a garbled tale reminiscent of *The Return of Martin Guerre*. As late as the 1970s the *Britannica* reprinted a variant of this legend in which the Lady Carrouges accused Le Gris of having "seduced" her while her husband was away, only to learn after Le Gris's death in the duel that another man confessed to having been "the seducer." The Carrouges–Le Gris affair finally disappeared from the *Britannica*'s fifteenth edition without correction.

A few modern commentators, including a French jurist who offered a public reappraisal of the case at Caen in 1973, have affirmed Le Gris's guilt and the truth of Marguerite's charges. But most have repeated the old tale of unjust accusation and belated confession. One of the most influential authorities, R. C. Famiglietti, writes in his *Tales of the Marriage Bed from Medieval France* (1992) that the Carrouges–Le Gris affair is "one of the most sinister cases of abuse recorded." Famiglietti claims that Carrouges, after learning that Marguerite was raped, "resolved to turn the rape to his own advantage" and "forced his wife to agree to accuse Le Gris of having been the man who raped her." Citing the court record but accepting Le Gris's version of events, Famiglietti reduces Marguerite's charges to nothing more than her husband's "script" for destroying his hated rival. Thus the lady accuses the wrong man not in honest error but in knowing collusion with her husband. Famiglietti also repeats the old legend that another man later confessed to the crime, and that Marguerite, "her perjury exposed," retreated to a convent in shame. But again no further evidence is cited for the oft-told tale of a last-minute confession by the "true" culprit.

This dubious legend, born soon after the celebrated case and given new life by chroniclers and historians down through the centuries, will doubtless live on as long as the famous affair of the knight, the squire, and the lady continues to be told, debated, and refought in the pages of history.

Acknowledgments

❦

This book has been ten years in the making—from the time I first stumbled across the story of the Carrouges–Le Gris quarrel in Froissart's *Chronicles*, through thousands of hours of research and writing, several trips to Europe, and countless exchanges with the many people who helped turn this book from a dream into a reality.

Above all, I am thankful to my wonderful wife, Peg, who explored the archives with me, took photos documenting the research, carefully read the entire manuscript several times, offered many crucial suggestions, and lovingly supported this project every step of the way. I never could have done it without her, and the book is gratefully dedicated to her.

I owe another huge debt to my superb editor, Charles Conrad, vice president and executive editor of Broadway Books at Random House. Charlie guided this book from early draft to finished product, offering brilliant strategic advice, many pages of editorial notes, and enthusiastic support all the way. I am very fortunate to have worked with—and learned from—him.

I also wish to thank my terrific literary agents, Glen Hartley, Lynn Chu, and Katy Sprinkel, at Writers' Representatives, who envisioned this book's wider possibilities, enthusiastically took it on, and skillfully guided its first-time commercial author through the literary marketplace.

At Broadway, a great team turned the manuscript into a finished book. Alison Presley oversaw the complicated flow of text, photos, maps, and permissions. Luisa Francavilla smoothly managed the production process. Janet Biehl skillfully copyedited the manuscript and Sean Mills was the production editor. Deborah Kerner designed the book's interior. Jean Traina created the beautiful jacket. And John Burgoyne drew the superb maps. I am also grateful to Gerry Howard, Jackie Everly-Warren, and Oliver Johnson for their early enthusiasm.

Much further back in the book's genesis, my parents took me to see castles in Europe when I was a small boy and later wisely refused to let me drop eighth-grade French, enabling my high school French teacher, Madame Morden, to give me a thorough grounding in the language. My mother, Marilyn, who died twenty-five years ago this year, would—I know—have been proud of this book. And it has been a joy to share the finished manuscript with my father, Marvin, a history enthusiast.

I am also indebted to many friends and colleagues. Professor Henry A. Kelly of UCLA generously read and annotated the entire manuscript, sharing his vast erudition in medieval law, religion, Latin, and other specialized areas, and saving me many slips. Any remaining errors are, of course, my own.

Andrea Grossman, founder and director of Writers Bloc, in Los Angeles, introduced me to people in the book business, enthusiastically read the manuscript, offered savvy publishing advice, and has been a generous friend to Peg and me.

Catherine Rigaud, whose Normandy *gîte* we stayed at during a cold and rainy March, showed us châteaux, old fortified farms, and other medieval sites. Jack Maneuvrier, a local historian who has written on the Carrouges–Le Gris affair, kindly hosted us at his home with his wife, Danie, answering many questions about the region's history, providing valuable leads, and even posting new finds to me in California.

Tom Wortham, chair of UCLA's English department, and Lynn Batten, vice chair, arranged a timely sabbatical leave and an optimal teaching schedule. Carolyn See kindly gave me expert publishing advice at an early stage. Professor Richard Rouse gave valuable advice about using the Paris archives. Other UCLA colleagues shared their varied expertise, including Chris Baswell, Al Braunmuller, Jonathan Grossman, Gordon Kipling, Del Kolve, Robert Maniquis, Claire McEachern, David Rodes, Debora Shuger, and Stephen Yenser. Jeanette Gilkison, Doris Wang, Nora Elias, and Rick Fagin helped with many logistical details. Christina Fitzgerald and Andrea Fitzgerald Jones tracked down elusive library items and checked out promising leads.

I am also grateful to the late Howard Schless of Columbia University, at whose prompting I first read Froissart; to Jim Shapiro and Andy Delbanco, also of Columbia, for sharing their publishing experience; and to Margaret Rosenthal (USC), Howard Bloch (Yale), Michael Davis (Mount Holyoke), John Langdon (Alberta), Kelly DeVries (Loyola-Baltimore), Martin Bridge (University College London), and Stuart W. Pyhrr and Donald LaRocca of the Department of Arms and Armor at the Metropolitan Museum of Art. Stella Paul, also of the Metropolitan, and James Bednarz of Long Island University—both longtime friends—provided valuable research leads and professional contacts. Mark Vessey and his colleagues at the University of British Columbia offered a friendly forum for a lecture drawn from the book in progress, and warm hospitality.

Many archivists in Paris and Normandy kindly allowed me to examine essential documents. I am especially grateful to Françoise Hildesheimer and Martine Sin Blima-Barru of the Archives Nationales (CARAN); the professional staff of the Bibliothèque Nationale; the Archives Départementales of Calvados (Caen), Eure (Évreux), and the Orne (Alençon); Monique Lacroix, Françoise Guindollet, and Marie-Françoise Bellamy of L'Association Paris Historique (Marais); Laurent Boissou of the Château de Vincennes; and Thierry Devynck of the Bibliothèque Forney. Photos and permissions were provided by Pierre Sozanski d'Alancaisez of the Bodleian Library; Dominik Hunger of the Universitätsbibliothek Basel; Isabelle Le Mée and Isabelle Pantanacce of the Centre des Monuments Nationaux; Rebecca Akan of the Metropolitan Museum; and Christine Campbell of the British Library.

Many UCLA librarians also helped crucially: Victoria Steele, Head of Special Collections at the Young Research Library; Barbara Schader of the Biomedical Library; Christopher Coleman of the YRL's Reference Department; Jonnie Hargis and David Deckelbaum of the Henry J. Bruman Map Collection; and Octavio Olvera of Special Collections. UCLA's efficient Interlibrary Loan Office made many rare sources available.

Dr. Terence Bertele provided valuable medical information. Boris Kushnir of the Beverly Hills Fencers Club helped me to get a sense—with mask and foil—of what it's like to cross swords with a skilled opponent on the attack. Col. George Newberry (USAF) provided information about military maps. Many people in publishing, film, and law shared professional advice: Nadia Awad, Philippe Benoit, Therese Droste, Randy Fried, Rick Grossman, Lisa Hamilton, Dave Johnson, Joe Johnson, Sarah Kelly, Kerrin Kuhn, and Kathleen McDermott.

Finally, I am grateful to my students at UCLA. A continual inspiration, they have taught me a few things about conveying the wonder, excitement, and danger of life in the Middle Ages.

ERIC JAGER
LOS ANGELES
APRIL 2004

Notes

The notes are arranged by chapter and topic (or quotation), with citations keyed to the list of sources appearing after the notes. Printed sources are cited by author and page (or article), with abbreviated titles given when the list of sources contains more than one work under the same name. Manuscript sources are cited by archive, series, shelf mark (i.e., call number), and folio. Thus "AN X 2A10, fol. 232r" refers to Archives Nationales (Paris), series X, manuscript 2A10, folio 232 recto (v = verso). Citations from PP, the summary of the testimony before the Parlement of Paris, include a manuscript folio followed by the corresponding page of the transcript in Buchon's edition of Froissart's *Chroniques*, vol. 10 (= *Collection des chroniques nationales françaises*, vol. 20). Thus "PP 208r/512" refers to AN X 2A11, fol. 208r / Froissart-Buchon, 10:512. A parenthetical note on the testimony's source (C = Carrouges, L = Le Gris) is added when relevant and not otherwise clear. The following abbreviations are used throughout the notes:

AD	Archives Départmentales
AN	Archives Nationales
BN	Bibliothèque Nationale de France
CG	*Cérémonies des gages de bataille*
Fr-Br	Froissart, *Chronicles* (trans. Brereton)
Fr-Bu	Froissart, *Chroniques* (ed. Buchon)
Fr-J	Froissart, *Chronicles* (trans. Johnes)
Fr-L	Froissart, *Chroniques* (ed. Lettenhove)
Fr-M	Froissart, *Chroniques* (ed. Mirot)
JJU	Jean Juvénal des Ursins, *Histoire de Charles VI*
MS.	Manuscript
n.s.	new style (year beginning January 1)
P.O.	Pièce originale
PP	Parlement of Paris, written testimony
RSD	Religieux de Saint-Denis, *Chronique du religieux de Saint Denys*

Route to China: John of Monte Corvino, a Franciscan friar who founded a church in Cambalec (now Beijing) in the 1290s, wrote that the overland route from Europe might take "five or six months" (Yule, 37), an optimistic estimate. *Muslims, Spain, Sicily, Crusades:* Cantor, 136–37, 289–303. *Travel times (in France):* Gilles le Bouvier, quoted in Boyer, 597.

Anglo-French war: Fr-Br, 55–62, 68–110, 120–45, 151–60; Contamine, 5–13, 27–43; Sumption, 1:489–586 (Crécy, Calais), 2:195–249 (Poitiers), 2:294–350 (popular revolts), 2:447 (king's ransom); Seward, 41–102. *Crops, weather, plague, population:* Braudel, 157–61; Fagan, 79–84; Ziegler, 63–83. *Schism:* Keen, *Medieval Europe,* 284–88. *English "crusade" in France:* Autrand, *Charles VI,* 145–46. Routiers, *fortified France:* Sumption, 2:28–30, 38–44, 351–484. *Breton nuns:* Seward, 125.

Charles VI (age, dates): Van Kerrebrouck, 114–29. *Royal family, France in 1380:* Contamine, 46–72; Autrand, *Charles VI,* 9–19, 39–53. *The three estates:* Adalbero of Laon (ca. 1025), cited in Duby, *Orders,* 4–5. *Feudalism:* Bloch, *Feudal Society,* 1:145–254; Bishop, 109–41 ("No lord without land," 110). *Normandy:* Mabire and Ragache, 15–199.

Carrouges family history: BN, P.O. 605, Carrouges, nos. 1–21; Fr-M, 13:xxxi–xxxiii (excerpts); *Cartulaire de Marmoutier,* 74–77 (no. 57); *Dictionnaire de la noblesse,* 4:738–39; Odolant-Desnos, 1:439–47; Diguères, 161–63; Rousseau, 3–9; Le Prevost, *Eure,* 3:479, 481; Le Prevost, *Tilleul,* 64, 124; Tournouër, 355–59; Terrier and Renaudeau, 6. *Count Ralph:* Vanuxem, *Veillerys,* 40–43. *Family arms:* BN, Dossier bleu 155, Carrouges, no. 1; Le Prevost, *Tilleul,* 64 (illustrated).

Lost portrait of Jean IV: Malherbe, 3:537–38 (letter no. 203). *Career and character:* Fr-Br, 309; PP 206r/503–4 (C), 208r/512–13 (L); BN P.O. 605, Carrouges, nos. 4–10, 17–18; Canel, 642; Desmadeleines, 36; Dewannieux, 34; Vanuxem, "Le duel," 198. *Jean's illiteracy:* Fr-L, 20:507. *Knighthood (in general):* Wise, 21; France, 58–59. *Income estimate based on 1424 figures:* Tournouër, 357. *Jean IV's siblings:* Rousseau, 7; Nortier, 110–111, no. 463; Diguères, 163.

Carrouges (place): Lagrange and Taralon; Terrier and Renaudeau, 6–8, 41, 57; Rousseau, 4; Tournouër, 356; La Noë, 4–5. *Bellême:* Mériel, 46–47; Pernoud, 131–33.

Jean IV's wife, son: PP 206r/503; Le Prevost, *Eure,* 3:479 (three surviving children, all by Jean's second wife); La Noë, 5. *Chambois:* Deschamps, 293–300.

Alençon family: Van Kerrebrouck, 412–19; Autrand, *Charles V,* 648–54; Fr-L, 20:22–23; Vanuxem, "Le duel," 197–99. *Pierre as hostage:* BN MS. fr. 23592, fols. 62r–65r. *Argentan:* Odolant-Desnos, 1:418–39; Prieur; Barbay, 48–49, 51. *Jean as chamberlain:* Canel, 642; Dewannieux, 34.

Le Gris, chamberlain: BN n.a. 7617, fol. 265v. *Friendship with Carrouges:* PP 206r/503

(C); Dewannieux, 35. *Le Gris at Count Robert's court:* PP 208r/512. *Family history, character:* Fr-Br, 309; Fr-L, 22:85; Caix, 367, 370; Canel, 642; Vérel, 167–68 (with arms); Dewannieux, 34–35; Guenée, 331–32.

Le Gris's physique: Fr-Bu, 10:278; Fr-L, 12:32. *Captain of Exmes, 1370:* Nortier, 136–37 (no. 569). *Education:* Le Coq, 110; Desmadeleines, 36. *Children:* Le Coq, 112; Contades and Macé, 87 ("Guillaume Legris fils"). *Alleged seductions:* PP 206v/504 (C); Canel, 645; Ducoudray, 404; Dewannieux, 35. *Le Gris, godfather:* PP 206r/503 (C); PP 208r/512 (L). *Family bond:* PP 206r/503 (C); Canel, 642; Desmadeleines, 36; Dewannieux, 35. *Baptism oaths:* Bishop, 118.

Aunou-le-Faucon: BN n.a. 7617, fols. 265v–266v; Odolant-Desnos, 1:439. *Robert de Thibouville:* Le Prevost, *Tilleul,* 56–57. *Jean's jealousy of Le Gris:* Canel, 642.

Jeanne's death: PP 206r/503 (C); PP 208r/512 (L), implying that the child was born *after* the two squires joined Count Pierre's court in 1377, and thus that Jeanne died between 1377–80. *Child's early death:* La Noë, 5; Rousseau, 7. *Childbirth, mortality:* Gottlieb, "Birth," 232–33; Verdon, 43–47.

The 1379–80 campaign: De Loray, 133–48. *Jean's military service:* BN P.O. 605, Carrouges, nos. 4–10; excerpted in Fr-M, 13:xxxi. *Feudal marriage:* Duby, *Marriage,* 1–22; Verdon, 22–33.

Chapter 2: The Feud

Jean and Marguerite's marriage ca. 1380: Le Prevost, *Tilleul,* 63; La Noë, 5. *Marguerite's birth, age:* Le Prevost, *Tilleul,* 56. *Beauty, character:* Fr-Bu, 10:277; JJU, 371; PP 206v/504 (C), 209v/518 (L). *Lost portrait:* Malherbe, 3:537–38 (letter no. 203). *Female beauty, clothing: Romance of the Rose,* 37–38 (lines 523–72); Verdon, 13–21; Horne, 39–40. *Household, manners, morals:* La Tour Landry; Bishop, 116–18; Ariès and Duby, 348–56. *Chastity:* Duby, *Marriage,* 7. *Youth and age:* Chaucer, 158. *Marriage ages:* Verdon, 28–29.

Thibouville estates: Le Prevost, *Eure,* 2:115–18, 3:248–49; Keats-Rohan, 732–33 (with refs.). *Family history:* BN, P.O. 2825, Thibouville, nos. 1–13; AD Eure, Série E. 2703, Seigneurie de Carsix (copy of will, 11 Jan. 1451); Le Prevost, *Tilleul,* 47–65 (arms, 54), 121–23, and *Eure,* 3:424–34, 472–80; Charpillon, 2:201–202. *Robert V's treason:* Le Prevost, *Tilleul,* 52–56 (and note E); Mauboussin, ch. 2; La Roque, 4:1899–1906. *Charles the Bad:* Sumption, 2:365–73, 418–19. *Robert V's 1360 pardon:* La Roque, 4:1426. *Robert V in 1370:* Charpillon, 2:973 (s.v. "Vernon"). *Guillaume de Thibouville:* Le Prevost, *Eure,* 3:478. *Thibouville hostage:* BN MS. fr. 23592, fol. 66v.

Sainte-Marguerite-de-Carrouges: Tournouër, 388–90; Rousseau, 4. *Saint Margaret:* Ferguson, 131. *Marriage rituals and dotation:* Stevenson, 68–76; Léonard, 188–94; Verdon, 31–33; Le Prevost, *Tilleul,* 95–97; Ducoudray, 791–96.

Quarrel over Aunou-le-Faucon: La Noë, 5; Odolant-Desnos, 1:439. *Charter of May 29, 1380:* BN n.a. 7617, fols. 265r–269r. Le Gris clearly did not attend Jean and Marguerite's wedding (1380), for even if he lied about visiting Capomesnil on January 18, 1386, he would not have risked his credibility in court by claiming to have first seen Marguerite in 1384 if he had actually—and very publicly—attended the wedding four years earlier.

Le Gris in Paris, August 1381: Le Fèvre, 8–9. *As royal squire:* PP 208r/512. *Bellême quarrel, lawsuit:* PP 208r/512 (L); Odolant-Desnos, 1:439; Dewannieux, 35. *Cuigny and Plainville:* PP 208r/513 (L); Odolant-Desnos, 1:442–43; La Noë, 5–6; Dewannieux, 35. *Jean "bon soldat, mais mauvais courtisan":* Vanuxem, "Le duel," 198. *Carrouges blames Le Gris:* PP 208r/512 (L); Caix, 369; La Noë, 6; Dewannieux, 35. *Carrouges briefly in Flanders (1383):* La Noë, 6 (citing August 23, 1383, *quittance*); Autrand, *Charles VI,* 146–47 (*montre* of August 15).

Crespin gathering: PP 206v/504 (C), 208v/513 (L); Canel, 645; Dewannieux, 35. *Crespin as forester:* Le Prevost, *Tilleul,* 105n. *The reconciliation:* the occasion, company, greeting, and kiss are all from the sources; some details of setting and gesture are added. La Noë, 6, claims Carrouges merely feigned peace. *Le Gris's interest in Marguerite:* Canel, 645.

CHAPTER 3: BATTLE AND SIEGE

The 1385 Scottish expedition: Fr-J, 2:35–37, 47–50, 52–57; RSD, 1:361–70, 384–92; JJU, 364–66; *Westminster Chronicle,* 120–33; *Book of Pluscarden,* 1:246–47; De Loray, 179–205; Palmer, 59–60. *Jean de Vienne:* De Loray, 79–85. *Carrouges in Scotland:* PP 206r/503–4; De Loray, cviii. *Carrouges and adventure:* Fr-L, 12:30. *War, plunder, ransom:* essays in Keen, *Medieval Warfare,* esp. Rogers, 136–60, and Jones, 163–85.

Marguerite at Fontaine-le-Sorel, good relations with Jean: PP 206r/503–4 (C); Dewannieux, 35. *Robert de Thibouville:* De Loray, cviii. *Sluys:* Fr-Br, 305. *Armor, money, cannons:* De Loray, 185–87, cxxxviii. *Carrouges's pay:* De Loray, cviii. *Scottish complaints, King Robert's demands:* Fr-J, 2:35–36.

Northumberland: Fr-J, 2:47–50. *Wark:* Long, 166–67; Fr-J, 2:49; RSD, 1:366–69 ("Dovart"); JJU, 365 ("Drouart"). *Escalade (in general):* Wise, 174–76. *"promptly transfixing every head . . .":* Warner, 39 (adapted from similar siege). *"murder, pillage and fire":* RSD, 1:366, 370. *English counterattack:* Westminster Chronicle, 120–33; Fr-J, 2:52–54. *Scots grant free passage, French decamp, English at Edinburgh:* RSD, 1:388–91. *Cumberland:* Fr-J, 2:53–54; White, 47–48. *Carlisle:* Summerson, 1:313–15. *Siege of Carlisle, Percy's raid:* Westminster Chronicle, 132–35. *Revue of October 28:* De Loray, cviii. *New Scottish outrages:* Fr-J, 2:55–56. *Admiral's affair:*

RSD, 1:390–92; JJU, 366. *Impoverished French:* Fr-J, 2:56–57; JJU, 366. *Disastrous expedition:* Autrand, *Charles VI,* 148.

Le Gris allegedly told Marguerite that he knew her husband had returned from abroad with little or no money; see PP 207r/506 (C); Dewannieux, 36. *Jean's illness:* Le Coq, 111; Fr-L, 12:367 (emending Le Coq); JJU, 371. *Jean's knight-hood:* De Loray, cviii. *Trip to Capomesnil:* PP 206r-v/504; Dewannieux, 35. *Winter weather, 1385–86:* JJU, 363.

CHAPTER 4: THE CRIME OF CRIMES

Hints of estrangement: Nicole's separate domicile; Jean's assumption that his wife and his mother quarreled in his absence (PP 207v/509). *Roman roads:* Talbert, plates 7, 11; Loth, 22–23. *Medieval routes:* Cassini de Thury, *Carte,* nos. 61–2; Mariette de La Pagerie. *Terrain:* IGN maps, Série Top 100, no. 18 (Caen/Alençon); Série bleue France 17130 (Livarot). *Capomesnil:* Hippeau, 58. *Dwellings:* PP 209v/519 (L). *Remoteness:* PP 206v/504 (C). *Rooms:* PP 207r/507. *Donjon:* Asse, 132. *Riverbank site:* Le Fort, 98. *Demolition:* Le Prevost, *Tilleul,* 105n2.

Carrouges stopped at Argentan while going to Paris on business or legal matters (negotiis)*:* PP 206v/505 (C). *His instructions to maidservant:* PP 208v/514 (L). *Argentan:* Barbay, 48–60. *Jean's encounter with Le Gris and others:* PP 206v/505 (C).

Adam Louvel's character: PP 206v/504–5 (C); Odolant-Desnos, 1:440; Desmadeleines, 37; Caix, 367. *An "Adam Louet" served under Carrouges in 1379–80:* BN P.O. 605, Carrouges, no. 18 (cf. Louvel as "Louvet," AN X 2A10, fol. 233r). *Le Gris's lust-ful motives:* PP 207v/504 (C); Fr-Br, 309–10; Ducoudray, 404. *Le Gris a widower (in 1386):* Le Coq, 110.

Nicole summoned: PP 206v/505 (C); 208v/514 (L). *Le Gris notified by Louvel:* PP 206v/505 (C); Canel, 645. *Marguerite left "virtually alone"* (quasi solam): PP 206v/505 (C). *Report of one remaining maidservant:* Le Coq, 112.

My account of what allegedly happened at Capomesnil on January 18, 1386, closely follows Carrouges's court brief, based on his wife's sworn testimony: PP 206v–207v / 505–509. Indirect speech is sometimes rendered as dialogue, and some details are added for continuity (e.g., Louvel's excuses about the cold).

"Haro": Wolfthal, 42–43. *"Against her will":* Fr-Br, 310; Fr-Bu, 10:278; PP 207r/508 (C). *Weeping, disheveled clothing:* Wolfthal, 43. *Le Gris's threats, Marguerite's vows, sack of coins:* PP 207v/509; Fr-Br, 310. The brief exchange between Le Gris and Louvel is my own addition.

Medieval rape law and attitudes: Gravdal, 1–20, 122–44; Wolfthal, 1–6, 99–107, 127–29; Saunders, 48–75, 141–42, 173–77. Beaumanoir, no. 824. *Caen, 1346:*

Fr-Br, 76–77. *"The crime of crimes"*: Rougement, 222. *Edward III:* Saunders, 173–75. "Sorrow": Pisan, 161. *Clerics:* Gravdal, 124–27; Wolfthal, 54.

Marguerite's sorrow: Fr-Br, 311; Wolfthal, 45–46. *Female honor:* La Tour Landry, 3–4. *Husband's prerogative:* Bloch, *Law,* 55. *"She fixed firmly in her memory":* Fr-Br, 311. *Jean's return from Paris:* PP 208v/514 (L). *Marguerite's depression:* PP 207v/509 (C). *Bedchamber scene:* Fr-Br, 311. *Sleeping customs:* Bishop, 127. *Marguerite tells Jean the whole story:* PP 207v/509 (C). *Family council:* PP 207v/510 (C); Fr-Br, 311–12; RSD, 1:464. *Pregnancy:* Le Coq, 111 *(puerperium);* La Noë, 6.

CHAPTER 5: THE CHALLENGE

Count Pierre hears news, investigates: PP 208v/515 (L). *Pierre's quandary:* Vanuxem, "Le duel," 197–99. *Tribunal, no plaintiff, Louvel's arrest:* PP 209r/515–16 (L); Dewannieux, 36. *Case dismissed:* PP 209r/516 (L). *"She must have dreamt it":* Fr-Br, 312.

Appeal procedure: Ducoudray, 528–38, 664–68; Bloch, *Law,* 136–39; Shennan, 71. *Count writes king:* PP 209r/516 (L). *Fury at Carrouges:* Fr-Br, 313. *Jean's friends in Paris:* La Noë, 6. *Le Gris favored, prejudice against Marguerite:* Le Prevost, *Tilleul,* 103.

History of judicial duels, attempts to suppress them: Bongert, 228–51; Ducoudray, 375–406; Neilson; Lea, 101–247, 255–59; Monestier, 7–97; Bloch, *Law,* 18–28, 119–21; Bartlett, 103–26; Cohen, 55–61. *Tempting God:* Lea, 207; Guenée, 333. *Philip IV's 1306 decree:* CG, 1–35; *Ordonnances,* 1:434–41.

Medieval Paris: Favier; Couperie, 19–26; Sumption, 1:1–9; Horne, 42–64; Autrand, *Charles VI,* 233 (map). *Student brawls:* Haskins, 25–26 (quoting Jacques de Vitry).

Carrouges's lawyers: AN X 2A10, fol. 243v ("Jehan de Bethisy"); Le Coq, 99 (bailiff).

Château de Vincennes: Chapelot; De Pradel de Lamase. *Bureau de La Rivière:* Autrand, *Charles VI,* 156–58. *Assassination attempt (1385):* JJU, 364; De Loray, 183–84. *Appeal wording* adapted from *Abrégé du livre des assises de la Cour des Bourgeois,* as cited in Cohen, 62. *King writes Parlement:* PP 210v/522. *Parlement's role in appeals:* Shennan, 78.

Le Gris's legal counsel: Le Coq, 110. *Biographical details:* Boulet (ed.) in Le Coq, vi–xvii; Ducoudray, 223–25; Delachenal, 345–46. *Benefit of clergy:* Ducoudray, 593–600. *Lawyer's advice, Le Gris's refusal:* Le Coq, 110. *Legal expenses, delays:* Ducoudray, 959–71.

Carrouges's, Le Gris's lodgings: AN X 2A10, fol. 239r. *Locations:* Hillairet, *Rues,* s.v. "Saint-Antoine (rue)"; "Baudoyer (place)"; "Louvre (rue du)". *Palais de Justice:* Ducoudray, 11–21; Shennan, 98–109; Sumption, 2:196. *Events of 1356–58:* Sumption, 2:254–55, 312–13. *Ushers:* Ducoudray, 285–94; Shennan, 48–49. *Grand' Chambre:* Shennan, 106–7. *Arnold de Corbie:* Delachenal, 170n.

Session of July 9, 1386: AN X 1A1473, fol. 145v; Le Coq, 95n. *Speeches adapted from 1306 formulaire:* CG, 7–9; *Ordonnances,* 1:435–36. Rapporteur: Shennan, 64–65. Arrêt *of July 9, 1386 (listing pledges):* AN X 2A10, fols. 232r-v; Fr-L, 12:368–69. *Waleran de Saint-Pol:* Fr-L, 23:77–78. *Count of Eu (Philip of Artois): Dictionnaire de biographie française,* 13:231–32.

CHAPTER 6: THE INQUIRY

Marguerite's testimony: PP 210v/523. *Marguerite in court:* PP 208v/513. *Jean's testimony based on Marguerite's:* Le Prevost, *Tilleul,* 103 ("sous sa dictée"). *Scribes:* Ducoudray, 257–61; Shennan, 45–46.

Summary of case: AN X 2A11, fols. 206r–210v. I have examined this manuscript at the Archives Nationales (Paris), checking the accuracy of the transcript in Fr-Bu, 10:503–26. Partial transcript (Carrouges's side only) in Le Prevost, *Tilleul,* 104–9.

Carrouges says (PP 206v/505) that Nicole was summoned to Saint-Pierre *by* the Viscount of Falaise (Regnaut Bigaut). Le Gris, giving different but not inconsistent information, says (PP 208v/514) she appeared there *before* the bailiff of Caen (Guillaume de Mauvinet) at the request of one Robert Seurel. Le Gris names only Seurel; for Bigaut and Mauvinet, see Dupont-Ferrier, 1:496 (art. 4541), 1:450 (art. 4232).

"Scarcely two leagues": PP 208v/514. *The league (2.75–3.0 miles):* Chardon, 133. From Capomesnil to Saint-Pierre it is 5.5 miles as the crow flies, and so somewhat farther by the road that Nicole likely took west along the Vie and then southwest to Saint-Pierre (Mariette de La Pagerie). A league of three miles gives a travel distance of six miles each way, which seems about right.

Capomesnil (49° 5′ N, 0° 5′ E) saw sunrise and sunset on January 18 at 7:23 A.M. and 4:36 P.M. (data from U.S. Navy tables, adjusted for ten-day Gregorian shift and a solar day). Civil twilight (usable light) begins about thirty minutes before sunrise and ends about thirty minutes after sunset.

"By the morning meal": PP 208v/514. The large meal of the day was eaten between nine A.M. and noon, ten A.M. being typical (Bishop, 134). Nicole thus could have returned as late as noon, or even after, given Le Gris's qualification. *"Prime":* originally six A.M. (or sunrise) but usually about nine A.M. by the fourteenth century (*Oxford English Dictionary,* s.v.). *"A seamstress and two other women":* PP 208v/514. *Beating with fists:* PP 208v/515. *Attitudes toward wife-beating:* Verdon, 38–39.

It is about twenty-three miles from Argentan to Capomesnil as the crow flies, but considerably farther by road. If a league was three miles, then the nine leagues were twenty-seven miles, a reasonable estimate. Mariette de La Pagerie shows a likely route proceeding north from Argentan to Trun and past Montpinçon nearly to Livarot and then west past Saint-Julien-le-Faucon to Capomesnil. A typical day's travel (ca. 1400) was twenty to thirty miles, with trips of fifty miles possible only for men able to requisition horses; see Boyer, 606.

Injuries as evidence of rape: Saunders, 63 (noting forty-day limit in medieval England); Gravdal, 129–30 (citing medical exams in fourteenth-century France). *"Ten or twelve houses":* PP 209v/519 (L). Nicole's death: PP 209v/519.

Carrouges's reply: PP 210r-v/521–22. *Risk of dishonor for woman bringing rape charges:* La Marche, 51. *Marguerite's child:* Le Coq, 111, placing its birth between July 9 and December 29. *Rape and conception:* Gottlieb, "Pregnancy," 157; Saunders, 73–75.

Berengier's expense receipts: BN MS. fr. 26021, nos. 899, 900; Moricet, 207 (excerpts). *Adam Louvel summoned (July 20):* AN X 2A10, fol. 233r. *Jour d'avis (explained):* Bloch, *Law,* 126–27. *Thomin du Bois challenges Adam Louvel (July 22):* AN X 2A10, fol. 233r-v; Le Coq, 97n.

Further arrests (August 20): AN X 2A10, fol. 235r; Le Coq, 97n (excerpts). *Adam Louvel and maidservant questioned under torture:* Le Coq, 112. *Judicial torture and methods:* Ducoudray, 506–19; Peters, 67–69. *Jeanne de Fontenay:* AN X 2A10, fol. 239v. *Beloteau arrested:* AN X 2A10, fol. 236r-v; Le Coq, 99.

French invasion plans: Fr-Br, 303–8; Fr-L, 11:456–57 (Burgundy's influence); Fr-J, 2:174–77, 195–200 (king's vow, 196); Palmer, 67–87.

"No one really knew": Le Coq, 111–12. *Le Coq's suspicions:* Odolant-Desnos, 1:445n; Le Prevost, *Tilleul,* 104. *Record of September 15, 1386, arrêt:* AN X 2A10, fols. 238v–239r; Fr-L, 12:369–70. *Latin text of the* arrêt: AN X 2A11, fols. 206r–210v; Fr-Bu, 10:503–23. *Arnold de Corbie's signature:* fol. 210v. *Sack,* rapporteur: Shennan, 64–65. *Duels disallowed (1330–83):* Ducoudray, 396–406. *Duel authorized for rape in 1354:* Diderot and d'Alembert, s.v. "Duel." *Original date of duel (November 27):* AN X 2A10, fol. 239v.

Parlement's rationale, controversy, Le Gris's illness: Le Coq, 96–97, 110–111. *"The squire fell ill":* AN X 2A10, fol. 239v. *Marguerite to be burned if perjury proven:* Fr-Br, 314; Fr-M, 13:107. *Burning of women for perjury:* Ibelin, 175, cited by Reinhard, 187; La Marche, 16, 51; Lea, 172–73.

CHAPTER 7: THE JUDGMENT OF GOD

Saint-Martin-des-Champs: Biver and Biver, 27–29; Hillairet, *Rues,* s.v. "Bailly (rue)," "Montgolfier (rue)," "Saint-Martin (rue)." *Saint Martin:* Ferguson, 133. *New city wall (1356–83):* Couperie, 19; Autrand, *Charles VI,* 233. *Aqueduct:* Lacordaire, 219–21. *Tribunal, prison:* Hillairet, *Gibets,* 233–39. *Court records: Registre criminel,* 220–22, 227–28.

Battlefield location: Chronographia, 85; Le Coq, 110; Hillairet, *Gibets,* 236, and *Rues,* s.v.

"Montgolfier (rue)," "Saint-Martin (rue)," no. 292. *Size of field:* CG, 20–21 (40 by 80 paces); Pisan, *Traité du droit d'armes,* as cited in Fr-L, 20:508–9 (24 by 96 paces, corrected from "94"). *A pace (2.5 feet): Oxford English Dictionary,* s.v. "pace," 3. *"the lists . . . that were made . . . ":* Pisan (as above); Le Coq, 110; Desmadeleines, 41. *Walls, fittings:* Jaille, 142–44; CG, 31. *"Big stands . . . ":* Fr-Br, 313. *Sand:* Jaille, 142; Fr-J, 2:229.

Homer, *Iliad* 3.310–80 (Lattimore, 108–10). *Duels on islands:* Lea, 111–12. *Royal challenges:* Huizinga, 107–8; Autrand, *Charles VI,* 146–47. *Dog-man duel:* Bullet, 70–71; Monestier, 82; Cohen, 60–61.

Itinerary of Charles VI: Petit, 28–32; Lehoux, 2:194. *Storms, omens, invasion canceled:* Fr-J, 2:201–3; RSD, 1:457–62; Palmer, 77–81.

Charles avid for jousts, consults uncles: Fr-J, 2:28, 205, 440. *Parlement, November 24:* AN X 2A10, fol. 243v (*not* September 24 as stated in Fr-Bu, 10:289). *King in Paris:* Petit, 31–32.

Royal marriage: Fr-Br, 252–59; RSD, 1:357–61; Autrand, *Charles VI,* 152–58. *Isabeau (dates):* Van Kerrebrouck, 115. *"Toute nue":* Fr-L, 10:345. *Dauphin's birth, death:* RSD 1:456; Van Kerrebrouck, 115; Autrand, *Charles VI,* 171. *Duel as highlight of Christmas court:* Lehoux, 2:196–97. *Marguerite in childbirth:* Le Coq, 111.

CHAPTER 8: OATHS AND LAST WORDS

Prayers, fasting, mass: Le Coq, 111; Dewannieux, 32; Bloch, *Law,* 24; Monestier, 71, 74 (citing a special *missa pro duello*).

Armor, weapons, horse-fittings: Lobineau, 2:672–77 (Brittany duel, December 19, 1386); CG, 10 (lance, sword, dagger, shield); Fr-M, 13:107 *(lances, espées)*; Brantôme, 51–52 ("masses qu'on nomme *becs de corbin* [probably axes, *haches*], et une forte courte espée [short sword] en façon de grand dague"); Malherbe, 3:537–38 (both men "à cheval . . . [avec] lances"). Dewannieux, 41–42, citing Brantôme, gives each man an ax *(hache).*

Additional information: Wise, 66–87 (lance, sword, dagger); Hewitt, 2:261–65 (axes); Davis, 11–29, 55–58, 67 (warhorses, lances); Monestier, 57–58 (swords); Ayton essay in Keen, *Medieval Warfare,* 186–208; Viollet-le-Duc, s.v. "armure," "bacinet," "chanfrein," "chausses," "cotte," "dague," "ecu," "épée," "gantelet," "hache," "harnois," "lance," etc. *Bread, wine, money:* CG, 19–20; Jaille, 155; Lobineau, 2:676. Hillairet, *Rues,* s.v. "Montgolfier (rue)," says a nobleman who lost a duel and had to pay 60 livres.

Duel's notoriety, huge crowd: Fr-Br, 309, 313; RSD, 1:464; Dewannieux, 31. Sunrise in Paris (48° 48´ N, 2° 30´ E) on December 29, 1386 (adjusted for ten-day Gregorian shift), was about 7:45 A.M., with civil twilight (usable light) beginning shortly after 7 A.M. *Winter of 1386–87:* Lebreton, 72.

Royal procession: Jaille, 149–50. *Rules for combatants' arrival at field:* CG, 10–11, 15; Jaille, 153–54. One *formulaire,* perhaps drawn up expressly for the Carrouges-Le Gris duel (Guenée, 335), specifies that both combatants must arrive by noon *(mydi)* but that all ceremonies were to await the king; BN MS. fr. 2699, fol. 189r. *Pledges:* Fr-Br, 313. *Pledges listed:* AN X 2A10, fols. 243v–244r; Fr-L, 12:371.

Marguerite's clothes, carriage: Fr-Br, 313; Le Coq, 111; Brantôme, 51; La Marche, 16. *Sir Robert de Thibouville (in 1386):* Le Prevost, *Tilleul,* 57; *Eure,* 3:478. *Du Bois-Louvel duel disallowed:* AN X 1A 1473, fol. 224r; Le Coq, 97n.

Pre-duel ceremonies: CG, 12–29; Jaille, 153–65; Lobineau, 2:670–71 (Brittany duel); Villiers, 31–41; Ibelin, 165–75; Du Breuil, 101–23; *Summa,* 167–74; Beaumanoir, nos. 1828–50; Fr-Br, 313–14; BN MS. fr. 2699, fols. 188v–193r; BN MS. fr. 21726, fol. 189v (third oath). *Further information:* Cohen, 56–59; Monestier, 74–75; Bartlett, 121.

Marguerite ordered down from carriage: Le Coq, 111; Le Prevost, *Tilleul,* 111n. *Marguerite at duel:* Fr-L, 12:37 ("[la] femme . . . là estoit"); cf. La Marche, 16. *Scaffold:* Brantôme, 51.

"Leaving nothing to chance": Monestier, 70. *Le Gris knighted:* Le Coq, 111. *Dubbing:* Bloch, *Feudal Society,* 2:312–16; Keen, *Chivalry,* 64–82. *Health of combatants:* Le Coq, 111; Fr-L, 12:367 (emending Le Coq); JJU, 371.

Altar: CG, 23; Jaille, 148. *Third oath:* Cohen, 57–58. *Marguerite's words:* Fr-Br, 313–14; Fr-Bu, 10:383–84; Le Coq, 111 *(dicendo . . . in die duelli). Marguerite's prayers, death by burning* (Betisac): Fr-Br, 314, 369.

CHAPTER 9: MORTAL COMBAT

Altar removed, commands, glove, escoutes: CG, 30–31; Villiers, 39; Jaille, 164–65; Monestier, 75. *Possible outcomes:* CG, 32–33; Jaille, 165–66. *No quarter or courtesy:* Beaumanoir, no. 1843; Monestier, 71; Lea, 178; Bartlett, 111. *The 1127 duel:* Galbert of Bruges, 212–13 (widely cited).

Joust with lances: Fr-Bu, 10:284; Fr-L, 12:38; Fr-M, 13:107. RSD, 1:464, says the two men dismounted after entering the field and fought on foot with swords. Le Coq, 111, says Le Gris attacked his mounted enemy on foot. JJU, 371, describes only a sword fight. *Chronographia,* 84–85, gives no combat details. Malherbe, 3:537–38, cites a mural (extant in 1621) showing both men mounted and armed with lances. Joust details are adapted from the Saint-Inglevert tournament (1390), also attended by Charles VI, Fr-J, 2:434–46. Cf. "pointed lances" used without injury, Fr-J, 2:229–30.

Speeds: a modern racehorse can average over 40 miles per hour in the quarter mile (440 yards), about twelve times the distance from one end of Saint-Martin's field to the middle. The slower, heavier medieval warhorse carried up to 300 pounds, but a top speed of 15 mph is plausible, for a closing speed of 30 mph, or nearly 45 feet per second. Averaging 10 mph during their charge, Carrouges and Le Gris would have met in midfield in about seven seconds.

Ax fights: Ax fights on horseback and foot were common in jousts of sport (e.g., Fr-J, 2:230), and *formulaires* for judicial combat mention axes (e.g., Jaille, 165). Brantôme, 52, mentions *becs de corbin,* suggesting a type of *hache* (ax), and axes appear in the only surviving image of the duel, British Library MS. Royal 14 E. iv, fol. 267v. Dewannieux, 41–42, has Carrouges and Le Gris fighting on horseback with axes *(haches),* a passage I quote, leading up to the deaths of the two horses, which I have added. *Ax-fighting tactics:* Hewitt, 2:261–65.

Sword fight details: Fr-Bu, 10:284–85; Fr-L, 12:38; Fr-M, 13:107; RSD, 1:464–66; JJU, 371. Both Froissart and RSD report Carrouges's thigh wound. *"Thrusting and striking and slashing":* Fr-Br, 314 (typical swordplay). Froissart says Carrouges threw Le Gris down; RSD, that Carrouges seized Le Gris's helmet, lunged backward, and threw him down; JJU, that Le Gris fell and Carrouges jumped on him. *Le Gris's heavy armor, Carrouges's difficulty penetrating it:* RSD, 1:466.

JJU's report that Carrouges climbed on top of Le Gris makes a coup de grâce with the dagger likely. *Helmet, visor:* Viollet-le-Duc, s.v. "bacinet." *Confession demanded, denied:* Fr-M, 13:107; JJU, 371; RSD, 1:466–67.

Knight's shout, crowd's reply: Fr-Bu, 10:285; Desmadeleines, 42. *Victor's wounds tended:* Jaille, 169. *Carrouges and king, rewards, reunion with wife, Notre-Dame:* Fr-Br, 314. *Medical aid ordered (adapted from Clisson story):* Fr-J, 2:525. *Knight's victory "like a miracle":* Le Coq, 111; Fr-L, 12:367 (emending Le Coq). *Victor's customary departure:* CG, 33–34; Jaille, 168–69.

Victor's right to loser's armor: Jaille, 169. *Armor donated:* Desmadeleines, 35. *Le Gris's body:* Fr-Br, 314; Jaille, 188–89. *Montfaucon:* Hillairet, *Gibets,* 31–39. *"Crowd of skeletons . . . ":* White, 51. *Fortune punishes Le Gris:* Fr-Br, 309; Fr-M, 13:107.

CHAPTER 10: CONVENT AND CRUSADE

Award of 6,000 livres: PP 211v–212r/523–26; Le Coq, 112–13. *Le Gris's lands sold:* Caix, 370. *Aunou-le-Faucon:* Odolant-Desnos, 1:439n; Van Kerrebrouck, 417. *Robert de Carrouges and siblings:* Le Prevost, *Eure,* 3:479.

Jean IV as chevalier d'honneur: BN P.O. 605, Carrouges, no. 11 (November 23, 1390). *Carrouges's 1391 trip to the East:* Fr-L, 12:39, 14:386. *Craon and Clisson, Brittany campaign, king's madness:* Fr-J, 2:521–35; RSD, 2:2–23 (four men slain); Autrand, *Charles VI,* 289–95. *Carrouges in Brittany:* Fr-L, 20:509. *Bal des Ardents:* Fr-J, 2:550–52; Autrand, *Charles VI,* 290–303.

Peace talks, Robert the Hermit, Richard and Isabelle: Fr-J, 2:584–88, 599–600. *Nicopolis:* Fr-J, 2:622–27; Nicolle, 33–71; Atiya. Carrouges's three reported companions (Fr-Br, 314–15) all died at Nicopolis, along with his old commander, Jean de Vienne, making it likely that he died there, too, as surmised by Le Prevost, *Tilleul,* 112n; Dewannieux, 43.

Another man's reported confession: RSD, 1:466; JJU, 371. *Marguerite's alleged suicide:* Minois, 20. *Her death (1419?), Robert's inheritance:* La Noë, 7. *Marguerite's estates:* AD Eure, E.2703, Seigneurie de Carsix (copy of will, January 11, 1451); Le Prevost, *Tilleul,* 63–65, and *Eure,* 3:481. *Contract with Saint-Martin's abbey (March 15, 1396, n.s.):* Contades and Macé, 83–92. *Le Gris's protesting descendants:* White, 42–56.

Carrouges-Le Gris duel as the last authorized by the Parlement, later combats: Morel, 613; Gaudemet, 131; Cohen, 59–60; Bartlett, 120–22; Neilson, 17, 204–5, 304–7, 328–31; Ducoudray, 405 (a 1388 wager disallowed by the king). *The 1455 duel at Valenciennes:* La Marche, 17–19; Monestier, 79. The 1547 duel between Jarnac and La Châtaigneraie, fought in Paris before King Henri II, was not a judicial duel per se (although preceded by oaths) but a duel of honor arising from a reported insult in the royal court: Monestier, 105–6. *The 1818 challenge (England):* Fr-Bu, 10:290n; Neilson, 328–31.

APPENDIX: THE QUARREL'S AFTERMATH

Rejoicing: Fr-M, 13:107. *Mixed responses:* Le Coq, 110. *Alleged confession by condemned man:* RSD, 1:466. *Sick man's confession:* JJU, 371. One early commentator, La Marche, 14–17, believes Le Gris was guilty, and a duel the only means of "proof." *Later accounts:* Diderot and d'Alembert, s.v. "Duel"; Voltaire, 119–20 (ch. 20); Du Bois, 1:257–61; Le Prevost, *Tilleul,* 102–4. *Le Gris's descendant, defender:* White, 42–56. *Modern accounts: Encyclopaedia Britannica,* 8:639a; Dewannieux (Caen 1973); Famiglietti, 137–41.

LIST OF SOURCES

This list is limited to the sources cited in the notes and does not include many general histories and specialized reference works consulted in the course of research. Manuscript sources are listed by city, archive, shelf mark, and folio where relevant. Printed sources are listed by author, title, city, and year of publication; subtitles are often omitted.

MANUSCRIPTS

Caen: Archives Départementales de Calvados (AD Calvados)
    Série F. 6279: Charter, Mesnil Mauger, 1394
Évreux: Archives Départementales de l'Eure (AD Eure)
    Série E. 2703: Carrouges-Thibouville will, 1451
Paris: Archives Nationales (AN)
    Série X—Parlement de Paris
        1 A 1473, fols. 145v, 224r-v, sessions of July 9, September 15 (microfilm)
        2 A 10, fols. 232r–244r, Criminal register, July 9, 1386–December 1, 1386 (microfilm)
        2 A 11, fols. 53r-v, 54v, 206r–210v, 211v–212r, *arrêts* and testimony, September 13, 1386–February 9, 1387
Paris: Bibliothèque Nationale (BN)
    Dossier bleu 155, Carrouges: notes on family history
    Manuscrits français:
        2258: copy of 1306 decree and duel *formulaire* (microfilm)
        2699, fols. 188v–193r: duel *formulaire*
        21726, fols. 188r–190v: duel *formulaire*
        23592: Alençon and Thibouville hostages for 1360 treaty
        26021, nos. 899, 900: receipts for Guillaume Berengier, July 1386
        n.a. 7617, fols. 265r–269r: Royal charter relating to Aunou-le-Faucon

Manuscrits Latins:

    4645: *Questiones Johannis Galli* (Jean Le Coq's casebook, Paris copy)

Pièces originales (P.O.):

    605, Carrouges, nos. 1–20: military records, etc.

    2825, Thibouville, nos. 1–16: family documents

Printed Primary Sources

Beaumanoir, Philippe de. *Coutumes de Beauvaisis.* Edited by Amédée Salmon. 2 vols. Paris, 1899–1900; rpt. 1970.

The Book of Pluscarden. Edited by Felix J. H. Skene. 2 vols. Edinburgh, 1877, 1880.

Brantôme, Pierre de Bourdeilles, Abbé et Seigneur de. *Discours sur les duels.* Edited by J.A.C. Buchon. Paris, 1838; rpt. Arles, 1997.

Cartulaire de Marmoutier pour le Perche. Edited by L'abbé Barret. Mortagne, 1894.

Cérémonies des gages de bataille selon les constitutions du Bon Roi Philippe de France. Edited by G. A. Crapulet. Paris, 1830.

Chaucer, Geoffrey. *The Canterbury Tales.* Edited by Larry D. Benson. Boston, 1987.

Chronographia regum francorum. Edited by H. Moranville. Vol. 3 (1380–1405). Paris, 1897.

Du Breuil, Guillaume. *Stilus curie parlamenti.* Edited by Félix Aubert. Paris, 1909.

Froissart, Jean. *Chroniques.* Edited by J. A. Buchon. 15 vols. (= *Collection des chroniques nationales françaises,* vols. 11–25). Paris, 1824–26.

———. *Chroniques.* Edited by Kervyn de Lettenhove. 25 vols. Brussels, 1867–76.

———. *Chroniques.* Edited by Léon and Albert Mirot, et al., 15 vols. (to date). Paris, 1869–.

———. *Chronicles.* Translated by Thomas Johnes. 2 vols. London, 1839.

———. *Chronicles* (selections). Translated by Geoffrey Brereton. London, 1968.

Galbert of Bruges. *The Murder of Charles the Good, Count of Flanders.* Edited and translated by James Bruce Ross. New York, 1960.

Homer. *Iliad.* Translated by Richmond Lattimore. Chicago, 1951; rpt. 1961.

Ibelin, Jean d'. *Assises de la haute cour.* Edited by Auguste-Arthur Beugnot. In *Assises de Jérusalem,* 1:7–432. Paris, 1841.

Jaille, Hardouin de la. *Formulaire des gaiges de bataille.* In Prost, 135–91.

Juvénal des Ursins, Jean. *Histoire de Charles VI.* Edited by J.A.C. Buchon. *Choix de chroniques et mémoires sur l'histoire de France,* 333–569. Paris, 1838.

La Marche, Olivier de. *Livre de l'advis de gage de bataille.* In Prost, 1–28, 41–54.

La Tour Landry, Geoffroy de. *Le livre du chevalier.* Edited by Anatole de Montaiglon. Paris, 1854.

Le Coq, Jean. *Questiones Johannis Galli.* Edited by Marguerite Boulet. Paris, 1944.

Le Fèvre, Jean. *Journal.* Edited by H. Moranville. Vol. 1. Paris, 1887.

Lobineau, Gui Alexis. *Histoire de Bretagne.* 2 vols. Paris, 1707; rpt. 1973.

Ordonnances des roys de France de la troisième race. Edited by Eusèbe Jacob de Laurière. Vol. 1. Paris, 1723.

Pisan, Christine de. *The Book of the City of Ladies.* Translated by Earl Jeffrey Richards. New York, 1982.

Prost, Bernard, ed. *Traités du duel judiciaire, relations de pas d'armes et tournois.* Paris, 1872.

Registre criminel de la justice de Saint-Martin-des-Champs à Paris au XIVe siècle. Edited by Louis Tanon. Paris, 1877.

Réligieux de Saint-Denis. *Chronique du réligieux de Saint-Denys (1380–1422).* Edited by L. Bellaguet. 6 vols. Paris, 1839–52.

The Romance of the Rose. By Guillaume de Lorris and Jean de Meun. Translated by Charles Dahlberg. Princeton, 1971; rpt. 1986.

Summa de legibus normannie in curia laicali. Edited by Ernest-Joseph Tardif. *Coutumiers de Normandie,* vol. 2. Paris, 1896.

Villiers, Jean de. *Le livre du seigneur de l'Isle Adam pour gaige de bataille.* In Prost, 28–41.

The Westminster Chronicle, 1381–1394. Edited and translated by L. C. Hector and Barbara F. Harvey. Oxford, 1982.

SECONDARY SOURCES

Anglo, Sidney. *The Martial Arts of Renaissance Europe.* New Haven, 2000.

Ariès, Philippe, and Georges Duby, eds. *A History of Private Life.* Vol. 2, *Revelations of the Medieval World.* Translated by Arthur Goldhammer. Cambridge, Mass., 1988.

Asse, Camille. *En pays d'Auge: St-Julien-le-Faucon et ses environs.* 2nd ed. Saint-Pierre-sur-Dives, 1981.

Atiya, Aziz Suryal. *The Crusade of Nicopolis.* London, 1934.

Autrand, Françoise. *Charles V: le sage.* Paris, 1994.

———. *Charles VI: la folie du roi.* Paris, 1986.

Barbay, Louis. *Histoire d'Argentan.* 1922; rpt. Paris, 1993.

Bartlett, Robert. *Trial by Fire and Water: The Medieval Judicial Ordeal.* Oxford, 1986.

Bishop, Morris. *The Middle Ages.* New York, 1968; rpt. 1987.

Biver, Paul, and Marie-Louise Biver. *Abbayes, monastères et couvents de Paris.* Paris, 1970.

Bloch, Marc. *Feudal Society.* 2 vols. Translated by L. A. Manyon. Chicago, 1961.

Bloch, R. Howard. *Medieval French Literature and Law.* Berkeley, 1977.

Bongert, Yvonne. *Recherches sur les cours laïques du Xe au XIIIe siècle.* Paris, 1949.

Boyer, Marjorie Nice. "A Day's Journey in Mediaeval France." *Speculum* 26 (1951): 597–608.

Braudel, Fernand. *The Identity of France.* Vol. 2, *People and Production.* Translated by Siân Reynolds. New York, 1990.

Bullet, Jean-Baptiste. *Dissertations sur la mythologie françoise.* Paris, 1771.

Caix, Alfred de. "Notice sur la chambrerie de l'abbaye de Troarn." *Mémoires de la société des antiquaires de Normandie* (ser. 3) 2 (1856): 311–87.

Canel, A. "Le Combat judiciaire en Normandie." *Mémoires de la société des antiquaires de Normandie* (ser. 3) 2 (1856): 575–655.

Cantor, Norman F. *The Civilization of the Middle Ages.* New York, 1994.

Cassini de Thury, César-François. *Carte de France.* Paris, ca. 1759.

Chapelot, Jean. *Le château de Vincennes.* Paris, 2003.

Chardon, Roland. "The Linear League in North America." *Annals of the Association of American Geographers* 70 (1980): 129–53.

Charpillon, M. *Dictionnaire historique de toutes les communes du département de l'Eure.* 2 vols. Les Andelys, 1868–79.

Cohen, Esther. *The Crossroads of Justice.* Leiden, 1993.

Contades, Gérard, and Abbé Macé. *Canton de Carrouges: essai de bibliographie cantonale.* Paris, 1891.

Contamine, Philippe. *La guerre de cent ans.* Paris, 1968.

Couperie, Pierre. *Paris au fils du temps.* Paris, 1968.

Davis, R.H.C. *The Medieval Warhorse.* London, 1989.

Delachenal, Roland. *Histoire des avocats au parlement de Paris, 1300–1600.* Paris, 1885.

De Loray, Terrier. *Jean de Vienne, Amiral de France, 1341–1396.* Paris, 1877.

De Pradel de Lamase, Martial. *Le château de Vincennes.* Paris, 1932.

Deschamps, Paul. "Donjon de Chambois." *Congrès archéologique de France, bulletin monumental* 111 (1953): 293–308.

Desmadeleines, A. Desgenettes. "Duel de Jean de Carouges et de Jacques Legris." *Bulletin de la société bibliophile historique* 3 (1837–38), no. 2: 32–42.

Dewannieux, André. *Le duel judiciaire entre Jean de Carrouges et Jacques Le Gris: le 29 décembre 1386.* Melun, 1976.

Dictionnaire de biographie française. Edited by J. Balteau et al. 20 vols. Paris, 1933–2003.

Dictionnaire de la noblesse. Edited by François-Alexandre Aubert de La Chesnaye Des Bois and Jacques Badier. 3rd ed. 19 vols. Paris, 1863–76.

Diderot, Denis, and Jean Le Rond d'Alembert, eds. *Encyclopédie.* 28 vols. Paris, 1751–72.

Diguères, Victor des. *Sévigni, ou une paroisse rurale en Normandie.* Paris, 1863.

Du Bois, Louis-François. *Archives annuelles de la Normandie.* 2 vols. Caen, 1824–26.

Duby, Georges. *Medieval Marriage.* Translated by Elborg Forster. Baltimore, Md., 1978.

———. *The Three Orders.* Translated by Arthur Goldhammer. Chicago, 1980.

Ducoudray, Gustave. *Les origines du Parlement de Paris et la justice aux XIII⁰ and XIV⁰ siècles.* 2 vols. Paris, 1902; rpt. 1970.

Dupont-Ferrier, Gustave. *Gallia regia.* 7 vols. Paris, 1942–66.

The Encyclopaedia Britannica. 11th ed. 29 vols. New York, 1910–11.

Fagan, Brian. *The Little Ice Age.* New York, 2000.

Famiglietti, R. C. *Tales of the Marriage Bed from Medieval France.* Providence, R.I., 1992.

Favier, Jean. *Paris: Deux mille ans d'histoire.* Paris, 1997.

Ferguson, George. *Signs and Symbols in Christian Art.* New York, 1954; rpt. 1975.

France, John. *Western Warfare in the Age of the Crusades.* Ithaca, N.Y., 1999.

Gaudemet, Jean. "Les ordalies au moyen âge: doctrine, legislation et pratique canoniques." In *La preuve.* Vol. 2, *Moyen âge et temps modernes,* 99–135. Brussels, 1965.

Gottlieb, Beatrice. "Birth and Infancy"; "Pregnancy." *Encyclopedia of the Renaissance,* 1:232–35, 5:155–57. New York, 1999.

Gravdal, Kathryn. *Ravishing Maidens.* Philadelphia, 1991.

Guenée, Bernard. "Comment le Réligieux de Saint-Denis a-t-il écrit l'histoire?" *Pratiques de la culture écrite en France au XVᵉ siècle,* 331–43. Edited by Monique Ornato and Nicole Pons. Louvain-la-Neuve, 1995.

Haskins, Charles H. *The Rise of Universities.* New York, 1923.

Hewitt, John. *Ancient Armour and Weapons in Europe.* 3 vols. 1860; rpt. Graz, 1967.

Hillairet, Jacques. *Dictionnaire historique des rues de Paris.* 9th ed. 2 vols. Paris, 1985.

———. *Gibets, piloris et cachots du vieux Paris.* Paris, 1956.

Hippeau, Célestin. *Dictionnaire topographique du département du Calvados.* Paris, 1883.

Horne, Alistair. *The Seven Ages of Paris.* New York, 2002.

Huizinga, Johan. *The Autumn of the Middle Ages.* Translated by Rodney J. Payton and Ulrich Mammitzsch. Chicago, 1996.

Keats-Rohan, K.S.B. *Domesday Descendants.* Vol. 2, *Pipe Rolls to Cartae Baronum.* London, 2002.

Keen, Maurice. *Chivalry.* New Haven, Conn., 1984.

———, ed. *Medieval Warfare: A History.* Oxford, 1999.

———. *The Penguin History of Medieval Europe.* London, 1991.

Lacordaire, Simon. *Les inconnus de la Seine.* Paris, 1985.

Lagrange, Louis-Jean, and Jean Taralon. "Le Château de Carrouges." *Congrès archéologique de France, bulletin monumental* 111 (1953): 317–49.

La Noë, René de [= Louis Duval]. *Robert de Carrouges.* Alençon, 1896.

La Roque de La Lontière, Gilles-André de. *Histoire généalogique de la maison de Harcourt.* 4 vols. Paris, 1662.

Lea, Charles Henry. *The Duel and the Oath.* (Orig. in *Superstition and Force,* 1866.) Edited by Edward Peters. Philadelphia, 1974.

Lebreton, Charles. "L'Avranchin pendant la guerre de cent ans, 1346 à 1450." *Mémoires de la société des antiquaires de Normandie* (ser. 3) 10 (1880): 12–172.

Le Fort, V. "L'Affaire de Carrouges." *La revue illustrée du Calvados* 7.7 (July 1913), 98–99.

Lehoux, Françoise. *Jean de France, duc de Berri.* 4 vols. Paris, 1966–68.

Leonard, John K. "Rites of Marriage in the Western Middle Ages." In *Medieval Liturgy,* edited by Lizette Larson-Miller, 165–202. New York, 1997.

Le Prevost, Auguste. *Histoire de Saint-Martin du Tilleul.* Paris, 1848.

———. *Mémoires et notes pour servir à l'histoire du département de l'Eure.* Edited by Léopold Delisle and Louis Passy. 3 vols. Évreux, 1862–69.

Long, Brian. *Castles of Northumberland.* Newcastle upon Tyne, 1967.

Loth, Yan. *Tracés d'itinéraires en Gaule romaine.* Dammarie-les-Lys, 1986.

Mabire, Jean, and Jean-Robert Ragache. *Histoire de la Normandie.* Paris, 1976.

Malherbe, François de. *Oeuvres.* Edited by M. L. LaLanne. 5 vols. Paris, 1862–69.

Maneuvrier, Jack. "L'affaire de Carrouges au Mesnil-Mauger." *Histoire et traditions populaires* 56 (December 1996): 29–35.

Mariette de La Pagerie, G. *Carte topographique de la Normandie.* Paris, ca. 1720.

Mauboussin, Christophe. *La première révolte de Godefroy d'Harcourt.* Master's thesis. Caen, 1993.

Mériel, Amédée. *Bellême: notes historiques.* 1887; rpt. Paris, 1992.

Minois, Georges. *Histoire du suicide.* Paris, 1995.

Monestier, Martin. *Duels: les combats singuliers des origines à nos jours.* Paris, 1991.

Morel, Henri. "La fin du duel judiciaire en France et la naissance du point d'honneur." *Revue historique de droit français et étranger* (ser. 4) 42 (1964): 574–639.

Moricet, Marthe. "Duel de Legris et de Carrouges." *Cahier des annales de Normandie* 2 (1963): 203–207.

Neilson, George. *Trial by Combat.* Glasgow, 1890; rpt. 2000.

Nicolle, David. *Nicopolis 1396.* Oxford, 1999.

Nortier, Michel. *Documents normands du règne de Charles V.* Paris, 2000.

Odolant-Desnos, Pierre Joseph. *Mémoires historiques sur la ville d'Alençon.* 2 vols. Alençon, 1787; rpt. 1976.

The Oxford English Dictionary. Edited by J. A. Simpson and E. S. C. Weiner. 2nd ed. 20 vols. Oxford, 1989.

Palmer, J. J. N. *England, France and Christendom, 1377–99.* London, 1972.

Pernoud, Régine. *Blanche of Castile.* Translated by Henry Noel. New York, 1975.

Peters, Edward. *Torture.* 2nd ed. Philadelphia, 1996.

Petit, Ernest. *Séjours de Charles VI: 1380–1400.* Paris, 1894.

Prieur, Lucien. "Château d'Argentan." *Congrès archéologique de France, bulletin monumental* 111 (1953): 84–90.

Reinhard, J. R. "Burning at the Stake in Mediaeval Law and Literature." *Speculum* 16 (1941): 186–209.

Rougemont, Denis de. *Love in the Western World.* Translated by Montgomery Belgion. Rev. ed. New York, 1956.

Rousseau, Xavier. *Le château de Carrouges.* 4th ed. La Ferté-Macé, 1955.

Saunders, Corinne. *Rape and Ravishment in the Literature of Medieval England.* Cambridge, England, 2001.

Seward, Desmond. *The Hundred Years' War.* London, 1978.

Shennan, J. H. *The Parlement of Paris.* Rev. ed. Stroud, 1998.

Stevenson, Kenneth. *Nuptial Blessing.* New York, 1983.

Summerson, Henry. *Medieval Carlisle.* 2 vols. Kendal, 1993.

Sumption, Jonathan. *The Hundred Years' War.* 2 vols. Philadelphia, 1990, 1999.

Talbert, Richard J. A., et al., eds. *Barrington Atlas of the Greek and Roman World.* Princeton, N.J., 2000.

Terrier, Claude Catherine, and Olivier Renaudeau. *Le château de Carrouges.* Paris, 2000.

Tournouër, H. "Excursion archéologique dans le Houlme." *Bulletin de la société historique et archéologique de l'Orne* 22 (1903): 349–95.

Van Kerrebrouck, Patrick, et al. *Les Valois.* Villeneuve d'Ascq, 1990.

Vanuxem, P.-F. "Le duel Le Grix–Carrouges." *Le pays d'Argentan* 6 (1934): 197–205, 236–43.

———. *Veillerys: légendes de Basse-Normandie.* Argentan, 1933; rpt. 1967.

Verdon, Jean. *La femme au Moyen Age.* Paris, 1999.

Vérel, Charles. "Nonant-le-Pin." *Bulletin de la société historique et archéologique de l'Orne* 22 (1903): 157–205.

Viollet-le-Duc, Eugène-Emmanuel. *Dictionnaire raisonné du mobilier français.* 6 vols. Paris, 1854–75; rpt. 1926.

Voltaire. *Histoire du Parlement de Paris.* Amsterdam, 1769.

Warner, Philip. *Sieges of the Middle Ages.* London, 1968.

White, F. Le Grix. *Forgotten Seigneurs of the Alençonnais.* Penrith, ca. 1880.

Wise, Terence. *Medieval Warfare.* New York, 1976.

Wolfthal, Diane. *Images of Rape.* Cambridge, Eng., 1999.

Yule, Henry, ed. and trans. *Cathay and the Way Thither.* 2nd ed. London, 1914.

Ziegler, Philip. *The Black Death.* New York, 1969; rpt. 1971.

INDEX

© ZinnPhoto

ABOUT THE AUTHOR

An award-winning professor of English at UCLA,
ERIC JAGER holds a Ph.D. from the University of
Michigan and has also taught at Columbia University.
He is the author of two previous books, *The Book of the
Heart* (a study of heart imagery in medieval literature),
and *Blood Royal: A True Tale of Crime and Detection in
Medieval Paris,* as well as numerous articles for acclaimed
academic journals. He lives in Los Angeles with his
wife, Peg.